"And thou, Capharnaum, shalt thou be 23
exalted to heaven? Thou shalt be thrust down
to hell! For if the miracles had been worked
in Sodom that have been worked in thee, it
would have remained to this day. But I tell 24
you, it will be more tolerable for the land of
Sodom on the day of judgment than for thee.

"He who hears you, hears me; and he who Luke 10
rejects you, rejects me; and he who rejects 16-22
me, rejects him who sent me."

Disciples Return with Joy

Now the seventy-two returned with joy, 17
saying, "Lord, even the devils are subject to
us in thy name." But he said to them, "I was 18
watching Satan fall as lightning from heaven. 19
Behold, I have given you power to tread upon
serpents and scorpions, and over all the might
of the enemy; and nothing shall hurt you. But 20
do not rejoice in this, that the spirits are subject to you; rejoice rather in this, that your
names are written in heaven."

Jesus Draws Men Gently to Himself

In that very hour he rejoiced in the Holy 21
Spirit and said, "I praise thee, Father, Lord of

heaven and earth, that thou didst hide these
things from the wise and prudent, and didst
reveal them to little ones. Yes, Father, for such
22 was thy good pleasure. All things have been
delivered to me by my Father; and no one
knows who the Son is except the Father, and
who the Father is except the Son, and him to
whom the Son chooses to reveal him.

Invites All to Be His Disciples

Matt. 11 28-30 "Come to me, all you who labor and are bur-
29 dened, and I will give you rest. Take my yoke
upon you, and learn from me, for I am meek
and humble of heart; and you will find rest
30 for your souls. For my yoke is easy, and my
burden light."

The good Samaritan

To GAIN ETERNAL LIFE

Mar. 2 or Sept. 1

AND TURNING to his disciples he said, Luke 10
"Blessed are the eyes that see what you 23-37
see! For I say to you, many prophets and kings 24
have desired to see what you see, and they
have not seen it; and to hear what you hear,
and they have not heard it."

The Great Commandment

25 And behold, a certain lawyer got up to test
him, saying, "Master, what must I do to gain
26 eternal life?" But he said to him, "What is
written in the Law? How dost thou read?"
27 He answered and said, "Thou shalt love the
Lord thy God with thy whole heart, and with
thy whole soul, and with thy whole strength,
and with thy whole mind; and thy neighbor
28 as thyself." And he said to him, "Thou hast
answered rightly; do this and thou shalt live."

"Who Is My Neighbor?"

29 But he, wishing to justify himself, said to
30 Jesus, "And who is my neighbor?" Jesus
answered, "A certain man was going down
from Jerusalem to Jericho, and he fell in with
robbers, who after both stripping him and
beating him went their way, leaving him half-
31 dead. But, as it happened, a certain priest
was going down the same way; and when he
32 saw him, he passed by. And likewise a Lev-
ite also, when he was near the place and saw
him, passed by.

33 "But a certain Samaritan as he journeyed
came upon him, and seeing him, was moved

with compassion. And he went up to him and 34
bound up his wounds, pouring on oil and
wine. And setting him on his own beast, he 35
brought him to an inn and took care of him.
And the next day he took out two denarii and
gave them to the innkeeper and said, 'Take
care of him; and whatever more thou spendest, I, on my way back, will repay thee.'

"Which of these three, in thy opinion, 36
proved himself neighbor to him who fell
among the robbers?" And he said, "He who 37
took pity on him." And Jesus said to him, "Go
and do thou also in like manner."

Martha and Mary

WISE CHOICE COMMENDED

MAR. 3 or Sept. 2

Luke 10 38-42 NOW IT CAME to pass as they were on their
journey, that he entered a certain vil-
lage; and a woman named Martha welcomed
39 him to her house. And she had a sister called
Mary, who also seated herself at the Lord's
40 feet, and listened to his word. But Martha was
busy about much serving. And she came up
and said, "Lord, is it no concern of thine that
my sister has left me to serve alone? Tell her
therefore to help me."

41 But the Lord answered and said to her,
"Martha, Martha, thou art anxious and

troubled about many things; and yet only one 42
thing is needful. Mary has chosen the best
part, and it will not be taken away from her."

Jesus Teaches a Method of Prayer

And it came to pass as he was praying in a Luke 11
certain place, that when he ceased, one of his 11-13
disciples said to him, "Lord, teach us to pray
even as John also taught his disciples." And he 2
said to them, "When you pray, say:
"'Father, hallowed be thy name. Thy kingdom come! Give us this day our daily bread, 3
and forgive us our sins, for we also forgive 4
everyone who is indebted to us. And lead us
not into temptation.'"

Persevering Prayer Rewarded

And he said to them, "Which of you shall 5
have a friend and shall go to him in the middle of the night and say to him, 'Friend, lend
me three loaves, for a friend of mine has just 6
come to me from a journey, and I have nothing to set before him'; and he from within 7
should answer and say, 'Do not disturb me;
the door is now shut, and my children and I
are in bed; I cannot get up and give to thee'?

8 "I say to you, although he will not get up
and give to him because he is his friend, yet
because of his persistence he will get up and
9 give him all he needs. And I say to you, ask,
and it shall be given to you; seek, and you
shall find; knock, and it shall be opened to
10 you. For everyone who asks receives; and he
who seeks finds; and to him who knocks it
shall be opened.

11 "But if one of you asks his father for a
loaf, will he hand him a stone? or for a fish,
12 will he for a fish hand him a serpent? or if he
asks for an egg, will he hand him a scorpion?
13 Therefore, if you, evil as you are, know how
to give good gifts to your children, how much
more will your heavenly Father give the Good
Spirit to those who ask him!"

JESUS REVEALS HE IS DIVINE

MAR. 4 or Sept. 3

NOW THERE took place at Jerusalem the John 10
feast of the Dedication; and it was win- 22-42
ter. And Jesus was walking in the temple, in 23
Solomon's portico. The Jews therefore gath- 24
ered round him, and said to him, "How long
dost thou keep us in suspense? If thou art the
Christ, tell us openly."

Jesus answered them, "I tell you and you do 25
not believe. The works that I do in the name
of my Father, these bear witness concerning
me. But you do not believe because you are 26
not of my sheep. My sheep hear my voice, 27
and I know them and they follow me. And I 28
give them everlasting life; and they shall never
perish, neither shall anyone snatch them out
of my hand. [1]What my Father has given me is 29

---

1. *What . . . is greater than all:* this gift may have been Christ's power, the work of redemption, or the flock itself. Generally, however, it is understood to be Christ's divine nature. It is taken in this sense by the Lateran Council.

greater than all; and no one is able to snatch
30 anything out of the hand of my Father. I and
the Father are one."

Men Stone Their God

31 The Jews therefore took up stones to stone
32 him. Jesus answered them, "Many good works
33 have I shown you from my Father. For which
of these works do you stone me?" The Jews
answered him, "Not for a good work do we
stone thee, but for blasphemy, and because
thou, being a man, makest thyself God."
34 [1]Jesus answered them, "Is it not written in
35 your Law, 'I said you are gods'? If he called
them gods to whom the word of God was
addressed (and the Scripture cannot be bro-
36 ken), do you say of him whom the Father has
made holy and sent into the world, 'Thou blas-
phemest,' because I said, 'I am the Son of God'?

Proof of His Divinity

37 "If I do not perform the works of my Father, do
38 not believe me. But if I do perform them, and

1. The judges who administered the Law were called gods, because they represented God. If they, merely men, and so often unfaithful to their duties, as in Ps.81, could enjoy this title, how much more right to it has He who was made holy, i.e., especially set aside for God's work!

if you are not willing to believe me, believe
the works, that you may know and believe that
the Father is in me and I in the Father."

They sought therefore to seize him; and he 39
went forth out of their hands.

And again he went away beyond the Jor- 40
dan, to the place where John was at first baptizing; and there he stayed. And many came 41
to him; and they were saying, "John indeed
worked no sign. All things, however, that 42
John said of this man were true." And many
believed in him.

Lesson from a lamp

JESUS CALUMNIATED

MAR. 5 or Sept. 4

Luke 11 14-15 AND HE, was casting out a devil, and the
same was dumb; and when he had cast out
the devil, the dumb man spoke. And the crowds
15 marvelled. But some of them said, "By Beelzebub, the prince of devils, he casts out devils."

Luke 11 17-23 But he, seeing their thoughts, said to
them: "Every kingdom divided against itself
is brought to desolation, and house will fall
18 upon house. If, then, Satan also is divided
against himself, how shall his kingdom stand?
Because you say that I cast out devils by Beel-
19 zebub. Now, if I cast out devils by Beelzebub,
by whom do [1]your children cast them out?
Therefore they shall be your judges.

20 "But if I cast out devils by the finger of God,
then the kingdom of God has come upon you.

1. The "children" of the Pharisees are their disciples. They taught them formulas and practices to cast out devils.

When the strong man, fully armed, guards his 21
courtyard, his property is undisturbed. But 22
if a stronger than he attacks and overcomes
him, he will take away all his weapons that
he relied upon, and will divide his spoils. He 23
who is not with me is against me; and he who
does not gather with me scatters.

[1]"But when the unclean spirit has gone Matt. 12
out of a man, he roams through dry places in 43-45
search of rest, and finds none. Then he says, 44
'I will return to my house which I left'; and
when he has come to it, he finds the place
unoccupied, swept and decorated. Then he 45
goes and takes with him seven other spirits
more evil than himself, and they enter in and
dwell there; and the last state of that man
becomes worse than the first. So shall it be
with this evil generation also."

He Who Both Hears and Heeds

Now it came to pass as he was saying these Luke 11
things, that a certain woman from the crowd 27-28
lifted up her voice and said to him, "Blessed is

---

1. Jesus warns that a devil cast out may return with reinforcements, to an individual or to a society; here there is a warning to those who are rejecting Him. He uses a parable to present the idea: the impure spirit is like a robber who goes into the desert, etc.

the womb that bore thee, and the breasts that
28 nursed thee." But he said, "Rather, blessed are
they who hear the word of God and keep it.

Luke 11 33-36 "No one lights a lamp and puts it in a cel-
lar or even under the measure, but upon the
lamp-stand, that they who enter in may see
the light.

The Eye of Worldly-mindedness

34 "The lamp of thy body is thy eye. If thy eye be
sound, thy whole body will be full of light.
35 But if it be evil, thy body also will be full of
36 darkness. Take care, therefore, that the light
that is in thee is not darkness. If, then, thy
whole body is full of light, having no part in
darkness, it will all be illumined, as when a
bright lamp illumines thee."

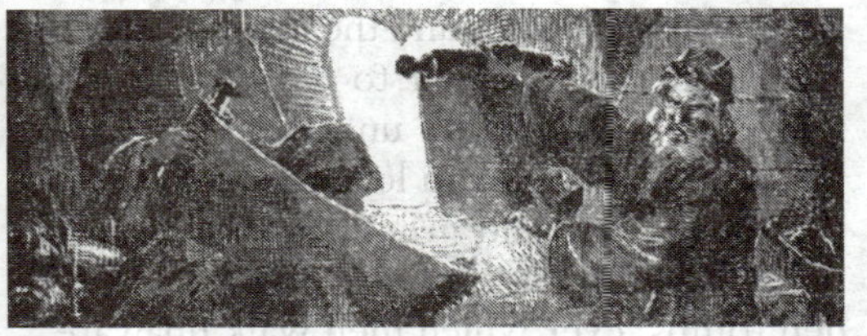

JESUS DENOUNCES HYPOCRISY

MAR. 6 or Sept. 5

NOW AFTER he had spoken, a Pharisee Luke 11 37-54
asked him to dine with him. And he
went in and reclined at table. But the Pharisee 38
began to ponder and ask himself why he had
not washed before dinner.

But the Lord said to him, "Now you Phari- 39
sees clean the outside of the cup and the dish,
but within you are full of robbery and wickedness. Foolish ones! did not he who made 40
the outside make the inside too? [1]Neverthe- 41
less, give that which remains as alms; and
behold, all things are clean to you.

"But woe to you Pharisees! because you 42
pay tithes on mint and rue and every herb,

1. Worldly possessions should be used for good purposes; the hearts of the Pharisees as well as their vessels will be clean, if they use them so.

and disregard justice and the love of God. But
these things you ought to have done, while
43 not leaving the others undone. Woe to you
Pharisees! because you love the front seats in
the synagogues and greetings in the market
44 place. Woe to you! because you are like hidden tombs, over which men walk unaware."
45 But one of the lawyers, answering, said
to him, "Master, in saying these things, thou
insultest us also."

Rebukes Those Who Burden Mankind

46 But he said, "Woe to you lawyers also! because
you load men with oppressive burdens and
you yourselves with one of your fingers do
47 not touch the burdens. Woe to you! for you
build the tombs of the prophets, whereas
48 your fathers killed them. So then you are witnesses and approve the deeds of your fathers;
for they indeed killed them, and you build
their tombs.

And Persecute His Messengers

49 "For this reason also the wisdom of God has
said, 'I will send them prophets and apostles;
and some of them they will put to death and

persecute, that the blood of all the prophets 50
that has been shed from the foundation of the
world may be required of this generation, 51
from the blood of Abel unto the blood of
Zacharias, who was slain between the altar
and the temple.' Yes, I say to you, it shall be
required of this generation. Woe to you law- 52
yers! because you have taken away the key
of knowledge; you have not entered yourselves and those who were entering you have
hindered."

After he had said these things to them, the 53
Pharisees and the lawyers began to press him
hard and to provoke him to speak on many
things, setting traps for him and plotting to 54
seize upon something out of his mouth, that
they might accuse him.

Fear only him who kills the soul

BEWARE of HYPOCRISY

MAR. 7 or Sept. 6

Luke 12 1-12 NOW WHEN immense crowds had gathered
together, so that they were treading on

one another, he began to say to his disciples,
"Beware of the leaven of the Pharisees, which
is hypocrisy. But there is nothing concealed 2
that will not be disclosed, and nothing hidden
that will not be made known. For what you 3
have said in darkness will be said in the light;
and what you have whispered in the inner
chambers will be preached on the housetops.

Fear Only Him Who Kills the Soul

"But I say to you, my friends: Do not be afraid 4
of those who kill the body, and after that have
nothing more that they can do. But I will show 5
you whom you shall be afraid of; be afraid of
him who, after he has killed, has power to cast
into hell. Yes, I say to you, be afraid of him. 6
"Are not five sparrows sold for two far-
things? And yet not one of them is forgotten
before God. Yes, the very hairs of your head 7
are all numbered. Therefore do not be afraid,
you are of more value than many sparrows.

Confess Your Faith Courageously

"And I say to you, everyone who acknowledges 8
me before men, him will the Son of Man also
acknowledge before the angels of God. But

9 whoever disowns me before men will be dis-
10 owned before the angels of God. And everyone
who speaks a word against the Son of Man, it
shall be forgiven him; but to him who blas-
phemes against the Holy Spirit, it will not be
forgiven.

11 "And when they bring you before the synagogues and the magistrates and the authorities, do not be anxious how or wherewith you
12 shall defend yourselves, or what you shall say,
for the Holy Spirit will teach you in that very
hour what you ought to say."

BEWARE OF AVARICE

MAR. 8 or Sept. [illegible]

NOW ONE out of the crowd said to him, Luke 12
"Master, tell my brother to divide the 13-31
inheritance with me." But he said to him, 14
"Man, who has appointed me a judge or arbi-
trator over you?" And he said to them, "Take 15
heed and guard yourselves from all covetous-
ness, for a man's life does not consist in the
abundance of his possessions."

Parable of the Rich Fool

But he spoke a parable to them, saying, "The 16
land of a certain rich man brought forth
abundant crops. And he began to take thought 17
within himself, saying, 'What shall I do, for I
have no room to store my crops?'
"And he said, 'I will do this: I will pull down 18
my barns and build larger ones, and there will

19 store up all my grain and my goods. And I will
say to my soul, Soul, thou hast many good things
laid up for many years; take thy ease, eat, drink,
20 be merry.' But God said to him, 'Thou fool, this
night do they demand thy soul of thee; and the
things that thou hast provided, whose will they
21 be?' So is he who lays up treasure for himself,
and is not rich as regards God."

Oversolicitous for Temporal Things

22 But he said to his disciples, "Therefore I say
to you, do not be anxious for your life, what
you shall eat; nor yet for your body, what you
23 shall put on. The life is a greater thing than the
food, and the body than the clothing.

24 "Consider the ravens: they neither sow nor
reap, they have neither storeroom nor barn;
yet God feeds them. Of how much more
25 value are you than they! But which of you by
being anxious about it can add to his stature
26 a single cubit? Therefore if you are not able
to do even a very little thing, why are you
anxious concerning the rest?

What to Seek

27 "Consider how the lilies grow; they neither
toil nor spin, yet I say to you that not even
Solomon in all his glory was arrayed like one

of these. But if God so clothes the grass which 28
flourishes in the field today but tomorrow is
thrown into the oven, how much more you,
O you of little faith!

"And as for you, do not seek what you 29
shall eat, or what you shall drink; and do not
exalt yourselves (for after all these things the 30
nations of the world seek); but your Father
knows that you need these things. But seek 31
the kingdom of God, and all these things shall
be given you besides."

BE READY for YOUR FINAL HOUR

MAR. 9 or Sept. 8

Luke 12 32-48 "DO NOT be afraid, little flock, for it has
pleased your Father to give you the
33 kingdom. Sell what you have and give alms.
Make for yourselves purses that do not grow
old, a treasure unfailing in heaven, where nei-
34 ther thief draws near nor moth destroys. For
where your treasure is, there also will your
heart be.

35 "Let your loins be girt about and your
36 lamps burning, and you yourselves like men
waiting for their master's return from the
wedding; so that when he comes and knocks,
37 they may straightway open to him. Blessed

are those servants whom the master, on
his return, shall find watching. Amen I say
to you, he will gird himself, and will make
them recline at table, and will come and serve
them. And if he comes in the second watch, 38
and if in the third, and finds them so, blessed
are those servants!

"But of this be assured, that if the house- 39
holder had known at what hour the thief was
coming, he would certainly have watched,
and not have let his house be broken into. You 40
also must be ready, because at an hour that
you do not expect, the Son of Man is coming."

Blessed Are They Who Prepare

And Peter said to him, "Lord, dost thou speak 41
this parable for us or for all alike?" And the
Lord said, "Who, dost thou think, is the faith- 42
ful and prudent steward whom the master
will set over his household to give them their
ration of grain in due time?

"Blessed is that servant whom his master, 43
when he comes, shall find so doing. Truly I 44
say to you, he will set him over all his goods.
But if that servant says to himself, 'My mas- 45
ter delays his coming,' and begins to beat

the menservants and the maids, and to eat
46 and drink, and to get drunk, the master of
that servant will come on a day he does not
expect, and in an hour he does not know, and
will cut him asunder and make him share the
lot of the unfaithful.

47 "But that servant who knew his master's
will, and did not make ready for him and did
not act according to his will, will be beaten
48 with many stripes. Whereas he who did not
know it, but did things deserving of stripes,
will be beaten with few. But of everyone to
whom much has been given, much will be
required; and of him to whom they have
entrusted much, they will demand the more."

Be ready for opposition in following Christ. ". . . They will be divided, father against son . . . mother against daughter."

BE READY for OPPOSITION

MAR. 10 or Sept. 9

Luke 12 49-59 "I HAVE COME to cast fire upon the earth,
and what will I but that it be kindled?
50 But I have a baptism to be baptized with; and
how distressed I am until it is accomplished!
51 "Do you think that I came to give peace
52 upon the earth? No, I tell you, but division. For
henceforth in one house five will be divided,
53 three against two, and two against three. They
will be divided, father against son and son
against his father; mother against daughter
and daughter against the mother; mother-in-
law against her daughter-in-law and daughter-
in-law against her mother-in-law."

Time for Reconciliation

54 And he said also to the crowds, "When you see
55 a cloud rising in the west, you say at once, 'A
shower is coming,' and so it comes to pass. And
when you see the south wind blow, you say,
'There will be a scorching heat,' and so it comes
56 to pass. You hypocrites! you know how to judge
the face of the sky and of the earth; but how is it
57 that you do not judge this time? But why even
of yourselves do you not judge what is right?

"And when thou art going with thy oppo- 58
nent to the ruler, take pains to be quit of him
on the way; lest he deliver thee to the judge,
and the judge to the officer, and the officer
cast thee into prison. I say to thee, thou wilt 59
not come out from it until thou hast paid the
very last mite."

The NECESSITY of REPENTANCE

MAR. 11 or Sept. 10

Luke 13 1-17 NOW THERE came at that very time some
who brought him word about the Galileans, whose blood Pilate had mingled with
their sacrifices.
2 And he answered and said to them, "Do
you think that these Galileans were worse sinners than all the other Galileans, because they
3 have suffered such things? I tell you, no; but
unless you repent, you will all perish in the
4 same manner. Or those eighteen upon whom
the tower of Siloe fell and killed them; do you
think that they were more guilty than all the
5 other dwellers in Jerusalem? I tell you, no;
but unless you repent, you will all perish in
the same manner."

Parable of the Fruitless Fig Tree

And he spoke this parable: "A certain man had 6
a fig tree planted in his vineyard; and he came
seeking fruit thereon, and found none. And 7
he said to the vine-dresser, 'Behold, for three
years now I have come seeking fruit on this fig
tree, and I find none. Cut it down, therefore;
why does it still encumber the ground?'

"But he answered him and said, 'Sir, let it 8
alone this year too, till I dig around it and
manure it. Perhaps it may bear fruit; but if 9
not, then afterwards thou shalt cut it down.'"

Jesus Heals an Invalid Woman

Now he was teaching in one of their synagogues 10
on the Sabbath. And behold, there was woman 11
who for eighteen years had had a sickness caused
by a spirit; and she was bent over and utterly
unable to look upwards. When Jesus saw her, 12
he called her to him and said to her, "Woman,
thou art delivered from thy infirmity." And he 13
laid his hands upon her, and instantly she was
made straight, and glorified God.

Hypocrisy Uncovered

But the ruler of the synagogue, indignant that 14
Jesus had cured on the Sabbath, addressed the
crowd, saying, "There are six days in which

one ought to work; on these therefore come
15 and be cured, and not on the Sabbath." But
the Lord answered him and said, "Hypocrites!
does not each one of you on the Sabbath loose
his ox or ass from the manger, and lead it
16 forth to water? And this woman, daughter of
Abraham as she is, whom Satan has bound, lo,
for eighteen years, ought not she to be loosed
from this bond on the Sabbath?"

17 And as he said these things, all his adversar-
ies were put to shame; and the entire crowd
rejoiced at all the glorious things that were
done by him.

"Depart from me, . . . workers of iniquity."

MIGHTY MUSTARD SEED

MAR. 12 or Sept. 11

HE SAID therefore, "What is the kingdom Luke 13
of God like, and to what shall I liken 18
it? The kingdom of heaven is like a grain of Matt. 13
mustard seed, which a man took and sowed in 31-32
his field. This indeed is the smallest of all the 32
seeds; but when it grows up it is larger than
any herb and becomes comes a tree, and puts Mark 4 32

out great branches, so that the birds of the air
can dwell beneath its shade."

The Mighty Leaven

Luke 13 And again he said, "To what shall I liken the
20 Matt. 13 kingdom of God? The kingdom of heaven is
33 like leaven, which a woman took and buried
in three measures of flour, until all of it was
leavened."

Are They Few That Are Saved?

Luke 13 And he passed on through towns and villages,
22-30 teaching and making his way towards Jerusa-
23 lem. But someone said to him, "Lord, are only
24 a few to be saved?" But he said to them, "Strive
to enter by the narrow gate; for many, I tell
you, will seek to enter and will not be able.
25 But when the master of the house has entered
and shut the door, you will begin to stand outside and knock at the door, saying, 'Lord, open
for us!' And he shall say to you in answer, 'I
26 do not know where you are from.' Then you
shall begin to say, 'We ate and drank in thy
presence, and thou didst teach in our streets.'
27 "And he shall say to you, 'I do not know
where you are from. Depart from me, all you

workers of iniquity.' There will be the weep- 28
ing, and the gnashing of teeth, when you shall
see Abraham and Isaac and Jacob and all the
prophets in the kingdom of God, but you
yourselves cast forth outside.

The First Will Be Last

"And they will come from the east and from 29
the west, from the north and from the south,
and will feast in the kingdom of God. [1]And 30
behold, there are those last who will be first,
and there are those first who will be last."

1. Many Gentiles will be called to salvation and take the place destined for the chosen people of Israel.

"Jerusalem, thou who killest the prophets"

HEROD THREATENS JESUS

MAR. 13 or Sept. 12

Luke 13
31-35 ON THAT same day certain Pharisees came
up, saying to him, "Depart and be on

thy way, for Herod wants to kill thee." And 32
he said to them, "Go and say to that fox,
'Behold, I cast out devils and perform cures
today and tomorrow, and the third day I am
to end my course. Nevertheless, I must go 33
my way today and tomorrow and the next
day, for it cannot be that a prophet perish
outside Jerusalem.'

"Jerusalem, Jerusalem, thou who killest 34
the prophets, and stonest those who are sent
to thee! How often would I have gathered
thy children together, as a hen gathers her
young under her wings, but thou wouldst
not! Behold, your house is left to you. And I 35
say to you, you shall not see me until the time
comes when you shall say, 'Blessed is he who
comes in the name of the Lord!'"

Watching Jesus to Ensnare Him

And it came to pass, when he entered the Luke 14
house of one of the rulers of the Pharisees on 1-6
the Sabbath to take food, that they watched
him. And behold, there was a certain man 2
before him who had the dropsy. And Jesus 3
asked the lawyers and Pharisees, saying, "Is it
lawful to cure on the Sabbath?"

4 But they remained silent. And he took and
5 healed him and let him go. Then addressing
them, he said, "Which of you shall have an ass
or an ox fall into a pit, and will not immedi-
6 ately draw him up on the Sabbath?" And they
could give him no answer to these things.

"Friend, go up higher"

EXHORTS to PERSONAL HUMILITY

MAR. 14 or Sept. 13

BUT HE also spoke a parable to those Luke 14
invited, observing how they were 7-24
choosing the first places at table, and he said
to them, "When thou art invited to a wedding 8
feast, do not recline in the first place, lest perhaps one more distinguished than thou have
been invited by him, and he who invited thee 9
and him come and say to thee, 'Make room
for this man'; and then thou begin with shame
to take the last place.

"But when thou art invited, go and recline 10
in the last place; that when he who invited
thee comes in, he may say to thee, 'Friend, go
up higher!' Then thou wilt be honored in the
presence of all who are at table with thee. For 11
everyone who exalts himself shall be humbled,
and he who humbles himself shall be exalted."

Also to Social Charity

12 But he also said to him who had invited him,
"When thou givest a dinner or a supper, do
not invite thy friends, or thy brethren, or thy
relatives, or thy rich neighbors, lest perhaps
they also invite thee in return, and a recom-
13 pense be made to thee. But when thou givest
a feast, invite the poor, the crippled, the lame,
14 the blind; and blessed shalt thou be, because
they have nothing to repay thee with; for thou
shalt be repaid at the resurrection of the just."
15 Now when one of those who were at
table with him had heard this, he said to him,
"Blessed is he who shall feast in the kingdom
of God."

Worldlings Ask to Be Excused

16 But he said to him, "A certain man gave a great
17 supper, and he invited many. And he sent his
servant at supper time to tell those invited to
18 come, for everything is now ready. And they
all with one accord began to excuse themselves. The first said to him, 'I have bought a
farm, and I must go out and see it; I pray thee
19 hold me excused.' And another said, 'I have
bought five yoke of oxen, and I am on my way

to try them; I pray thee hold me excused.'
And another said, 'I have married a wife, and 20
therefore I cannot come.'
"And the servant returned, and reported 21
these things to his master. Then the master of
the house was angry and said to his servant,
'Go out quickly into the streets and lanes of
the city, and bring in here the poor, and the
crippled, and the blind, and the lame.' And 22
the servant said, 'Sir, thy order has been carried out, and still there is room.'

God Ever Sending His Messengers

"Then the master said to the servant, 'Go out 23
into the highways and hedges, and make them
come in, so that my house may be filled. For I 24
tell you that none of those who were invited
shall taste of my supper.'"

Christ's disciple must be a cross-bearer

READY for SACRIFICE

MAR. 15 or Sept 14

Luke 14 25-35 NOW GREAT CROWDS were going along with him. And he turned and said to

them, "If anyone comes to me and does not 26
[1]hate his father and mother, and wife and children, and brothers and sisters, yes, and even
his own life, he cannot be my disciple. And he 27
who does not carry his cross and follow me,
cannot be my disciple.

Counting the Cost

"For which of you, wishing to build a tower, 28
does not sit down first and calculate the out-
lays that are necessary, whether he has the
means to complete it? Lest, after he has laid 29
the foundation and is not able to finish, all
who behold begin to mock him, saying, 'This 30
man began to build and was not able to finish!'

Life a Warfare

"Or what king setting out to engage in battle 31
with another king, does not sit down first and
consider whether he is able with ten thousand
men to meet him who with twenty thousand is
coming against him? Or else, whilst the other 32
is yet at a distance, he sends a delegation and

1. *Hate:* i.e., love less. Jesus does not command us to have a feeling of hatred towards our relatives, but teaches that we should pay no attention to their requests if these are detrimental to our spiritual welfare.

33 asks the terms of peace. So, therefore, every
one of you who does not renounce all that he
possesses, cannot be my disciple.

Salt as an Illustration

34 "Salt is good; but if even the salt loses its
35 strength, what shall it be seasoned with? It
is fit neither for the land nor for the manure
heap, but must be thrown out. He who has
ears to hear, let him hear."

"Rejoice with me, because I have found my sheep that was lost"

JOY over SINNER'S PENANCE

MAR. 16 or Sept. 15

Luke 15 1-10 NOW THE publicans and sinners were
drawing near to him to listen to him.
2 And the Pharisees and the Scribes murmured,
saying, "This man welcomes sinners and eats
with them."
3 But he spoke to them this parable, saying,
4 "What man of you having a hundred sheep,
and losing one of them, does not leave the
ninety-nine in the desert, and go after that
5 which is lost, until he finds it? And when he
has found it, he lays it upon his shoulders
rejoicing.
6 "And on coming home he calls together
his friends and neighbors, saying to them,
'Rejoice with me, because I have found my
7 sheep that was lost.' I say to you that, even
so, there will be joy in heaven over one sinner
who repents, more than over ninety-nine just
who have no need of repentance.

How He Seeks the Sinner

8 "Or what woman, having ten drachmas, if she
loses one drachma, does not light a lamp and
sweep the house and search carefully until

she finds it? And when she has found it, she 9
calls together her friends and neighbors, saying, 'Rejoice with me, for I have found the
drachma that I had lost.' Even so, I say to you, 10
there will be joy among the angels of God
over one sinner who repents."

The PRODIGAL SON

MAR. 17 or Sept. 16

Luke 15 AND HE SAID, "A certain man had two
11-32
12 sons. And the younger of them said to
his father, 'Father, give me the share of the
property that falls to me.' And he divided his
means between them.

13 "And not many days later, the younger son
gathered up all his wealth, and took his journey into a far country; and there he squan-
14 dered his fortune in loose living. And after he
had spent all, there came a grievous famine
over that country, and he began himself to
15 suffer want. And he went and joined one of
the citizens of that country, who sent him to
16 his farm to feed swine. And he longed to fill
himself with the pods that the swine were eating, but no one offered to give them to him.

17 "But when he came to himself, he said,
'How many hired men in my father's house
have bread in abundance, while I am perish-
18 ing here with hunger! I will get up and go to
my father, and will say to him, Father, I have

sinned against heaven and before thee. I am 19
no longer worthy to be called thy son; make
me as one of thy hired men.'

Father Welcomes Repentant Son

"And he arose and went to his father. But 20
while he was yet a long way off, his father saw
him and was moved with compassion, and ran
and fell upon his neck and kissed him. And the 21
son said to him, 'Father, I have sinned against
heaven and before thee. I am no longer worthy to be called thy son.' But the father said 22
to his servants, 'Fetch quickly the best robe
and put it on him, and give him a ring for his
finger and sandals for his feet; and bring out 23
the fattened calf and kill it, and let us eat and
make merry; because this my son was dead, 24
and has come to life again; he was lost, and is
found.' And they began to make merry.

Elder Brother Becomes Jealous

"Now his elder son was in the field; and as he 25
came and drew near to the house, he heard
music and dancing. And calling one of the 26
servants he inquired what this meant. And he 27
said to him, 'Thy brother has come, and thy

father has killed the fattened calf, because he
28 has got him back safe.' But he was angered
and would not go in.

"His father, therefore, came out and began
29 to entreat him. But he answered and said to his
father, 'Behold, these many years I have been
serving thee, and have never transgressed one
of thy commands; and yet thou hast never
given me a kid that I might make merry with
30 my friends. But when this thy son comes, who
has devoured his means with harlots, thou hast
killed for him the fattened calf.'

The Father's Heart for Both

31 "But he said to him, 'Son, thou art always with
32 me, and all that is mine is thine; but we were
bound to make merry and rejoice, for this thy
brother was dead, and has come to life; he
was lost, and is found.'"

"You cannot serve God and mammon"

WE, TOO, MUST BE SHREWD

MAR. 18 or Sept. 17

AND HE SAID also to his disciples, "There Luke 16 1-13
was a certain rich man who had a stew-
ard, who was reported to him as squandering
his possessions. And he called him and said to 2
him, 'What is this that I hear of thee? Make an
accounting of thy stewardship, for thou canst
be steward no longer.'

"And the steward said within himself, 3
'What shall I do, seeing that my master is

taking away the stewardship from me? To dig
4 I am not able; to beg I am ashamed. I know
what I shall do, that when I am removed from
my stewardship they may receive me into
5 their houses.' And he summoned each of his
master's debtors and said to the first, 'How
6 much dost thou owe my master?' And he said,
'A hundred jars of oil.' He said to him, 'Take
thy bond and sit down at once and write fifty.'
7 Then he said to another, 'How much dost thou
owe?' He said, 'A hundred kors of wheat.' He
said to him, 'Take thy bond and write eighty.'
8 "And the master commended the [1]unjust
steward, in that he had acted prudently; for
the children of this world, in relation to their
own generation, are more prudent than the
children of the light.

How Material Wealth May Help

9 "And I say to you, make friends for yourselves
with [2]the mammon of wickedness, so that

1. The unjust behavior of the steward is not commended, but the master admires his worldly wisdom in providing for his future.

2. The Greek reading is, "when it shall fail." *Mammon of wickedness:* riches, which often lead men to sin. The disciples of Jesus during their short span of life are to use their wealth to relieve the poor and needy.

when you fail they may receive you into the
everlasting dwellings.
"He who is faithful in a very little thing is 10
faithful also in much; and he who is unjust in a
very little thing is unjust also in much. There- 11
fore, if in the case of the wicked mammon
you have not proved faithful, who will entrust
to you what is true? And if in the case of what 12
belongs to another you have not proved faithful, who will give you what is your own? No 13
servant can serve two masters; for either he
will hate the one and love the other, or else
he will stand by the one and despise the other.
You cannot serve God and mammon."

Lazarus and the rich man

JESUS CONDEMNS DIVORCE

MAR. 19 or Sept. 18

Luke 16 14-31 NOW THE PHARISEES, who were fond of
money, were listening to all these
things, and they began to sneer at him. And
15 he said to them, "You are they who declare
yourselves just in the sight of men, but God
knows your heart; for that which is exalted
in the sight of men is an abomination before
16 God. Until John came, there were the Law
and the Prophets; since then the kingdom of
God is being preached, and everyone is forc-
17 ing his way into it. Yet it is easier for heaven
and earth to pass away than for one tittle of
the Law to fail.

18 "Everyone who puts away his wife and
marries another commits adultery; and he
who marries a woman who has been put away
from her husband commits adultery.

Unmerciful Rich Man in This Life

"There was a certain rich man who used to 19
clothe himself in purple and fine linen, and
who feasted every day in splendid fashion.

And Deserving Poor Man

"And there was a certain poor man, named 20
Lazarus, who lay at his gate, covered with
sores, and longing to be filled with the crumbs 21
that fell from the rich man's table; even the
dogs would come and lick his sores.

Both in the Next Life

"And it came to pass that the poor man died and 22
was borne away by the angels into Abraham's
bosom; but the rich man also died and was
buried in hell. And lifting up his eyes, being in 23
torments, he saw Abraham afar off and Lazarus
in his bosom. And he cried out and said, 'Father 24
Abraham, have pity on me, and send Lazarus
to dip the tip of his finger in water and cool
my tongue, for I am tormented in this flame.'

"But Abraham said to him, 'Son, remember 25
that thou in thy lifetime hast received good
things, and Lazarus in like manner evil things;
but now here he is comforted whereas thou

26 art tormented. And besides all that, between
us and you a great gulf is fixed, so that they
who wish to pass over from this side to you
cannot, and they cannot cross from your side
to us.'

All Have Means to Know and Do

27 "And he said, 'Then, father, I beseech thee
28 to send him to my father's house, for I have
five brothers, that he may testify to them, lest
29 they too come into this place of torments.'
And Abraham said to him, 'They have Moses
and the Prophets, let them hearken to them.'
30 But he answered, 'No, father Abraham, but if
someone from the dead goes to them, they
31 will repent.' But he said to him, 'If they do
not hearken to Moses and the Prophets, they
will not believe even if someone rises from
the dead.'"

LAZARUS TAKEN SICK

MAR. 20 or Sept. 19

NOW A CERTAIN man was sick, Lazarus of John 11
Bethany, the village of Mary and her 1-16

2 sister Martha. Now it was Mary who anointed
the Lord with ointment, and wiped his feet
dry with her hair, whose brother Lazarus was
3 sick. The sisters therefore sent to him, saying,
"Lord, behold, he whom thou lovest is sick."
4 But when Jesus heard this, he said to them,
"This sickness is not unto death, but for the
glory of God, that through it the Son of God
5 may be glorified." Now Jesus loved Martha
6 and her sister Mary, and Lazarus. So when he
heard that he was sick, he remained two more
7 days in the same place. Then afterwards he said
to his disciples, "Let us go again into Judea."
8 The disciples said to him, "Rabbi, just now
the Jews were seeking to stone thee; and dost
9 thou go there again?" Jesus answered, "Are
there not twelve hours in the day? If a man
walks in the day, he does not stumble, because
10 he sees the light of this world. But if he walks
in the night, he stumbles, because the light is
not in him."

Jesus Declares Lazarus Is Dead

11 These things he spoke, and after this he said
to them, "Lazarus, our friend, sleeps. But
12 I go that I may wake him from sleep." His

disciples therefore said, "Lord, if he sleeps,
he will be safe." Now Jesus had spoken of his 13
death, but they thought he was speaking of
the repose of sleep. So then Jesus said to them 14
plainly, "Lazarus is dead; and I rejoice on your 15
account that I was not there, that you may
believe. But let us go to him."

Thomas, who is called the Twin, said 16
therefore to his fellow-disciples, "Let us also
go, that we may die with him."

SORROW of MARTHA and MARY

MAR. 21 or Sept. 20

John 11 17-31 JESUS THEREFORE came and found him already four days in the tomb. Now Bethany was

close to Jerusalem, some fifteen stadia dis- 18
tant. And many of the Jews had come to Mar- 19
tha and Mary, to comfort them on account of
their brother. When, therefore, Martha heard 20
that Jesus was coming, she went to meet him.
But Mary remained at home.

Martha therefore said to Jesus, "Lord, if 21
thou hadst been here my brother would not
have died. But even now I know that whatever 22
thou shalt ask of God, God will give it to thee."

Predicts Resurrection of Lazarus

Jesus said to her, "Thy brother shall rise." 23
Martha said to him, "I know that he will rise 24
at the resurrection, on the last day." Jesus said 25
to her, "I am the resurrection and the life; he
who believes in me, even if he die, shall live;
and whoever lives and believes in me, shall 26
never die. Dost thou believe this?" She said
to him, "Yes, Lord, I believe that thou art the 27
Christ, the Son of God, who hast come into
the world."

The Call of Jesus

And when she had said this, she went away 28
and quietly called Mary her sister, saying,

29 "The Master is here and calls thee." As soon
as she heard this, she rose quickly and came
30 to him, for Jesus had not yet come into the
village, but was still at the place where Martha had met him.

31 When, therefore, the Jews who were with
her in the house and were comforting her,
saw Mary rise up quickly and go out, they
followed her, saying, "She is going to the tomb
to weep there."

At TOMB of LAZARUS
MAR. 22 or Sept. 21

WHERE, THEREFORE, Mary came where Jesus was, and saw him, she fell at his feet, and said to him, "Lord, if thou hadst been here, my brother would not have died." John 11 32-46

33 When, therefore, Jesus saw her weeping, and
the Jews who had come with her weeping, he
groaned in spirit and was troubled, and said,
34 "Where have you laid him?" They said to him,
"Lord, come and see."

Jesus Weeps

35-36 And Jesus wept. The Jews therefore said,
37 "See how he loved him." But some of them
said, "Could not he who opened the eyes of
the blind, have caused that this man should
not die?"
38 Jesus therefore, again groaning in himself,
came to the tomb. Now it was a cave, and a
39 stone was laid against it. Jesus said, "Take away
the stone." Martha, the sister of him who was
dead, said to him, "Lord, by this time he is
already decayed, for he is dead four days."

Belief Necessary to See God's Power

40 Jesus said to her, "Have I not told thee that
if thou believe thou shalt behold the glory of
41 God?" They therefore removed the stone. And
Jesus, raising his eyes, said, "Father, I give thee
42 thanks that thou hast heard me. Yet I knew
that thou always hearest me; but because of

the people who stand round, I spoke, that they
may believe that thou hast sent me." When he 43
had said this, he cried out with a loud voice,
"Lazarus, come forth!"

Lazarus Raised from the Dead

And at once he who had been dead came 44
forth, bound feet and hands with bandages,
and his face was tied up with a cloth. Jesus
said to them, "Unbind him, and let him go."

Many therefore of the Jews who had come 45
to Mary, and had seen what he did, believed
in him. But some of them went away to the 46
Pharisees, and told them the things that Jesus
had done.

The evil of scandal

RULERS PLAN to SLAY JESUS

MAR. 23 or Sept. 22

John 11 47-56 THE CHIEF PRIESTS and the Pharisees therefore gathered together a council, and
said, "What are we doing? for this man is
48 working many signs. If we let him alone as
he is, all will believe in him, and the Romans
will come and take away both our place and
our nation."

49 But one of them, Caiphas, being high priest
that year, said to them, "You know nothing at

all; nor do you reflect that it is expedient for 50
us that one man die for the people, instead of
the whole nation perishing." This, however, he 51
said not of himself; but being high priest that
year, he [1]prophesied that Jesus was to die for
the nation; and not only for the nation, but 52
that he might gather into one the children of
God who were scattered abroad. So from that 53
day forth their plan was to put him to death.

Jesus Withdraws to Safety

Jesus therefore no longer went about openly 54
among the Jews, but withdrew to the district
near the desert, to a town called Ephrem; and
there he stayed with his disciples.

Now the Passover of the Jews was at hand; 55
and many from the country went up to Jerusalem before the Passover, in order to purify
themselves. And they were looking for Jesus. 56
And as they stood in the temple they were
saying to one another, "What do you think,
that he is not coming to the feast?" But the
chief priests and Pharisees had given orders

1. Although Caiphas saw only the present, temporal significance of his words, he was led to make the statement by God who intended the higher sense. It was not necessary that Caiphas realize the prophetic character of his counsel.

that, if anyone knew where he was, he should
report it, so that they might seize him.

Avoid Scandal; Practise Charity

Luke 17 And he said to his disciples, "It is impossible
1-4 that scandals should not come; but woe to
2 him through whom they come! It were better for him if a millstone were hung about his
neck and he were thrown into the sea, than
that he should cause one of these little ones
to sin.
3 "Take heed to yourselves. If thy brother
4 sin, rebuke him; and if he repent, forgive him.
And if seven times in the day he sin against
thee, and seven times in the day turn back to
thee, saying, 'I repent,' forgive him."

"Were not the ten made clean?"

LORD, INCREASE OUR FAITH!

MAR. 24 or Sept. 23

AND THE APOSTLES said to the Lord, "Increase Luke 17
our faith." And the Lord answered, "If 5-19 6

you have faith even like a mustard seed, you will say to this mulberry tree, 'Be uprooted and be planted in the sea,' and it will obey you.

We Are Unprofitable Servants

7 "But which of you is there, having a servant
plowing or tending sheep, who will say to
him on his return from the field, 'Come at
8 once and recline at table!' But will he not say
to him, 'Prepare my supper, and gird thyself
and serve me till I have eaten and drunk; and
afterwards thou thyself shalt eat and drink'?
9 Does he thank that servant for doing what he
10 commanded him? I do not think so. Even so
you also, when you have done everything that
was commanded you, say, 'We are unprofit-
able servants; we have done what it was our
duty to do.'"

Jesus Heals Ten Lepers

11 And it came to pass as he was going to Jerusalem, that he was passing between Samaria
12 and Galilee. And as he was entering a certain village, there met him ten lepers, who
13 stood afar off and lifted up their voice, crying,
14 "Jesus, master, have pity on us." And when he

saw them he said, "Go, show yourselves to the
priests." And it came to pass as they were on
their way, that they were made clean.

Only One Expresses Gratitude

But one of them, seeing that he was made 15
clean, returned, with a loud voice glorifying
God, and he fell on his face at his feet, giving 16
thanks; and he was a Samaritan.
But Jesus answered and said, "Were not 17
the ten made clean? But where are the nine?
Has no one been found to return and give 18
glory to God except this foreigner?" And he 19
said to him, "Arise, go thy way, for thy faith
has saved thee."

GOD'S JUDGMENT

MAR. 25 or Sept. 24

Luke 17 20-37 AND ON BEING asked by the Pharisees,
"When is the kingdom of God com-
ing?" he answered and said to them, "The
21 kingdom of God comes unawares. Neither
will they say, 'Behold, here it is,' or 'Behold,
there it is.' [1]For behold, the kingdom of God
is within you."

---

1. *Within you:* i.e., in the midst of you and within your power to reach through faith, justice and love. It has already begun and the Pharisees might recognize it if they had eyes to see and ears to hear. The Messias is already reigning.

Beware of False Christs

But he said to the disciples, "The days will 22
come when you will long to see one day of
the Son of Man, and will not see it. And they 23
will say to you, 'Behold, here he is; behold,
there he is.' Do not go, nor follow after them. 24
For as the lightning when it lightens flashes
from one end of the sky to the other, so will
the Son of Man be in his day. But first he must 25
suffer many things and be rejected by this
generation.

Unbelievers Will Be Punished

"And as it came to pass in the days of Noe, 26
even so will it be in the days of the Son of
Man. They were eating and drinking, they 27
were marrying and giving in marriage, until
the day when Noe entered the ark, and the
flood came and destroyed them all. Or as it 28
came to pass in the days of Lot. They were
eating and drinking, they were buying and
selling, they were planting and building; but 29
on the day that Lot went out from Sodom, it
rained fire and brimstone from heaven and
destroyed them all.

God's Judgment Will Come Suddenly

30 "In the same wise will it be on the day that the
31 Son of Man is revealed. In that hour let him
who is on the housetop and his goods in the
house, not go down to take them away; and
likewise let him who is in the field not turn
32-33 back. Remember Lot's wife. Whoever tries
to save his life will lose it; and whoever loses
34 it will preserve it. I say to you, on that night
there will be two on one bed; one will be
35 taken, and the other will be left. Two women
will be grinding together; one will be taken,
and the other will be left. Two men will be
in the field; one will be taken, and the other
will be left."

36 And they answered and said to him,
37 "Where, Lord?" He said to them, "Wherever
the body is, there will the eagles be gathered
together."

Humility versus pride

PRAY PERSEVERINGLY

MAB. 26 or Sept. 25

AND HE also told them a parable—that Luke 18
they must always pray and not lose 1-14

2 heart—saying, "There was a judge in a cer-
3 tain town who did not fear God and did not
respect man. Now there was a certain widow
in that town, and she kept coming to him,
saying, 'Do me justice against my adversary.'
4 And he would not for a long time. But afterwards he said within himself, 'Although I
5 do not fear God, nor even respect man, yet
because this widow bothers me, I will do
her justice, lest by her continual coming she
finally wear me out.'"
6 And the Lord said, "Hear what the unjust
7 judge says; and will not God avenge his elect,
who cry to him day and night? And will he
8 be slow to act in their case? I tell you that he
will avenge them quickly. Yet when the Son of
Man comes, will he find, do you think, faith
on the earth?"

Be Not Self-righteous

9 But he spoke this parable also to some who
trusted in themselves as being just and
10 despised others. "Two men went up to the
temple to pray, the one a Pharisee and the
11 other a publican. The Pharisee stood and
began to pray thus within himself:

"'O God, I thank thee that I am not like the
rest of men, robbers, dishonest, adulterers,
or even like this publican. I fast twice a week; 12
I pay tithes of all that I possess.' But the pub- 13
lican, standing afar off, would not so much
as lift up his eyes to heaven, but kept striking
his breast, saying, 'O God, be merciful to me
the sinner!'

"I tell you, this man went back to his home 14
justified rather than the other; for everyone
who exalts himself shall be humbled, and he
who humbles himself shall be exalted."

MARRIAGE INDISSOLUBLE

MAR. 27 or Sept. 26

Matt. 19 AND IT CAME TO PASS when Jesus had
1 brought these words to a close, that he
departed from Galilee and came to the district
Mark 10 of Judea beyond the Jordan; and crowds again
1 flocked to him. And as had been his custom,
Matt. 19 he again began to teach them, and he cured
2-3 them there. And there came to him some
Pharisees, testing him, and saying, "Is it lawful
for a man to put away his wife for any cause?"
Mark 10 But he answered and said to them, "What
3-4 4 did Moses command you?" [1]They said, "Moses

1. *Moses permitted us . . . to put her away:* the Mosaic Law permitted divorce for certain causes. In the verses immediately following here, Jesus abrogates divorce and declares the indissolubility of marriage.

permitted us to write a notice of dismissal,
and to put her away."
But he answered and said to them, "Have Matt. 19
you not read that the Creator, from the begin- 4-9
ning, made them male and female, and said,
'For this cause a man shall leave his father and 5
mother, and cleave to his wife, and the two
shall become one flesh'? Therefore now they 6
are no longer two, but one flesh. What therefore God has joined together, let no man put
asunder."
They said to him, "Why then did Moses 7
command to give a written notice of dismissal, and to put her away?" He said to them, 8
"Because Moses, by reason of the hardness of
your heart, permitted you to put away your
wives; but it was not so from the beginning.
And I say to you, that whoever puts away 9
his wife, except for immorality, and marries
another, commits adultery; and he who marries a woman who has been put away commits
adultery."
And in the house, his disciples again asked Mark 10
him concerning this. And he said to them, 10-12 11
"Whoever puts away his wife and marries
another, commits adultery against her; and if 12

the wife puts away her husband, and marries another, she commits adultery."

Excellence of Virginity

Matt. 19 10-12 His disciples said to him, "If the case of a
man with his wife is so, it is not expedient
11 to marry." And he said, "Not all can accept
this teaching; but those to whom it has been
12 given. For there are eunuchs who were born
so from their mother's womb; and there are
eunuchs who were made so by men; and there
are eunuchs who have made themselves so for
the sake of the kingdom of heaven. Let him
accept it who can."

JESUS with CHILDREN

MAR. 28 or Sept. 27

LITTLE CHILDREN were brought to him then Matt. 19 13
that he might lay his hands on them and Mark 10 13-16

pray; but the disciples rebuked those who
14 brought them. But when Jesus saw them, he
was indignant, and said to them, "Let the little
children come to me, and do not hinder them,
15 for of such is the kingdom of God. Amen I say
to you, whoever does not accept the kingdom
of God as a little child will not enter into it."
16 And he put his arms about them, and laying
his hands upon them, he began to bless them.

Discusses Eternal Life with Young Man

Matt. 19 15 *And* he departed from that place. †And as he
was going forth on his journey, a certain man
running up fell upon his knees before him,
Matt. 19 16-17 and asked him, "Good Master, what good
work shall I do to have eternal life?" He said
17 to him, "Why dost thou ask me about what is
Luke 18 19 good? Why dost thou call me good? No one
is good but only God.

Who Observed Commandments

Matt. 19 17-18 "But if thou wilt enter into life, keep
18 the commandments." He said to him,
Mark 10 19 "Which?" And Jesus said, "Thou knowest the

† Mark 10, 17

commandments: Thou shalt not commit adultery, Thou shalt not kill, Thou shalt not steal, Thou shalt not bear false witness, Thou shalt
not defraud, Honor thy father and mother, Matt. 19
and, Thou shalt love thy neighbor as thyself." 19-20
The young man said to him, "All these I 20
have kept; what is yet wanting to me?"

"Come, Follow Me"

And Jesus, looking upon him, loved him, and Mark 10
said to him, "One thing is lacking to thee; go, 21
sell whatever thou hast, and give to the poor, and thou shalt have treasure in heaven; and
come, follow me." But when the young man Matt. 19
heard the saying, he went away sad, for he had 22
great possessions.

DANGER of RICHES

MAR. 29 or Sept. 28

Luke 18 24 Mark 10 23-28 BUT JESUS, seeing him become sad said to his disciples, "With what difficulty will

they who have riches enter the kingdom of
God!" But the disciples were amazed at his 24
word. But Jesus again addressed them, saying,
"Children, with what difficulty will they who
trust in riches enter the kingdom of God! [1]It 25
is easier for a camel to pass through the eye
of a needle, than for a rich man to enter the
kingdom of God."

But they were astonished the more, saying 26
among themselves, "Who then can be saved?"
And looking upon them, Jesus said, "With 27
men it is impossible, but not with God; for
all things are possible with God."

Rewards for Following Jesus

Peter began to say to him, "Behold, we have 28
left all and followed thee; what then shall we Matt. 19 27-29
have?" And Jesus said to them, "Amen I say to 28
you that you who have followed me, in the
regeneration when the Son of Man shall sit on
the throne of his glory, shall also sit on twelve
thrones, judging the twelve tribes of Israel.

1. Our Lord does not condemn riches as essentially evil. He expresses in a paradoxical way the idea that it is very difficult for a rich man to be saved; v. 27 shows that it is not impossible with the help of God.

29 "And everyone who has left house, or
Mark 10 brothers, or sisters, or father, or mother, or
29-31 wife, or children, or lands, for my name's
30 sake, and for the gospel's sake, . . . shall . . .
receive now in the present time a hun-
dredfold as much, houses, and brothers,
and sisters, and mothers, and children, and
lands—along with persecutions, and in the
31 age to come life everlasting. But many who
are first now will be last, and many who are
last now will be first."

PARABLE of the WORKERS

MAR. 30 or Sept. 29

"FOR THE kingdom of heaven is like a Matt. 20 1-16
householder who went out early in
the morning to hire laborers for his vineyard.
[1]And having agreed with the laborers for a 2
denarius a day, he sent them into his vineyard.

1. The laborers in the vineyard all receive the same reward, a denarius. God is master of His gifts and His grace may make one who has served Him only for a short time as worthy of supernatural rewards as one who has borne the burden of the day and the heat.

3 And about the third hour, he went out and
saw others standing in the market place idle;
4 and he said to them, 'Go you also into the
vineyard, and I will give you whatever is just.'
5 "So they went. And again he went out
about the sixth, and about the ninth hour, and
6 did as before. But about the eleventh hour he
went out and found others standing about,
and he said to them, 'Why do you stand here
7 all day idle?' They said to him, 'Because no
man has hired us.' He said to them, 'Go you
also into the vineyard.'

Workers Receive Their Pay

8 "But when evening had come, the owner of
the vineyard said to his steward, 'Call the
laborers, and pay them their wages, beginning
9 from the last even to the first.' Now when they
of the eleventh hour came, they received each
10 a denarius. And when the first in their turn
came, they thought that they would receive
more; but they also received each his denarius.

Murmurings

11 "And on receiving it, they began to murmur
12 against the householder, saying, 'These last

have worked a single hour, and thou hast put
them on a level with us, who have borne the
burden of the day's heat.'

Reply of Divine Employer

"But answering one of them, he said, 'Friend, 13
I do thee no injustice; didst thou not agree
with me for a denarius? Take what is thine and 14
go; I choose to give to this last even as to thee.
Have I not a right to do what I choose? Or art 15
thou envious because I am generous?' Even 16
so the last shall be first, and the first last; for
many are called, but few are chosen."

PROPHESIES HIS SUFFERINGS

MAR. 31 or Sept. 30

Mark 10 THEY WERE now on their way, going up to
32 Jerusalem; and Jesus was walking on in
front of them, and they were in dismay, and
those who followed were afraid. And again
taking the Twelve, he began to tell them what
would happen to him.

Luke 18 "Behold, we are going up to Jerusalem,
31-32 and all things that have been written by the
prophets concerning the Son of Man will be
32 accomplished. For he †will be betrayed to the
chief priests and the Scribes; and they will
condemn him to death, and will deliver him
34 to the Gentiles; and they will mock him, and
Luke 18
33-34 spit upon him, and scourge him; and after
they have scourged him, they will put him to
death; and on the third day he will rise again."

† Mark 10, 33-34

And they understood none of these things 34
and this saying was hidden from them, neither did they get to know the things that were
being said.

Worldly Ambition of Mother

And James and John, the sons of Zebedee, Mark 10
came to him, saying, "Master, we want thee 35-36
to do for us whatever we ask." But he said to 36
them, "What do you want me to do for you?"
Then the mother of the sons of Zebedee Matt. 20
came to him with her sons; and worship- 20 21
ping, she made a request of him. He said to 21
her, "What dost thou want?" She said to him,
"Command that these my two sons may sit,
one at thy right hand and one at thy left hand,
in thy kingdom."
And they said, "Grant to us that we may sit, Mark 10
one at thy right hand and the other at thy left 37-39
hand, in thy glory." But Jesus said to them, "You 38
do not know what you are asking for. Can you
drink of the cup of which I drink, or be baptized with the baptism with which I am to be
baptized?" And they said to him, "We can." 39
And Jesus said to them, "Of the cup that I
drink, you shall drink; and with the baptism

with which I am to be baptized, you shall be
Matt. 20 baptized; but as for sitting at my right hand
23 and at my left, that is not mine to give you,
but it belongs to those for whom it has been
prepared by my Father."

Lesson in Humility and Service

Mark 10 41-45 And when the ten heard this, they were at
42 first indignant at James and John. But Jesus
called them and said to them, "You know that
those who are regarded as rulers among the
Gentiles lord it over them, and their great
43 men exercise authority over them. But it is
not so among you. On the contrary, whoever
wishes to become great shall be your servant;
44 and whoever wishes to be first among you
45 shall be the slave of all; for the Son of Man
also has not come to be served but to serve,
and to give his life as a ransom for many."

"TRYING to SEE JESUS"

APR. 1 or Oct. 1

AND HE entered and was passing through Luke 19 1-10
Jericho. And behold there was a man 2
named Zacchæus; and he was a leading publican, and he was rich. And he was trying to see 3
Jesus, who he was, but could nct, on account
of the crowd, because he was small of stature. So he ran on ahead and climbed up into 4
a sycamore tree to see him, for he was going
to pass that way.

5 And when Jesus came to the place, he
looked up and saw him, and said to him,
"Zacchæus, make haste and come down; for I
must stay in thy house today."

Seeing Jesus in the Poor

6 And he made haste and came down, and wel-
7 comed him joyfully. And upon seeing it all
8 began to murmur, saying, "He has gone to be
the guest of a man who is a sinner." But Zacchæus stood and said to the Lord, "Behold,
Lord, I give one-half of my possessions to the
poor, and if I have defrauded anyone of anything, I restore it fourfold."
9 Jesus said to him, "Today salvation has
come to this house, since he, too, is a son of
10 Abraham. For the Son of Man came to seek
and to save what was lost."

"That I May See": Faith Rewarded

Mark 10 46-52 And as he was leaving Jericho with his disciples and a very great crowd, Bartimeus, a
blind man, the son of Timeus, was sitting by
47 the wayside, begging. And hearing that it was
Jesus of Nazareth, he began to cry out and
say, "Jesus, Son of David, have mercy on me!"

My Meditation on the Gospel

And many angrily tried to silence him. But 48
he cried out all the louder, "Son of David,
have mercy on me!" Then Jesus stopped and 49
commanded that he should be called. And
they called the blind man and said to him,
"Take courage. Get up, he is calling thee." And 50
throwing off his cloak, he sprang to his feet
and came to him. And Jesus addressed him, 51
saying, "What wouldst thou have me do for
thee?"

And the blind man said to him, "Rabboni,
that I may see." And Jesus said to him, "Go 52
thy way, thy faith has saved thee." And at once
he received his sight, and followed him along
the road.

PARABLE of GOLD PIECES

APR. 2 or Oct. 2

Luke 19 11-28 NOW AS THEY were listening to these
things, he went on to speak a parable,
because he was near Jerusalem, and because
they thought that the kingdom of God was
going to appear immediately.

"Trade till I Come"

12 He said therefore, "A certain nobleman went
into a far country to obtain for himself a king-
13 dom and then return. And having summoned
ten of his servants, he gave them ten gold
pieces and said to them, 'Trade till I come.'
14 "But his citizens hated him; and they sent a
delegation after him to say, 'We do not wish

this man to be king over us.' And it came to 15
pass when he had returned, after receiving
the kingdom, that he ordered the servants to
whom he had given the money to be called to
him in order that he might learn how much
each one had made by trading.

Industrious Servants Rewarded

"And the first came, saying, 'Lord, thy gold 16
piece has earned ten gold pieces.' And he said 17
to him, 'Well done, good servant; because
thou hast been faithful in a very little, thou
shalt have authority over ten towns.'

"Then the second came, saying, 'Lord, thy 18
gold piece has made five gold pieces.' And he 19
said to him, 'Be thou also over five towns.'

"And another came, saying, 'Lord, behold 20
thy gold piece, which I have kept laid up in
a napkin; for I feared thee, because thou art 21
a stern man. Thou takest up what thou didst
not lay down, and thou reapest what thou
didst not sow.'

Slothful Servant Punished

"He said to him, 'Out of thy own mouth I judge 22
thee, thou wicked servant. Thou knewest that

I am a stern man, taking up what I did not lay
23 down and reaping what I did not sow. Why,
then, didst thou not put my money in a bank,
so that I on my return might have gotten it
24 with interest?' And he said to the bystanders,
'Take away the gold piece from him, and give
25 it to him who has the ten gold pieces.' But they
said to him, 'Lord, he has ten gold pieces.'
26 "I say to you that to everyone who has shall
be given; but from him who does not have,
even that which he has shall be taken away.

Enemies Punished More Severely

27 "But as for these my enemies, who did not
want me to be king over them, bring them
here and slay them in my presence."
28 And when he had said these things, he
went ahead, going up to Jerusalem.

ANONTING at BETHANY

APR. 3 or Oct. 3

JESUS THEREFORE, six days before the Pass- John 12 1-3
over, came to Bethany where Lazarus,
whom Jesus had raised to life, had died. And 2
they made him a supper there; and Martha

served, while Lazarus was one of those reclining at table with him.
3 Mary therefore took a pound of ointment,
genuine nard of great value, and anointed
the feet of Jesus, and with her hair wiped
his feet dry;†and breaking the alabaster jar,
she poured it on his head ‡as he reclined at
table.*And the house was filled with the odor
of the ointment.

Jesus Rebukes Judas

4 Then one of his disciples, Judas Iscariot, he
5 who was about to betray him, said, "Why
was this ointment not sold for three hun-
6 dred denarii, and given to the poor?" Now he
said this, not that he cared for the poor, but
because he was a thief, and holding the purse,
Mark 14 6-9 used to take what was put in it. But Jesus said,
"Let her be. Why do you trouble her? She has
done me a good turn.

Her Charity Memorialized

7 "For the poor you have always with you, and
whenever you want you can do good to them;
8 but you do not always have me. She has done

† Mark 14, 3
‡ Matt. 26, 7
* John 12, 3-6

what she could; she has anointed my body
in preparation for burial. Amen I say to you, 9
wherever in the whole world this gospel is
preached, this also that she has done shall be
told in memory of her."

Crowds Believe Because of Lazarus

Now the great crowd of the Jews learned that John 12
he was there; and they came, not only because 9-11
of Jesus, but that they might see Lazarus,
whom he had raised from the dead. But the 10
chief priests planned to put Lazarus to death
also. For on his account many of the Jews 11
began to leave them and to believe in Jesus.

PART III

+++ The Passion and

The Prelude of the Passion

Holy Week

palm sunday:
triumphal entry into jerusalem

monday:
the barren fig tree

tuesday:
the last parables and prophecies

wednesday:
the treachery of judas

thursday:
the last supper
the last discourses of jesus

Death of Christ + + +

The Passion and Death

a night of agony

jesus goes to meet judas

jesus accused falsely

jesus now silent

barabbas or jesus

jesus scourged, crowned

sentenced to crucifixion

jesus crucified

jesus is blasphemed

his last words

christ's side is pierced

jesus buried

"Behold, thy king comes to thee, meek and seated upon an ass, and upon a colt, the foal of a beast of burden."

PREPARING TRIUMPHAL ENTRY

APR. 4 or Oct. 4

AND WHEN they drew near to Jerusalem, Matt. 21
and came to Bethphage, on the Mount 1-2
of Olives, then Jesus sent two disciples, saying
to them, "Go into the village opposite you, 2
and immediately on entering it you will find Luke 19 30
a colt of an ass tied, upon which no man ever
yet sat; loose it and bring it.

"And if anyone say to you, 'What are you Mark 11
doing? Why are you loosing it?' you shall 3 Luke 19
answer him thus, 'Because the Lord has need 31
of it.' †And immediately he will send it here."

And they who were sent went away and Luke 19
found the colt standing, ‡tied at a door out- 32
side in the street.

And as they were loosing the colt, its own- Luke 19
ers said to them, "Why are you loosing the 33-34
colt?" And they replied, "Because the Lord has 34
need of it." And they let them go. And they Mark 11 6-7
brought the colt to Jesus, and throwing their Luke 19
cloaks over the colt they set Jesus on it, *and 35
he sat upon it.

---

† Mark 11, 3
‡ Mark 11, 4
* Mark 11, 7

Prophecy Now Fulfilled

Matt. 21 Now this was done that what was spoken
4-5 5 through the prophet might be fulfilled, "Tell
the daughter of Sion: Behold, thy king comes
to thee, meek and seated upon an ass, and
upon a colt, the foal of a beast of burden."

John 12 These things his disciples did not at first
16 understand. But when Jesus was glorified,
then they remembered that these things were
written about him, and that they had done
these things to him.

Jesus weeps over Jerusalem

The CROWDS ACCLAIM JESUS

APR. 5 or Oct. 5

AND AS HE WENT, †most of the crowd Luke 19
spread their cloaks while others were 36

† Matt. 21, 8

upon the road, while others were cutting
branches from the trees, and strewing them
Luke 19 on the road. And when he was drawing near,
37 being by now at the descent of the Mount of
Olives, the whole company of the disciples
began to rejoice and to praise God with a loud
voice for all the miracles that they had seen.

Mark 11 And those who went before him, and
9 those who followed, kept crying out, saying,
‡"Hosanna to the Son of David! Blessed is he
who comes in the name of the Lord! *Blessed
is the kingdom of our father David that comes!
**Peace in heaven, and glory in the highest!"

Envy of the Rulers

John 12 The crowd therefore, which was with him
17-19 when he called Lazarus from the tomb and
raised him from the dead, bore witness to
18 him. And the reason why the crowd also went
to meet him was that they heard that he had
19 worked this sign. The Pharisees therefore said
among themselves, "Do you see that we avail

‡ Matt. 21, 9
* Mark 11, 10
** Luke 19, 38

My Meditation on the Gospel

By

Rev. James E. Sullivan

ILLUSTRATED

1962

Msgr. Austin P. Bennett. JCD, P.A.
Director of the

CONFRATERNITY OF THE PRECIOUS BLOOD

5300 FORT HAMILTON PARKWAY, BROOKLYN, N.Y. 11219
102

NIHIL OBSTAT:
THOMAS W. SMIDDY, S. T. L.
Censor Librorum

IMPRIMATUR:
✠ BRYAN IOSEPHUS McENTEGART, D. D., LL. D.
Episcopus Bruklyniensis

Bruklyni,
Die xxii maii, 1962.

Printed and bound in India.

Foreword

THE Confraternity of the Precious Blood is privileged to add another volume to its little spiritual library for the Catholic family.

"MY Meditation on the Gospel" offers short but fruitful reflections on the life and teachings of Christ. "Let us meditate on the Gospels," urges Pope John XXIII. "Amidst the confusion of so many human words, the Gospel is the only voice that enlightens, draws, comforts, quenches thirst."

THIS BOOK must be read not only with the head but with the heart. We must think and pray. To understand the Gospel fully, we must live the Gospel. To learn Christ we must live Christ.

(Rt. Rev. Msgr.) Joseph B. Frey

Feast of St. Joseph the Worker

May 1, 1962.

How to Use this Book

IN THE Gospels the Holy Spirit has painted for us a perfect Heart — the Heart of Christ the King! When we study His words and actions, and ponder over them in meditation, we get an insight into His ideals, His motives, His sense of values — His Heart!

This is the purpose of these meditations. In the first point we use our *memory* to recall what Jesus did and said, as though we were back in His time and standing with the crowd. In the second point we use our *understanding* to grasp the ideal that He is teaching in the particular incident. And in the third we use our *will* and our *affections* to relish what He holds dear, to despise what He despises — to achieve, finally, a union of hearts.

In using the meditations it is of *prime importance* that we first read carefully the texts from the Gospels. They are the inspired and the truest portrait of Jesus. We must never get away from them. A particular meditation may not suggest the lesson we need at the moment. But a prayerful reading of the Gospel will never fail to give us a fresh and inspiring insight into His Mind and Heart. The Gospel passages are given with each meditation.

Prologue

THE WORD MADE FLESH

John 1:18

1. *The Infant Jesus lying in a manger.*
2. *The grace, my Lord, to love the Gospel story with all my heart.*

IN THIS introduction to his Gospel St. John the Apostle sounds a chord of haunting sadness which occurs again and again in the great symphony of Sacred Scripture: God loving man so much; man appreciating God so little. In the beginning God gave Adam and Eve a garden of paradise with untold joys and the promise of heaven. And Adam and Eve chose the forbidden fruit in complete defiance. During the wanderings in the desert God sent the Chosen People food from heaven, water from the rock, guided them by day and night, and in their blindness they longed for the luxury and sin of Egypt and raised their golden idol. And now that God sent His own Son into the world, it seemed to be the same story: "the world was made by Him and the world knew Him not. He came unto His own and His own received Him not."

AND YET, dear Lord, interwoven with that sad theme of man's ingratitude is one happy chord. Some men will accept God's love. And O, my King, the reward! "To as many as received Him, He gave the power of becoming the sons of God." It seems that all God wants is a response, a return of love. And then His gifts flow in torrents. He gives back sanctifying grace, making men His adopted sons. And as they cooperate with His grace, He gives them more and more. "Of His fulness we have all received, grace for grace."

JESUS, my King, as much as I hate to admit it, have I not been among the ungrateful ones? In these pages of the Gospel I have You as You came unto Your own—as You talked and acted and felt. You, the Son of God! I should love every page of it—every word. I should love to pore over it and find You there, thrill to listen to Your every word! And yet, my King, the Gospel has been a closed book for me. I listen to a little part of it at Sunday Mass—and that's the end of it! You came unto Your own, and Your own received You not.

Dear Jesus, I resolve here and now to change. I promise with all my heart to read every day part of the Gospel story—to read it and meditate upon it. Come again unto Your own, my Saviour, and let me receive You!

ANNUNCIATION OF THE BIRTH OF THE BAPTIST—FAITH

Luke 1:5-25

1. *Zachary standing dumbstruck before the angel Gabriel.*
2. *The grace of deep faith to believe even when truths are buried in mystery.*

ZACHARY was overjoyed when he was chosen to offer the incense at the morning sacrifice. A chance like this might come only once in a lifetime. A large concourse of people were assembled. All of Jerusalem stopped for a moment to unite in spirit with the morning service to God. Then, accepting the golden bowl of incense, Zachary went through the outer curtain and entered the Holy Place. It seemed dark at first—except for the flickering light from the seven-branched candlestick. There at the center before the Holy of Holies was the golden altar of incense. He approached it and spread the incense over the glowing embers and enjoyed the sweet odor that ascended to God. And then the startling vision, the bright glow, the handsome young man in white, the tremendous message: "Your petition has been heard ... Elizabeth shall bear thee a son." And such a son, the one promised by Malachias 400 years before to usher in the Messianic Age in the spirit and power of Elias, "to prepare for the Lord a perfect people." Doubts crept into Zachary's heart. He was so old, Elizabeth also. "How shall I know this? For I am an old man and my wife is advanced in years?" The stern rebuke from the angel and a punishment—Zachary could no longer speak!

DEAR MASTER, Zachary was a good priest and had faith. He even prayed for a son. But his faith was weak. He prayed for a son because that was the thing to do, but he never really believed his prayer would be answered. Both he and Elizabeth were old and that's all there was to it. How he had forgotten Abraham and Sara, and what God said to Sara when she laughed at conceiving in her old age: "Is anything impossible with God?" How he had forgotten Anna, the mother of Samuel. Or perhaps he just thought that those things only happened to saints and God would not work any special favors for him. How wrong he was, dear Master! The Father loves us all personally, and sends us what is best for us, even if it seems impossible to us!

DEAR LORD, I'm very much like Zachary. I'm almost afraid to ask any favors in prayer for fear that I won't get them and my weak faith will be hurt even more. I, too, have the notion that only the saints get special care. I know that I'm wrong; help me to realize it, dear Jesus! Make my faith so strong that when things look most impossible, then I'll love and trust and believe even more. Let me say often: "O, my God, is anything impossible for You?"

ANNUNCIATION OF THE BIRTH OF JESUS—TRUE GREATNESS

Luke 1:26-38

1. *The beautiful picture of Gabriel, an archangel, saluting the little girl who was about to become his Queen.*
2. *The grace to seek to be holy, perfectly resigned to God's Holy Will.*

THE MOST wonderful part of the great drama of redemption was about to begin, and the scene was so humble! A little girl some thirteen years of age knelt in prayer in a simple, one-room house in the little village of Nazareth. God was choosing a mother for the human nature He was about to assume, and He sent Gabriel not to the palace of the

Empress at Rome or to the wealthy villas along the Tiber, not to the sophisticated ladies of Athens or the richly dressed women of Egypt. It was to the little girl in the one-room cottage.

Mary was wide-eyed in amazement that a messenger from heaven should come to her. She was more startled when he told her that she was to be a mother, she who was the wife of Joseph but who had taken a vow of virginity. She asked what God wanted her to do, and Gabriel told her about the virgin birth. He was pleased—this archangel who had to face a Zachary who doubted about a natural birth—he was pleased, in telling Mary things more wondrous by far, to hear no doubts but only: "Behold the handmaid of the Lord. Be it done unto me according to thy word."

DEAR LORD, You teach us with great clarity in this scene that what counts with You is not riches or power or even great deeds —what counts with You is being a good person. Mary was chosen above all others because with Your grace she was the most beautiful soul. Being holy, her very presence made the little house at Nazareth a palace more fitting for You and more beautiful than any in the world. Her purity was more beau-

tiful than marble floors; her patience and gentleness gave an odor more delightful than incense; her charity gave a warmth and a welcome more sincere and more true than the cheers of a thousand servants.

O MY KING, when will I come to realize that to please You I need only be a holy person. I don't have to erect great buildings or discover new vaccines. I don't have to win thunderous ovations at Carnegie Hall, or even win great numbers of converts—for all success in drawing hearts comes from Your grace. What I must do is to go along each day, doing my work as best I can and trusting completely that You will do the rest. I must welcome Your Holy Will as Mary did, in all the messages You send by Your other angels—the persons I meet and work and live with, the things that happen to me, and even the mistakes I make. Then I shall be holy and pleasing to You and happy.

THE VISITATION— LOVE AND SYMPATHY OF MARY

Luke 1 : 39-56

1. *Mary riding on a donkey along the banks of the Jordan, a beautiful smile on her face.*
2. *The grace of knowing and loving your ready and motherly sympathy, my Mother.*

ONCE the angel Gabriel had departed from her, Mary realized that her elderly cousin Elizabeth would need help during these last three months of her pregnancy. So Mary got permission from her parents to make the long journey to Judea. She probably went along with one of the caravans, her father Joachim making the arrangements. The three-day journey was a most joyous one for her. She enjoyed the countryside, was thrilled by the sight of the Holy City with its magnificent Temple, was overwhelmed at God's goodness in making her a temple—for He was more truly present in her spotless womb than He was there in the very Holy of Holies. She must have uttered the Magnificat many times to ease the pressures of joy on her heart. At Ain Karim she cared for Elizabeth, did all the heavy work, suffered the pain with Elizabeth and rejoiced in her joy when John was born.

DEAR Blessed Lady, your heart was unspeakably generous. Your first thought once the angel departed was not for yourself or the dignity conferred on you. Your first thought was for Elizabeth. Elizabeth was old and needed help, so your heart went out to her. There was no one who suffered but that you felt the pain; no one that rejoiced but that you felt very glad. You were all love and sympathy and goodness. To think of yourself and your own Child never entered your mind. The journey furnished you time to satisfy your thirst to praise Him for His goodness. The time at Ain Karim satisfied your longing to give affection and love to one who needed you.

O MY MOTHER, how unconscious I am of your beautiful solicitude and motherly care for me. I acknowledge it with my mind; I profess it as my faith, but how little I realize it. When sufferings come and anxieties arise, I imagine that I must face them alone and so I get upset. How easy they would be to bear if I only saw you there beside me, knowing that you understand, knowing that you care and suffer it with me. The same with my joys. How much more wonderful they would be if I told you about them and saw the interest in your face, the love in your eyes! It isn't just imagination; it's real. You care for me just as much as you loved Elizabeth. O Mary, help me to know and realize your all-embracing love and sympathy. And let me have all the trust and filial affection for you that you deserve. I renew once more my act of total devotion to you. Take whatever is good in me to use as you will for God's glory.

THE MAGNIFICAT— JOY IN GOD

Luke 1 : 46-55

1. *A look of joy and peace on Mary's face as she stands before Elizabeth, her arms crossed before her, her eyes closed, saying her beautiful Magnificat.*
2. *The grace to take all my joy in Thee, O my God, Who art so lovable and joy-inspiring.*

MARY was completely wrapped in silence and in God on her journey. It just thrilled her that the long waiting of her people and her loved ones was coming to an end. And she was to be the mother of the Saviour. How good God was to her! How worthy of

praise! How lovable that He should not forget His wayward people! Mary just enjoyed thinking about Him! She didn't have to talk to Him; her prayer was just the warmth in her as she felt His loving protection and care, as she admired His kindness and goodness and beauty.

DEAR MARY, at that time in your life absolutely no sorrow or anxiety could disturb your peaceful reflection or even make its way into your consciousness. Your heart was too happy enjoying God even to feel a worry or bit of nervousness, or hurt feelings that some one might not be thinking highly of you. "My soul magnifies the Lord and my spirit rejoices in God my Saviour." God was in His heaven; the big things were right! Who cared if little things went wrong!

O MY MOTHER, what a lesson you teach me. I'm so easily and quickly disturbed by little things: my failures and my faults, an unkind word from this person, a slight neglect or misunderstanding from the next person; disturbed because I can't do all that I want to do; hurt because I can't do anything to relieve the pain of a loved one, or win some one back to the Good Shepherd. How I miss your unclouded vision of God's goodness and providence! As if He didn't see it all, and know all about it; as if He wasn't letting it all happen for good reasons and to work out His beautiful plan in His own way! O Mary, pray for me that I may see His goodness, and feel its glowing warmth so much that my soul will be bathed continually in joy—joy in Him! Then nothing will distract me from Him and little things will never bother me!

BIRTH OF ST. JOHN THE BAPTIST—SILENCE

Luke 1 : 56-80

1. *Zachary, unable to speak to the people, wrapped in prayer and meditation.*
2. *The grace to pay the price for a true prayer life: silence, spiritual reading and self-examination.*

ZACHARY left the Temple after the vision with great interior humiliation at his doubt and his punishment. And yet there was joy and gratitude to God; joy over the wonderful news that he would have a son, and gratitude that God had taken him down a peg by striking him dumb for his pride and his doubts.

He had mixed feelings of sorrow and joy

as he wrote on the little clay tablet and made signs to explain it all to Elizabeth. He knew she would be so happy about the child and yet hurt that he had been punished. But once the trial of seeing her hurt was over, his soul was nothing but joy and gratitude. Elizabeth conceived; God was so faithful to His promise! And so very, very good! A new era was dawning, and his son was to announce it. God was preparing to send a Saviour, and Zachary's son was to be the forerunner! Zachary would sit for hours, eyes closed, just enjoying God's goodness and praising His name.

DEAR LORD, those months were like a retreat for Zachary. He prayed as he never prayed before; he became holy and possessed of the big vision of God's plan and God's goodness in so short a time. You show me what real prayer can do for a person. Then tell me further, dear Master, what made his prayer so fine? Was it not a combination of a great self-knowledge which came with his fault and humiliation, plus the silence, both exterior and interior, which let him concentrate on the things of God?

DEAR MASTER, prayer can make me holy also. But to pray well, I have to pay the price. I must take time out from work and distractions in order to enter the big spacious halls of silence where I can be alone with You. Not just exterior silence either! I must also banish the anxieties, the plans, the worries, the fretting and feverish activity inside. And alone and in peace meet You face to face. Spiritual reading may help me to see You more clearly in these moments, but the silence is an essential prerequisite.

I must also be firm in my daily examen of conscience. I must welcome humiliations, especially my own faults, and learn from them as Zachary did. Help me, dear Jesus! Pray for me, my Mother and my Queen!

THE TRIAL OF ST. JOSEPH— CONQUERING RESENTMENT

Matt. 1 : 18-25

1. *Joseph, distracted, tortured by thoughts of resentment.*
2. *The grace, my Lord, to conquer all resentment by an all-consuming humility like Joseph's.*

WHEN St. Joseph first began to realize that Mary was with child, his first reaction was just one of numbness. How could it be? She was so good . . . so pure! And yet, as the days went on, the insistent temptation kept torturing his mind that he was deceiving himself. And then the shock of such a thought would make him stop quickly and blame himself unmercifully for doubting her. And yet, after the blame, the doubt crept back again. He couldn't eat or sleep. His soul was tortured! What hurt him most of all was her continued silence. Whatever was the explanation about the child, he was being left in the dark, an outsider! The surge of resentment became so strong!

DEAR ST. JOSEPH, anyone else would have given in to that resentment. What better cause for anger and denunciation! However wonderful Mary had been, she was now treating you like a stranger—as though you had no right to know! As though you were unworthy of a confidence! And yet, you were so humble and so big! In every life there are misfortunes. In every love there are moments of misunderstanding. That's how life is on this earth! And humility means taking life as it is. Resentment, anger, hateful reprisals—they only complicate matters. So you pushed them right out of your heart.

DEAR ST. JOSEPH, how I love and admire your bigness and humility! And yet I can be so small at times, so picayune! I let the smallest slights annoy me. I resent being overlooked or refused a confidence. I am as quick as lightning to pay back insult with insult. Dear Joseph, make me like yourself. You fought all resentment toward Mary—and so you came out of this incident like a giant. Inspire me, great, manly saint. Bigness conquers all problems; humility wins all peace.

THE ANGEL APPEARS TO JOSEPH—TRUST

Matt. 1 : 18-25

1. *Joseph being awakened by an angel and told the good news about Mary.*
2. *The grace, my Lord, to hold my Father's Hand through every sorrow.*

FOR A FEW DAYS St. Joseph struggled with his doubts and fears. Suspicion tortured his mind. He couldn't work; he couldn't eat or sleep. It was only out of sheer exhaustion that he finally fell into fitful sleep. During that night, he was awakened by a soft voice—an angel of God! Joseph jumped up from the small mat to kneel before God's messenger.

"Fear not to take unto thee Mary thy wife," the angel said, "for the Child conceived by her is of the Holy Spirit." The news was startling! The relief it brought seemed to drain all the strength from his body. He sank back in his kneeling position, his face buried in his hands. "Thank God," he heard himself sobbing, "thank God!" She was as pure as an angel! This was her secret! No wonder she was silent! Joseph felt his strength come back now. He knelt up straight, his face lifted to heaven, eyes misty with tears of joy. His soul was lost in gratitude to God.

O MY FATHER in Heaven, how perfect and beautiful was the soul of Joseph at that moment! He had such a clear vision then of Your goodness and providence! And yet that vision would never have possessed his soul so completely unless the pain and the torturous doubt had come first. O Divine Sculptor, You show me how You work on the stubborn stone of our soul. You hammer unmercifully with hammer and chisel. You chip, You cut—but now I know why! It is only to change the rough, shapeless block into the beautiful image of Your Son. How else can we be formed in patience and trust except under the relentless chisel of suffering! How else can our lazy wills learn humility, self-discipline or charity! Forming saints is Your great work, my Father; suffering is only the tool.

MY FATHER, how often I experience that same utter confusion of anxious worry and sorrow. Conflicting thoughts torture my mind like the beating of a heavy pulse. I'm like a frightened child—alone, afraid, very hurt! And then, into that dark gloom, You send an angel of Your grace, and I realize that I am not alone, that my Father is near! Like St. Joseph, I begin to see that my life is not without plan and meaning; that all the struggles and sufferings and dark moments are not stumbling blocks, but stepping stones to bring me closer to Life Eternal.

Send me what You will, my Father! From now on I will trust as St. Joseph did—no matter how dark the night or bitter the sorrow. "He Who watches Israel slumbers not nor sleeps." I have a Father!

THE BIRTH OF JESUS— CONQUERING SELF-PITY

Luke 2 : 1-7

1. *The picture of a damp and uncomfortable stable, slightly lighted by a lantern, revealing the joyful face of a young mother holding her baby.*
2. *The grace, dear Jesus, to realize that all joy and warmth is from within.*

JOSEPH prepared to leave Nazareth for Jerusalem to enroll in the census at Bethlehem. Mary didn't have to go, but he urged her to come so that her reputation would not be hurt among those who didn't know about the Virgin Conception. He made such careful preparations so that she would be comfortable on the journey. He worked so hard beforehand to make extra money, so they could settle in Bethlehem until Jesus got to be two or three years old. It wasn't hard to work for Mary and Jesus; it was a labor of love.

When they arrived at Bethlehem, Joseph began to realize how crowded were all the homes and inns. It was an awfully bitter trial for him when door after door was closed. He tried to hide it from Mary; he looked as cheerful and hopeful as he could. Then finally she let him know that she understood. Any place would do. A stable or one of the caves would be fine. He built a fire; she cleaned up hurriedly. And there Jesus was born! Both Mary and Joseph were joyful. They had nothing and they had everything!

DEAR JOSEPH, you must have loved her so very much then. Any other girl would have had to fight back the tears of self-pity, no matter how brave she was or how resigned to God's Will. But you saw not a trace of a tear, for self-pity was never allowed the smallest place in her heart or your own. You took things as they came; you made the best of what you had, and you never questioned for a moment that this was anything except the best.

DEAR JOSEPH AND MARY, pray for me that I may have that same beautiful attitude of mind and heart. I notice insults so easily and rash judge and write people off for the slightest infractions—so often just imagined or exaggerated. I tend to think how bad things are and wonder why they couldn't be better, and thus waste my time in self-pity. I go over negative thoughts again and again, instead of taking people and events and things just as I find them and making the best of them. Teach me, O my Mother and St. Joseph, that all joy and warmth comes from within, that life is what I make it. Pray for me to be humble. St. Joseph, who loved the background, pray for me that I may be self-effacing and manly like you. Let me treat all negative thoughts like bad thoughts—out!

THE MESSAGE OF THE ANGELS—GOOD WILL

Luke 2 : 8-20

1. *The appearance over Bethlehem of the beautiful choirs of angels; the unearthly loveliness of their song.*
2. *The grace to be "of good will."*

JOSEPH AND MARY knelt beside the little manger and gazed with joy at their infant Who was God made man. They were breathless with wonder and peace. They stared at the Child Jesus as though they could hardly believe their eyes. The cold didn't bother them; the smell of the stable and the rude coarseness of the straw on which they knelt were hardly noticed. Their thoughts were lost in God. How good He was to come to save us! How kind He was to them that they should have a part in it! Their joy and wonder made the stable seem warm and beautiful.

The angels God sent to the shepherds must have caught the spirit of the stable. They almost sang the message: "Good news of great joy, which shall be for all the people." And even as they spoke, an untold multitude of angels took up the refrain as they appeared in the heavens and their song was like the melody of silver trumpets. It was almost as though they could no longer be silent. "Glory to God in the highest and on earth peace among men of good will."

DEAR ANGELS OF GOD, no wonder you sang of good will as you gazed on that lovely scene in the stable. It is our will that determines the degree of our love and the measure of our cheerfulness in sacrifice. The men of good will are those who love God sincerely, both in joy and in sorrow, in fervor and in dryness. Men of good will don't have to depend upon feelings to give themselves cheerfully to God's service; they don't live by mood or whim or caprice. They love God sincerely. And so whatever He sends they take with such cheerfulness and good grace! Like Joseph and Mary, they make the best of what they have! O Angels of God, what true peace comes to men of good will — a peace from within, the warmth and joy of their own splendid hearts!

DEAR FATHER of all, I want to love You in this manner—sincerely, completely! Teach me that love—true love—is in the will, not the feelings. Let me never give way to moods or self-pity, no matter how high the obstacles or how hard the work. Moods have been my undoing in the past. Self-pity has been a constant snare. And when I lived by the moods and whims, I had absolutely no peace or joy—no strong fresh sense of loving You, my Father — just an awful sickening emptiness of being small and loving self! Peace is for the men of good will—for no others! Teach me, my Father! Let me be like Joseph and Mary—no self-pity—taking all with good heart and cheer!

THE CIRCUMCISION OF JESUS—PERSONAL LOYALTY

Luke 2 : 21

1. *The happy gathering of friends and relatives at the circumcision of Jesus.*
2. *The grace of personal loyalty and devotion to Jesus the Saviour.*

A FEW DAYS after the birth of Jesus the crowds in Bethlehem went back to their homes and it was easy for Joseph to find a little shelter with some uncle or aunt. Like any couple with their first baby, Mary and Joseph prepared excitedly for the party for His circumcision. Mary prepared foods and wines and Joseph places for all to sit and be comfortable. It was only fairly distant relatives who were present, since all their close relatives and friends were at Nazareth. Mary welcomed them and, just by being genuinely interested in them as persons, made them feel perfectly at home and at ease.

Devoutly they prepared for the little ceremony—hymns and psalms of joy and thanksgiving to God. Then a few drops of the Precious Blood were shed for the first time and the Holy Child was given the sacred name of Jesus.

IT WAS FITTING, my King, that You should be called Jesus—Saviour—especially at that first shedding of Your Blood, the Blood by which You would redeem the world. All through the Old Testament names were important; they signified a man's mission or some important message from God to His people. So You are called Saviour because through You every good thing comes to us; through You we find our way back to heaven; through You all men can find peace and love and happiness.

HOW I should love Your Name, my Jesus! And what personal love and devotion I should feel for You! Yet I am cold. Your presence in the Eucharist doesn't move me; Your reflection in others I overlook. I pass so much of the day without any recollection of Your presence, Your nearness or Your goodness all around me. And I act on natural likes and dislikes when every affection of my heart should be loyally and lovingly dedicated to the King Who is my Saviour.

Teach me that personal love and devotion, my Jesus. Nourish it through recollection and thoughtfulness and the necessary amount of silence.

PRESENTATION OF THE CHILD JESUS—RECOLLECTION

Luke 2 : 22-38

1. *The holy, white-haired Simeon, holding the Child Jesus, his eyes raised to heaven.*
2. *The grace of recollection and the spiritual insight which it gives us.*

AS THE fortieth day after Jesus' birth approached, Mary and Joseph prepared joyfully for the five-mile journey to Jerusalem and the Temple. They loved God's law and wanted to fulfill it completely, to redeem their first-born Son, and to offer the sacrifice for Mary's purification. They walked with awe and silence across the majestic court of the Temple. Mary stood in line to wait her turn. Anxiously she and Joseph handed Jesus to the priest. The priest blessed Him. Joseph put the five shekels into the Treasury. And then Mary received back her Son.

She then gave the two pigeons for her purification, and the priest, going into the priests' court, ascended the altar and poured out their blood. She held Jesus close to her and put her head down toward His. Her Son was now hers again. She had ransomed Him. And then suddenly a venerable old man stood

before her. He held out his arms, and before she realized it she had given Jesus to him. His face was aglow; his eyes looked up to heaven. Mary and Joseph could barely hear his words: "Now Thou dost dismiss Thy servant, O Lord, according to Thy word, in peace; because my eyes have seen Thy Salvation . . . a light of revelation to the Gentiles, and a glory for Thy people Israel."

DEAR JESUS, there was something almost unearthly about Simeon. So docile was he to the Holy Spirit that he recognized You right away. In all that crowded court he picked You out. He almost didn't notice Mary and Joseph at first; his eyes were raised to heaven. Amidst all the noise and confusion of the crowd he was conscious of nothing save the beauty and nearness and goodness of God. What beautiful faith and docility to grace! What big thoughts of God!

DEAR MASTER, one of the biggest steps on the road to sanctity is this prayerful awareness of God's Beauty and Greatness, this devout preoccupation with God. How I have lacked it! No wonder my ideas of God are small and limited; no wonder that I get anxious and fail to have perfect trust. No wonder I fail to see His Holy Will in all that occurs. My Jesus, force me by Thy grace to do spiritual reading each day and make my holy hour faithfully. Teach me to love and glory in thoughts of God's goodness and greatness in creation and in the redemption and sanctification of the world.

THE MAGI (1)—
BEING PREPARED FOR GOD'S CALL

Matt. 2 : 1-12

1. *The three Magi consulting with each other about the meaning of the star.*
2. *The grace, my Jesus, to be ready for Your stars when they shine.*

WHEN the star of Bethlehem shone in the East there were many men who saw it. But its full meaning came only to a few. The Magi were scholars who sought for the truth with an avid hunger and thirst. They had studied the teachings of Zoroaster and the sciences. And they were fascinated by the holy books of the Jews and often spoke about their admirable belief in one Supreme Being. They realized, too, that the world was sick; that human nature so capable of good was also so prone to evil. And so the Jewish

idea of original sin and the promise of a Saviour made very good sense to them. They studied further: "A star shall arise out of Jacob" ... "Seventy weeks of years" from the time of Daniel. They talked about it and they prayed and they longed that they would see the day. And they scanned the sky. Then one night the star was there—bright, moving to the west, a new star! They met and discussed it. This must be it! Quickly they decided to follow.

DEAR LORD, the Wise Men understood the meaning of the star because they had studied and prayed. And the Wise Men followed the star because they were ready for it when it appeared. Prayer and meditation and study had made them deeply spiritual men, keen to see God's sign, thirsty for truth, and generous to give all and follow. The vision and generosity did not come all at once.

MY KING, I recognize with my mind the need for recollection and prayer, and yet I am so prone to excuse myself from spiritual reading and prayer because of work. Give me the grace to see the shortsightedness of this idea! Let me see that I shall only be ready for Your call when it comes if I am prepared beforehand. Otherwise I won't even recognize Your star! Millions saw the first one; only three followed it—the three who were ready.

Let me get back to the half-hour of spiritual reading every day! Let only the gravest excuses make me put it off!

THE MAGI (2)—
IDEALS

Matt. 2 : 1-12

1. *The Magi answering the vehement objections of family and loved ones.*
2. *The grace, my Lord, of seeing the right ideals and the courage to follow them.*

THE appearance of the star coincided with the wonderful workings of grace in the hearts of the three great followers of Zoroaster. They had read the prophecies of Daniel and recognized the sign of the star. But their enthusiasm was chilled a bit when their friends and families heard about their plans. Some were scornful and called them outright fools. Those more kind said that they were simply caught up with some religious mania and they should give themselves time to calm down and get back to reality. It was their families that placed the hardest obstacles. At first they pleaded with the Magi not to go. Then they cried, told them that they were selfish to leave their families, that it would be so much more pleasing to God if they stayed at home. And finally they threatened. If they went chasing a star, then they'd find no one home when they returned! And through it all the Magi were brave and true. They didn't shout back or raise a fuss. Quietly, peacefully they explained that they simply had to go, that the star was calling for them.

O MY KING, how I admire their courage and their strength of purpose. The pressure of human respect brought against them was strong enough to bend the strongest will. They were able, however, to withstand men's scorn and laughter. They were able to resist the pleas and emotional outbursts of loved ones, because they had the inner peace of knowing that they were right. Prayer and meditation had formed ideals, and the ideals were their steelwork and their strength. The arguments brought up by their families and friends were very good arguments. The Magi were able to resist only because they had thought out the whole thing in prayer.

MY KING, I am so prone to waver under pressure. Emotional stress from others, especially from loved ones, makes me so fearful that I may be wrong, so nervous about being strong. Laughter and scorn and even fear of ridicule can cause me such uneasiness also. For my will to be strong I must have a strong motivation, as did the Magi. I must have strong convictions and right ideals. These are formed by sincere and earnest thought and prayerful meditation, and forged into true steel by intelligent discussion and debate. Teach me the truth and give me the peace of respect for my ideals once I am sure that my ideals are right. Let prayer be my safeguard.

THE MAGI (3)—
TRUST IN GOD

Matt. 2 : 1-12

1. *The sad look on the faces of the Magi as the Jews at Jerusalem fled in terror from their question.*
2. *The grace, my Jesus, to trust in You, even when things seem hopeless.*

IT TOOK great preparations for the long journey—supplies, trusted soldiers and guides, gifts for the King, suitable wardrobes becoming their state. Finally all was ready. Then the long arduous trip; the constant vigilance for robber bands; the anxiety to see the King and to learn more about what He would do for the world. They were so filled with expectation. Then, after many weary weeks, they sighted Jerusalem. They camped outside for the night so that they would be fresh and clean for their meeting with the King in the morning. Nervously, expectantly, they entered with their long, impressive retinue through the eastern gate of the city. Crowds gathered and stared. The caravan halted and the chief officers of the Magi's guard asked where they could find the newborn King of the Jews. His words stiffened and terrified the crowd like an electric shock! If the tyrant Herod heard them even listening to such talk! No one spoke! Fearfully they slipped away and disappeared. The Magi could hardly believe their eyes. The King's own people didn't seem to know Him or to care! And suddenly they recalled that the star also had disappeared. It was all such a letdown!

O MY KING, how they were tempted to be disheartened at that moment! It all looked so black! How the taunts of their friends rang in their mind—"Star-chasers!" "Fools!" How they began to mistrust themselves and their judgment. But the star was reality and it was from You. So they trusted and waited, and finally someone came and led them to Herod. And there they found out about the King.

DEAR MASTER, this lesson is so important for me to see. It makes me realize that sometimes You deliberately let the star go out and let things look hopeless, only to make us trust You the more. I realize now that trust in You is just like loyalty to a friend; it's really counting on Your goodness all the way, no matter how things may seem to fall apart. You are so pleased by that kind of loyalty. Teach me then to love these opportunities for trust. Don't let me be fearful, even when I see great pride in myself or other faults. The dark hours can create in me true greatness of soul. Then send them, my King, in Your own good time. Only give me the grace to take them with loyalty and to please You completely!

THE MAGI (4)— APPRECIATION OF THE SPIRITUAL

Matt. 2 : 1-12

1. *The Magi standing in the spacious and beautiful throne room of Herod.*
2. *The grace, my Jesus, to appreciate and value the spiritual treasures You have given me.*

HEROD'S many spies soon reported to him about the Magi and their search for the new-born King. Herod immediately dispatched an emissary to lead them to the palace on the western side of the city. There they were received with courtesy; their guards were given quarters; their camels watered, and they themselves installed in beautiful accommodations in one of the many suites for guests. Presently they were summoned to meet Herod himself. They noticed the unusual splendor of the throne room as they waited for the King to come in, but they were surprised to see his wasted body and to smell the sickening odor of his decaying flesh even above the odor of the incense. They bowed respectfully, exchanged greetings, and then asked about the new-born King. Again they were amazed when Herod apparently knew

nothing about Him. So it was not Herod's son! The learned men of the Law were summoned, and they told that it was in Bethlehem, some five miles southwest of Jerusalem, where the King was to be born. Herod inquired about the time of the star and where they saw it. And he told them to go and find the Child and then tell him so that he too might adore. Sending his soldiers might cause suspicion and make people hide the Child. This way he could cover up his plan to kill the Child.

DEAR LORD, I love the way the Magi were completely unimpressed by the magnificence and splendor of Herod's palace, and how they left its sumptuous life in order to seek little, poor Bethlehem. For them Bethlehem held the real treasure and the real life! And I marvel at the Pharisees who were able to point out the way to the Saviour, but didn't go themselves! What coldness and lukewarmness! How careless they had become in things spiritual!

O MY KING, You know only too well how this is a danger for me. Familiarity with things spiritual can so easily lead us to value them less. Your presence in the Eucharist just a little distance away and yet how many excuses I find to neglect to make a visit. The same with the real treasure of spiritual reading and Sacred Scripture. Like the Pharisees, I urge these on others and show them the way—and then I fail to go that way myself! O my King, make me have a keen sense of spiritual values!

THE MAGI (5)— FAITH

Matt. 2 : 1-12

1. *The astonished looks on the faces of the simple people of Bethlehem as they saw the three Magi enter the simple house of Joseph.*
2. *The grace, my Jesus, of that deep, beautiful faith that sees beyond appearances to what is real.*

THE MAGI thanked King Herod, bowed and left his presence. The captain of their guard assembled the men and they started for Bethlehem. As soon as they left the palace grounds and went through the western gate of the city, the star shone again—even though it was daylight. Tears streamed down their faces and their lips moved silently in prayerful

thanks. It was not a fools' journey after all! God was just trying their faith, making it stronger through trials. The pressure of joy on their hearts almost hurt. It was no trial to them then when the star led to a little one-room house; no scandal to their great faith when they saw in the doorway a simple carpenter, with shavings of wood on his apron, and a little girl mother with her baby in her arms! The star was there. It was enough. At a signal their guard of honor dismounted and formed a double line to the little doorway. Mary and Joseph withdrew into the house. The Magi came in with their gifts. They were enthralled by her beauty and gracious simplicity as she made them welcome. They offered their gifts, and then falling down on their knees, they adored!

O MY KING, what a beautiful scene to see those great men on their knees before You! They didn't kneel before Herod for all his trappings of wealth and majesty. But they knelt before You in that simple, unadorned little room. "Faith is the substance of things to be hoped for; the evidence of things that are not seen." They now had the substance because they had You. Their faith was the evidence. It made them put aside all their

Eastern prejudice about wealth and external glory. Faith made them find You.

DEAR MASTER, faith is a light. With it I can see in the darkness of doubt, scepticism, cynicism and sorrow. Increase my faith; make bright my lamp that I may see. Let me be like the Magi and never be scandalized by appearances! Let me see and love You in the Eucharist, see and embrace You in the Sacrament of the present moment, see and praise You in the beauties of nature and persons. Let me see and love You in the sorrows and the joys that come my way!

THE FLIGHT INTO EGYPT (1)— OBEDIENCE

Matt. 2 : 13-15

1. *Joseph, a startled look on his face, as he tries to grasp the meaning of the angel's message.*
2. *The grace, my Lord, to see Your Will in the commands of my superiors.*

THE JOY and happiness of the Holy Family didn't last too long. Sometime after the Magi left, an angel appeared to Joseph during the middle of the night. "Arise," he said, "take the Child and His Mother and flee into Egypt . . . for Herod will seek the Child to destroy Him!" St. Joseph could hardly believe his ears. He tried desperately to shake off the heaviness of sleep to realize what was happening. Almost unbelievable! Herod would try to destroy the Child! Even now Herod was dying of a loathsome disease. He would be dead long before Jesus was even a young Boy! Why would he . . . ? Joseph stopped his thoughts; he would have to act soon. He sat up and lit the small oil lamp. Doubts and problems rushed in upon him like a raging stream. Egypt? In the middle of the night? With no light, no map, few provisions! And when day came, would not Herod's horsemen easily overtake them? Wouldn't it be safer to hide in the hills? He caught himself again. He must obey and stop questioning. God's plan is best! He looked over to the other side of the room where Mary lay asleep on her little mat—her face peaceful and beautiful. How he hated to awaken her! How he hated to give her this news!

DEAR BLESSED JOSEPH, doing God's Will probably never seemed so hard to you as it did at that moment! The task seemed close to impossible and the risk so great. Your natural instincts and reason kept telling you that your own plan was much better. And after all, it was only of the safety of the Child and His Mother that you were thinking! And yet the message was clear. "Egypt," the angel said. God's Will be done! Although it hurt so much, you went over and shook Mary gently and told her the sad news.

DEAR ST. JOSEPH, how I need your splendid example in that scene! So often the commands of my superiors sound senseless and meaningless. Sometimes I feel that obedience would actually hinder God's work, not help it. And so I try to cut corners, to put through my own plan and my own ideas. Certainly I am permitted to suggest my plan, but, dear Saint of God, when my ideas are rejected, then teach me to obey. Teach me to see that in obeying lawful authority, I serve not men but God! It is His plan—no matter how obscure the goal or unreasonable the means. And His plan is best—though it takes me through the dark night and the scorching sands of Egypt!

THE FLIGHT INTO EGYPT (2)— GOOD WILL

Matt. 2 : 13-15

1. *Mary seated on the donkey, holding the Child Jesus close to her.*
2. *The grace, my Jesus, to be of good will, to make the best of all that comes.*

JOSEPH felt that he knelt for minutes beside Mary before he made himself wake her. She had had such little sleep and peace since Simeon's prophecy. Only these last few days had she gotten back to her old self. And now —now he had to frighten her all over again. "Mary," he heard himself saying, "Mary, we have to take a journey!" She was awake immediately. Her large eyes looked into his questioningly. "There's nothing to be worried about," he said softly, trying to seem calm, "it's only a precaution—to make sure He'll be safe." There wasn't another word. She arose quickly and gathered some food and clothes for the Child. She spread a large cloth, put everything in the center and then tied up the ends. A skin of water and a small cask of oil—and she was ready. Joseph had the donkey ready. He nodded towards some of the nice objects she had made for the house, but she shook her head. Better to leave them—they weren't really necessary. Joseph put the little pack on the donkey. He lifted Mary and the Child on the faithful animal's back and then led him silently down the road. She held Jesus close to her and didn't turn to look back.

HOW GREATLY you admired her then, St. Joseph! The "good will" of which the angels sang at Christmas—how completely true it was of her! From the cold stable at Christmas you both had worked so hard to get a house. She cleaned and decorated with such exquisite taste—made it comfortable and homey. And now she had to leave it all! Yet there wasn't one trace of whining or regret or complaint! Good will is the will that cheerfully accepts God's Will. Good will means taking things as they come and making the best of what happens. That wonderful, cooperative, cheerful attitude of good will—how absolutely lovely it made her!

DEAR JOSEPH AND MARY, how I love and admire your good will. It makes you both so lovable. I love it, too, in people I meet, who are cheerful and serene even in great trials, who make the best of everything. And yet, when my plans go wrong, or thoughtless people cause me inconvenience, I complain, I show my resentment, I lose joy. Dear Joseph, let me see her as you saw her that night—and my heart will be so thrilled with the loveliness of good will that I'll be cheerful, too, and take what God sends with joy.

THE EXILE IN EGYPT—DEVOTION

Matt. 2 : 13-15

1. *The Holy Family in a little house near the great cities of Egypt.*
2. *The grace of constant devotion through times of dryness as well as times of fervor.*

ST. JOSEPH AND MARY settled in one of the ghettos where they would have some fellow countrymen for companions. But his work involved him very often in dealings with the pagan Egyptians. The whole tone of that culture was so foreign to anything he or Mary had ever experienced. The very worship of their pagan gods was accompanied by the basest and most disgusting orgies. Here there was no beautiful Temple to Yahweh; no trumpet call each morning and evening to lift up their minds and hearts to God at the

Temple sacrifices. Here there was no regard for the Sabbath rest; no sense of morality or modesty. It was a bleak exile!

DEAR JOSEPH AND MARY, what a cold feeling you must have had there in Egypt! You who loved God so much—what pain to see Him unknown and unloved! What a test of faith to see magnificent buildings dedicated to idols! And yet, no questions of "Why?" ever escaped your lips or even came to your mind. Rather than being a scandal to your faith and devotion, this paganism around you made you feel a greater need to pray for these people, a stronger desire to love and praise God for those who did not love Him. No matter how cold were your surroundings, in your hearts was the warmth of faith and love and ardent prayer!

O MY FATHER, how I need their loving devotion. I can so easily become discouraged by the tremendous number of people away from God! I can easily be tempted to despair when I consider the great number of Your enemies—bad books, laxity, indifference, divorce, birth control, materialism. I so easily forget in my pagan surroundings that You are all-powerful and all-good. Teach me to be like Joseph and Mary, my Father! Let the pagan atmosphere of the world only urge me to pray more and love more! And let me trust completely in You! In times of spiritual dryness also, let me remain faithful and true to my prayers, knowing that I can love and serve no matter how I feel—knowing that in Your own time You will lead me back from the dry sands of Egypt.

THE HOLY INNOCENTS—TRUST IN GOD

Matt. 2 : 14-18

1. *Soldier running his sword through a child.*
2. *The grace, my Jesus, of seeing God's good purpose in all the tragedies that happen.*

HEROD WAS nicely satisfied with himself. He had fooled the Magi into believing that he was a devout man, as anxious to worship the new King as they. He told his courtiers in a self-congratulatory way how his self-discipline and wisdom kept him from "letting the cat out of the bag." He explained how he found out so much more by being nice to them, than by having them punished for treason. But as the days went by and they did not return, he became more and more annoyed. He hated to be outfoxed; he hated particularly to have the courtiers notice that he had lost. His anger grew until in a furious rage he ordered his Idumean soldiers to go to Bethlehem and slay every male child two years of age and under. And if they were to see the Magi . . . !

The Idumeans were half-savage. It meant little to them to seize children from their screaming, fainting mothers, run their swords through them and then drop them on the ground. Fathers who protested were cut down. About thirty in all were killed before they rode back with their ghastly mission fulfilled.

O MY KING, what a temptation for those parents to deny that there was any God at all! Or if He existed, how could He be a good God and let men like Herod get their way. And yet, my King, we can see now that Herod didn't get his way. The Baby Jesus was on the way to Egypt and not slain. And the little babies who died in His place received Baptism of Blood and became little saints, the first glorious martyrs. Even Herod serves God's plan!

MY KING, I need that trust so very much. The Herods of our day seem so strong as they destroy the holy innocents—the increasing number of rotten books, bad movies, immodest dress, absolutely devilish ideas and philosophies that pervert the minds and hearts of so many. It's so easy to become disheartened and to feel that we'll never win the world for You! Such a temptation to say that it is an impossible task. Give me trust, my King. Let me see that these modern Herods serve Your ultimate purpose just as the Herod of old. In the end You will win back these souls, and being won back they will be stronger and more wonderful than if they had never strayed away. Let me work hard, but with peace and joy and trust. Give me the big vision!

THE RETURN TO NAZARETH—GRATITUDE

Matt. 2 : 19-23

1. *Holy Family stopping for a moment to view their beloved Nazareth from the hillside.*
2. *The grace, my Lord, of deep gratitude for You and for Your gifts!*

AFTER ABOUT two or three months in Egypt, an angel again appeared to St. Joseph and told him of Herod's death and bade him return to Israel. The news brought unspeakable joy to Joseph. This time there wasn't even the slightest delay in telling Mary. He could hardly wait. Their exile in the pagan land was over! God was so good! They settled their few affairs, said their goodbys to the other Jewish settlers who had been so good to them and started back. How different was the return! Daylight instead of darkness; the main road instead of the desert sands. And the difference in their feelings! They were going home, back to where they were known and loved! The Magnificat must have resounded again and again in her warm heart as they came nearer and nearer.

At the border Joseph learned that Archelaus now ruled and that he had just had 3,000 people killed in quelling a rebellion. He wouldn't trust the Holy Family there under such a ruler. Nor would Bethlehem be safe. For Jesus would be the only baby boy under two years of age and the unhappy mothers might blame Him for the massacre. Jesus was old enough now for them to return to Nazareth without anyone suspecting when He was born. So on they went up the Jordan valley, across the plain of Esdralon and then suddenly over a hill they could see Nazareth.

They stopped to watch it, and tears ran down their cheeks. They were home!

MY KING, I am sure Mary and Joseph never loved Nazareth so much, or felt so close to their faith and their fellow Jews than at that moment. We only truly appreciate Your great gifts when we have been deprived of them for a while. It is the sick man who is so grateful and happy at recovering his health; it is the thirsty man who appreciates water, and the hungry who thank You for food. When You deprive us of Your gifts for a time, it is only that we might appreciate and enjoy them more and through them grow in love for You, the Giver of all good gifts.

TEACH ME this lesson of gratitude, my Lord! Let me live in joy based on a deep appreciation of all Your unspeakable gifts—my faith, my health, my country, my loved ones. And when You choose to deprive me of any of them for a time, let me love You more, not less—let me see Your plan in all that happens. I am grateful, my Lord. With a heart brimming with joy and gratitude, I thank You for Yourself and all Your gifts!

THE HIDDEN LIFE AT NAZARETH—DOCILITY OF HEART

Luke 2 : 40

1. *The Boy Jesus helping St. Joseph at the carpenter's bench.*
2. *The grace to adapt myself cheerfully to any changing circumstances.*

ONCE BACK in Nazareth, the Holy Family received a warm welcome from their relatives and friends. For the grandparents it was an untold joy to see the Baby Jesus. Joseph made arrangements for a small, one-room house with a little extra room for a shop facing on the street. Mary sewed and decorated and fixed it with neat simplicity and beauty. And there the Baby Jesus grew into boyhood and young manhood. Nothing of the extraordinary or miraculous marked these hidden years. Jesus ate, slept, played games with the other boys—especially His cousins, James, Jude, Simon and Joseph. He went to the little school, sat like the other boys on the dirt floor and memorized the Shema, the Commandments and the Hallel. His friends liked Him; people noticed that He was a very good boy and very generous in being a help to Joseph in the carpenter shop.

DEAR LORD, Your life at Nazareth and Your growth were so natural that no one suspected that You were anything other than a good boy. Even Mary and Joseph began to think of You as their child and almost forgot Who You really were. What beautiful humility, my King! What perfect docility to the situation in which You found Yourself! What perfect adaptation to circumstances! You were so surpassingly brilliant, yet You contented Yourself with work in a carpenter shop. You had fearful, unlimited power, yet You walked through the streets of Nazareth, meek and gentle and unknown.

MY KING, I find it so hard to have that humility of adapting myself to changing circumstances in life. I develop certain habits of acting, certain ways of doing things, and I find it so hard to change. I resent it when others force me to change or when circumstances no longer permit my old way of acting. Teach me to adapt myself graciously to all changes. If a talkative person dominates the conversation, let me be silent graciously. If a fellow worker's thoughtlessness or lack of system makes it necessary for me to change all my plans and appointments, teach me to adapt with docility and patience.

BOY JESUS LOST IN JERUSALEM (1)—REVERENCE

Luke 2 : 41-50

1. *The reverent, joyful look on the face of Jesus as He looked upon Jerusalem.*
2. *The grace, my Lord, of deep reverence for all that is sacred.*

ST. JOSEPH was so proud as he brought the Boy Jesus over the top of Olivet and let Him look upon the magnificent Temple and Jerusalem for the first time. Mary, too, was thrilled. She watched His strong Face light with joy and wonder as He saw the one place on earth where His Father was truly honored. He knew it all as God, but now He was seeing it for the first time as Man. Joseph and Mary had almost come to think of Him now as their boy. They showed Him all through the beautiful porticos of the Temple. Mary showed Him where she had held Him when Simeon took Him from her arms. And then a twinge came as she recalled Simeon's prophecy.

In the home of their friends that night, Jesus celebrated the Passover meal with St. Joseph and the others. Their piety and love thrilled Him. As He looked on the slain lamb through His boyish eyes, He pictured the day when He would take the lamb's place and bleed to death for the sins of the world. Thoughts such as these brought Him back next day to the Temple. He sat and listened to the Doctors of the Law. How He loved "the beauty of God's house and the place where His Glory dwelleth!"

O MY KING, what unspeakable reverence You had for the things that pertained to Your Father! How You loved the Temple and those who worshipped there with sincere piety! The ceremonies and hymns and liturgy all gave You joy because of the honor they gave to the Father You loved so much. Reverence was another way of loving.

MY KING, reverence for holy things is a beautiful virtue. It is part of the virtue of humility and justice because it is seeing things as they are and giving all their due. How truly reverent I should be in the presence of the Blessed Sacrament! My every action should show how much You are to be honored and praised. I should reverence sacred objects, too—the crucifix, blessed articles, etc. Somehow they all speak of You and that very association makes them honorable. And, O my Jesus, what reverence I should have for persons — all persons, but particularly the aged and the sick and the disagreeable. Others may not see Your image in these latter persons, so I must strive to have respect and reverence for Your image in them. Teach me, my King!

THE BOY JESUS IN JERUSALEM (2)— HUMILITY

Luke 2 : 41-50

1. *Jesus sitting among the Doctors of the Law.*
2. *The grace, my Lord, to be true, to be humble.*

JESUS had gotten used to Jerusalem during the time they were there. He wandered each day to the Temple which was still under construction. He watched the workmen putting the stones in place and fixing the porticos. Silently He sat at the edge of the crowd that gathered about the Doctors of the Law as they explained various points. Then one day, the day that the caravan was due to return to Nazareth, the Boy Jesus stood very near to the Doctors. They were explaining some of the Messianic prophecies—perhaps Isaias about the glorious Messiah or the glories of the kingdom He would establish. Then Jesus raised His hand. What about Isaias' words describing the suffering Messiah? Why, those passages refer to the Jewish people, one of the Doctors answered. And again, the question: Is it not the same Servant of Jahweh that Isaias speaks about in both passages? And is not the taking away of our sins a greater mission than merely bringing material blessings? The Doctors were dumbfounded. What the young Boy said made such sense. And yet, how could their glorious Messiah be led "like a lamb to the slaughter"! It was unthinkable! Maybe God has different standards of greatness, the young Boy suggested. Maybe by suffering bravely, the Messiah will show us how to bear our own sufferings. The Doctors were overcome with wonderment, especially when they questioned Him about His parents and His schooling. They brought up difficult questions and found themselves trying to solve them at the feet of a young Boy from Nazareth.

I LOVE this scene, my King! I love it not only because it shows Your glory and Your divinity, but because it shows so clearly Your true humility. In all honesty, You knew these answers, so You didn't pretend that You did not. You shared Your learning with these sincere Doctors of the Law and You proposed questions that would lead them on to greater truths and more earnest study! There were times, such as the hidden years at Nazareth, when Your mission called for You to remain unknown. And this You did beautifully and humbly. Now was the time to show all future generations that You were always conscious of Your divinity. So this, too, You did simply, directly, humbly. Humility means being true.

DEAR MASTER, there are times when my talents and abilities are ignored, when my most sincere offers of kindness and thoughtfulness are misunderstood. In those times, let me feel no resentment. You are inviting me then to share the hidden life. I am what I am, whether others notice it or not. I please You by being glad to be the living fulfillment of Your Will—whether or not others benefit from my service or recognize my talents.

And when those times come that I should step up and let my ideas be known and my talents seen, then let me do so graciously and humbly and without fear. Boy Saviour, humble, unpretentious, true—make me like Yourself!

JESUS IN JERUSALEM (3)— SPIRITUAL TRIALS

Luke 2 : 41-50

1. *Anxious look in the eyes of Mary as she searched for Jesus.*
2. *The grace, my Jesus, not to be discouraged by dryness, but only to seek You the more!*

MARY AND JOSEPH saw Jesus the morning the caravan prepared to go back to Nazareth, so when He wandered off, they didn't miss Him. A twelve-year-old who had just become a man before the Law could still travel with the women. So Joseph thought He was with Mary, and Mary that He was with Joseph. It was evening before He was missed. They had walked a whole day and were terribly weary. "Where's Jesus?" Mary asked. "Wasn't He with you?" said St. Joseph. And then a terrible fear gripped both of them. They search through the entire camp. Not a sign. They were almost sick with the thought of all that could have happened. Joseph begged Mary to eat something. The little she took was just to please him. He would go back with some of the men, he told her. The Passover moon was still in the sky, so they could see their way. But she wouldn't hear of not going also. She was womanly and let Joseph make the decisions. But now she begged him to let her go with him.

Joseph packed a few things and before the sun had set they started back for Jerusalem. It was in the early hours of the morning that they reached the city. For a few hours until dawn they tried to sleep. Then at dawn the search—all through the city—asking everyone they saw—trying to follow up every lead. The worst anxiety for both was the haunting thought that they had been careless, that they had lost Him through their own fault.

MY KING, it wasn't the fault of Joseph and Mary that they lost You in Jerusalem. There are times when You send us spiritual trials for our own good—times when the sense of losing You and feeling that You are far away makes us need and desire You more. At such times we should act like Joseph and Mary, seek You, want You, long for You —and You will come to us again.

MY JESUS, we are surprised at first to see Mary and Joseph without You and heartbroken seeking for You! We have that same surprise when You send moments of dryness and weariness, moments when everything spiritual seems flat and uninteresting. Let me not be surprised or discouraged at these times. Let me think of Joseph and Mary and, like them, seek You again with all my heart. No self-blame! No discouragement! You are not far away or unconcerned! You want me to thirst in order to be filled, to desire in order to embrace and love the more!

JESUS IN JERUSALEM (4)— SORROW

Luke 2 : 41-50

1. *The look of surprise on the face of Mary as she sees Jesus with the Doctors in the Temple.*
2. *The grace, my Lord, to see sorrow as a friend and use it according to Your purpose.*

JOSEPH was almost afraid that Mary would have a nervous collapse. She just seemed to stare without seeing. And when he spoke reassuring words to her, there was no answer —she didn't hear him. Her thoughts were tortured and far away. Finally, Joseph thought of the Temple again. This would be the most likely place, for the Boy Jesus seemed so thrilled and enchanted by it when they first showed it to Him. So they went to the Temple across the courtyard. And as they entered one of the finished meeting rooms in the portico of Solomon's Porch, they saw a fairly large group. There was silence except for one voice. It was the voice of Jesus. They could see Him standing there in the midst of the Doctors, answering a question. Mary and Joseph just stood still. Their relief was overwhelming. For the first time since He was lost, she cried and tears rolled down her cheeks. She realized then how tired she was. Joseph found her a place to sit. And there they sat and waited until Jesus was finished. He came over to them then. He didn't seem repentant or act as though anything had happened out of the ordinary. She was tired and this seemed too much for her. She couldn't restrain the words of mild rebuke: "Son, why hast Thou done so to us? Behold, in sorrow thy father and I have been seeking Thee." "How is it that you sought Me?" He replied. "Did you not know that I must be about My Father's business?"

MY KING, You knew that Your answer then was only a partial answer. Yes, it is true that it was the first place they should have looked for You. But that didn't answer the

bigger question she was asking—the question about the anguish and pain You had caused them by not letting them know. Why had You done this? You didn't answer, my King, because You had done this deliberately! Deliberately and knowingly You had caused them anguish and sorrow—because sorrow could do things for their souls that nothing else could do. They couldn't fully understand this then, so You didn't answer directly. But You loved them dearly and would never hurt them except to help them. Your love was so strong that it wouldn't stop from hurting, when the hurt would make them more beautiful and thoughtful of soul.

MY KING, I think this is one of the most difficult lessons for me to understand. I recognize in theory how suffering and sorrow can deepen and enrich a soul. In theory I admit that there never has been any greatness without sorrow. And yet when You send it, my "why" is so loud. Not that I say the word—but my "why" comes with my resentment, my anger, my failure to be docile and to learn. Lord, teach me that sorrow accepted and used is a friend and a blessing!

YOUNG MANHOOD OF JESUS (1)— ENDING QUARRELS

Luke 2 : 50-52

1. *Jesus carrying the water for His Mother.*
2. *The grace, my Lord, to end quickly misunderstandings and useless quarrels.*

MARY AND JOSEPH didn't question Jesus any further. Jesus also let the subject drop. Together they started back for Nazareth. He spoke freely and smiled readily as they walked along. He spoke about the beauty of the Temple, the Feast, and the journey home. There were times of silence, too, as they enjoyed the beautiful countryside and the golden sunlight. Jesus let them know in so many little ways that He loved them — a smile, a willingness to talk, an interest in listening, an offer to help, even asking them to help Him. But there was no mention of the incident in the Temple or the long search or the misunderstanding.

DEAR JESUS, there are points of honest disagreement and misunderstanding even among the holiest and best of people. You had been misunderstood by Mary, who was always most understanding. And the misunderstanding hurt Joseph, who loved you both so dearly. You show me so clearly, my King, that I have to expect misunderstandings and disagreements even among my closest friends and acquaintances. It doesn't necessarily mean that either they or myself are to blame. It's just a case, as with You and Your parents, that one party can't see fully the plan and purpose of the other party. You teach me what to do in such cases—drop it!! Forget about it and talk about some other subject. Further talk in such cases can only rub salt in the wounds.

O MY LORD, I need that lesson so badly! I'm reluctant to admit that there can be honest misunderstandings in which no one is really to blame. Too easily do I conclude that my friends are being unkind or rude or careless. Too easily do I also blame myself and become discouraged and upset. And then I keep going over and over the whole thing in my mind and in my speech. And the more I talk, the worse it gets!

Teach me, my King, that most of our clashes are honest misunderstandings where both parties have good will and where no one is to blame. If I can't see the reasons, nor clear up the misunderstanding, then teach me to act like You—to drop it! And start on something new! To be kind and cheerful as though nothing happened! And misunderstanding will give way to love.

YOUNG MANHOOD OF JESUS (2)—OBEDIENCE

Luke 2 : 50-52

1. *Jesus listening attentively as St. Joseph instructs Him in carpentry.*
2. *The grace, my Lord, of sincere, cheerful obedience and docility.*

WHEN the Holy Family arrived at Nazareth, they were greeted joyfully by their relatives and friends. They all asked what had happened to Jesus. He had just remained on in the Temple a while, Joseph explained, without mentioning the startling impression Jesus made on the Doctors of the Law. Jesus seemed to prefer to be considered one of the ordinary boys of Nazareth so Joseph never mentioned the extraordinary.

The whole life of Jesus now was ordinary. Since He was twelve and considered a man in the eyes of the Law, He took a greater part in the work at the carpenter shop. St. Joseph showed Him how to make tables and chairs, how to measure accurately and saw the wood straight, how to plane and smooth and polish. Jesus listened attentively; carefully He followed all the instructions. And St. Joseph was proud to see that He became a good carpenter.

When Mary called for dinner, He left His work and went in to meals. He helped her with the water and went on messages and errands for St. Joseph. Everyone at Nazareth knew that Jesus was a dutiful Son.

LORD, I love You in that role of apprentice-carpenter and faithful Son. What lessons You show me in obedience and docility! You had fashioned the universe so You knew a thousand better ways to make a bench than St. Joseph, but You did it his way! With Your eternal wisdom, You were far better able to arrange the activities and plans of the Holy Family. But You let Joseph and Mary do it! And You did what they wanted. This was Your role now, to be a Son, so You would be one perfectly! Can I possibly miss the lesson that the better way is not always the wisest way—the better way is the way of obedience and love!

DEAR LORD, how different from You am I! I resent orders! I smart under direction! "I know! I know!" I say with evident annoyance. And so often go on to do it wrongly and show that I don't know at all! And when I am convinced that a certain way of doing things is the best way, doesn't it irk me when those in authority say, "No! Do it the other way!" I get angry, I speak unkindly about superiors; I'm even tempted to sulk and give up the project. And why, my King? Because I forget You and Your magnificent example of obedience. I forget that cheerful obedience is the best way, that it is the way of humility and love. It is Your way! Let me love obedience, my King, cheerful, ready, whole-hearted obedience!

YOUNG MANHOOD OF JESUS (3)— SANCTIFYING THE ORDINARY

Luke 2 : 50-52

1. *Beads of perspiration on the Sacred Face of Jesus.*
2. *The grace, my King, to do all things out of love.*

AS JESUS grew older He noticed St. Joseph growing more tired, so He took over more and more of the work. He did it gradually and unobtrusively, so that St. Joseph would always feel that he was still the head of the family and the main support. The days for Jesus now became very full of work and activity. He carried lumber, sawed, hammered, measured, fit together the finished products and carried them to those who ordered them. There were annoyances, too, as with all who serve the public. He had to change His plans to suit their convenience and accept complaints when they felt the work wasn't done correctly. And then there was the monotony of small-town living. He could feel Himself hemmed in by small talk and gossip, by small-town thinking and the wearisome routine. Often as He came to the edge of the hill that overlooked Esdralon, He thought of the world that was hungry for His coming. He thought of the crowds He could sway with His sermons, the miracles He could perform . . . And then He turned and went back to His work!

DEAR LORD, humanly speaking, how You longed to go out to that world that needed You so much! How tempted would anyone else have been to leave Nazareth and the carpenter shop, and simply blaze a trail of miracles from Jerusalem to Rome! But,

O my King, You were teaching us still that greatness does not consist in outward show but in faithful devotion and love. What a wonderful lesson for us! We couldn't imitate Your miracles, but we can follow You in Your faithful devotion to duty. You were just as great at Nazareth in performing the ordinary duties of a carpenter as You were in Your miracles and great sermons. It's not what we do, but how we do it that counts.

MY KING, what a lesson for me. The monotony of everyday life makes me so listless and discouraged. "If only I were doing big things and important things! But these petty, insignificant duties—what good do I accomplish with these?" And because I feel this way I become careless and unhappy. O my King, in these moments take me back to Nazareth! Show me there that nothing is ordinary when it is done in a spirit of Nazareth. The smallest, most insignificant duties are great when they are done with fidelity and love. Teach me that spirit of faithful love. Let me live Nazareth day by day, and then nothing will be ordinary.

JOSEPH, HEAD OF THE HOUSE (1)— TAKING RESPONSIBILITIES BRAVELY

Luke 2 : 51-52

1. *Joseph sending the Boy Jesus on an errand.*
2. *The grace, my Lord, to accept my responsibilities bravely.*

MANY NIGHTS St. Joseph would lie awake on his cot, lost in wonder at the treasures beneath his roof at Nazareth. God's own Son made Man was there, sleeping peacefully in a corner of the room—and His mother, the queen of angels and of men! And they were in Joseph's care. It was his responsibility to provide for their material needs, his place to make the decisions for the Holy Family. It was even his work to give direction to Jesus' study and prayer-life and apprenticeship as a carpenter. It filled Joseph with a sense of awe, almost bordering on fear. Often he fell off to sleep, begging Jahweh to make him less unworthy.

DEAR ST. JOSEPH, how easily you could have been tempted to run away from your responsibilities! How easy to let Mary take over the direction of the family, and particularly of the Boy Jesus! You could have found many excuses. Jesus was her Son, not yours. They were both much greater in dignity and grace than you. How dare you lead them! And yet, St. Joseph, you never gave way to that temptation. God had made you the head of the family, so you would fulfill the role perfectly. How well you knew that humility means being completely what we are! You were the head of the family, so you took the responsibility; you gave the orders. You gave them kindly and gently. But you gave them!

DEAR LORD, I need St. Joseph's noble example. When I have to give orders or make decisions, how tempted I am to dodge the responsibility. Especially those times when it is my duty to correct others or reprimand them. How cowardly I act! I run away from the task with false protestations of humility, and hope that someone else will do it for me. Dear Master, give me the courage of true humility. Teach me to see that giving commands and correction is just as truly humility for a superior as obeying is humility for a subject. Help me to fulfill my role; help me to be true!

JOSEPH, HEAD OF THE HOUSE (2)— GIVING ORDERS GRACIOUSLY

Luke 2 : 51-52

1. *Joseph watching Mary at her work.*
2. *The grace, my Lord, of great respect for each person I must command.*

ST. JOSEPH loved to watch Mary at her work, especially when she wasn't conscious of his glances. He had never seen anyone as graceful as she, or as cheerful, yet so recollected and absorbed in God. It gave him great joy just to watch her as one takes joy from watching a beautiful sunset. He loved to look out also from his shop on the street front and watch the Boy Jesus playing with the other boys. He couldn't help but marvel at the condescension of God. To think that this was God's Son; to realize that He was subject to him, Joseph of Nazareth, a simple man of ordinary ways! Joseph never lost his sense of dignity for Jesus and Mary. When he had to give directions or make decisions, it was always with kindness and gentleness, always with the reasons for his decisions so they would find it easier to obey.

DEAR JOSEPH, what splendid example you give me in your leadership of the Holy

Family! How clearly you show me that he rules best who rules least. He commands best who finds it harder to command than he finds it to obey—because he has such great respect for the dignity of his subjects. Only then does he command with gentleness and insight and understanding.

O MY LORD, how I need this lesson! I who tend to be so highhanded and gruff in my commands—without a real feeling for the temperament and problems and individual needs of each subject. Help me to realize that each person is an individual, with personal dignity and individual needs. Let me be so aware of each one's dignity, that I will command only when I have to; so conscious of each one's needs, that I will command each with a different approach.

It is respect and reverence for my subjects that give me the key, dear Master. Help me to have that healthy, wholesome respect for their dignity as human beings—and then my commands will be gracious.

DEATH OF ST. JOSEPH—TRUE SENSE OF VALUES

Tradition

1. *Joseph, his face bathed in sweat, smiling feebly at Jesus and Mary.*
2. *The grace, my Jesus, to live by the sense of values I will have on my deathbed.*

AS JESUS grew near to His thirtieth year, St. Joseph became very sick. Mary did everything she could to make him feel comfortable. She prepared a soft mat on which he could lie. She cooked the light broths that he could keep in his stomach. And for hours she sat down beside him, whether he was awake or asleep. She smiled and talked when he wanted to talk; and when he was weary, she was silent. Jesus, too, took time out from His work to keep him company. He helped Joseph recite some of the Psalms he loved so much. And when the end came, Jesus and Mary were both at his side, comforting, praying. In the heart of Joseph there was nothing but peace. His work was ended now. He smiled his appreciation to Jesus and Mary. With a willing heart he closed his eyes and surrendered his soul to God.

DEAR ST. JOSEPH, no wonder Our Holy Mother the Church has named you the patron of a happy death! You died in the arms of Jesus and Mary, surrounded by their loving care and affection. And you died with your work accomplished! Doing His Will had been hard at times, the reasons for it so often difficult to see. But you did His Will. And what peace it gave you at death!

DEAR ST. JOSEPH, how clearly we see life when we are about to leave it! At that time all riches and honors seem empty. Sin and neglect loom up as the horrible things they really are. And faithfulness to duty, struggle against temptations, the effort to do God's Will—what shining jewels, what true values are they! If only I could live my life in the light of the vision at the time of my death! This was how you lived, St. Joseph! Pray for me. Help me to picture my deathbed each day, and then live by that sense of values all day long—a man of good will.

JESUS LEAVES NAZARETH— DEPARTURES

Matt. 3 : 13

1. *Mary watching Jesus walk down the road out of Nazareth.*
2. *The grace, my Lord, of looking forward, not back.*

MARY WAS very proud of her tall, virtuous Son. After St. Joseph's death, He assumed the responsibility of head of the family. She looked to Him to make the decisions now and she wasn't disappointed.

Then one day news reached Nazareth about the new prophet God had sent to His people. John, Elizabeth's son, had left his desert retreat and was preaching that the Messiah was soon coming. Mary noticed a change in Jesus from that day forward. He seemed to be settling all His affairs at the shop, not accepting any further orders. She knew that His time was close at hand. Then one morning He held her at arm's length and looked intently at her as though to fix her face in His mind. He bent and kissed her on the forehead, and then turned and walked down the road to the south.

DEAR MARY, departures are always hard when they are departures from our loved ones. This was so hard on you. First Joseph; now Jesus. You were alone. You suspected you would see Him now and again in His public life, but it would never again be like Nazareth. There would be crowds and noise and hardly a chance to be alone with Him—not the warmth and closeness of these past years. Yet there were no tears, no complaints. You knew that life is a series of departures from the old familiar ways to the new unsure ways. You never tried to continue what God wanted to end.

MY MOTHER, help me to see that for me, too, life is a series of changes—departures from friends and loved ones, departures from home and customs and ways that I've grown to love. Teach me to make them bravely and cheerfully. Teach me not to waste time and energy on regrets or longings for the old ways. My King and my Mother, no departure was ever as sad as yours, yet you never looked back!

I will go forward, my King, to the new friends, the new surroundings, the new work!

JOHN'S PREPARATION FOR HIS WORK—SILENCE

Mark 1:1-6

1. *The lonely desert wastes of Judea and Transjordan; a solitary figure kneeling in prayer.*
2. *The grace to love silence and prayer and to retire to these as often as I can.*

FROM HIS early youth, John the Baptist was in the desert. Those chosen for great things must make great sacrifices, and they dare not be shallow. John gave up his parents and friends, wore the coarse clothing, ate the minimum and most distasteful of foods, spent many years of loneliness in the desert.

ST. JOHN, surely there were times when the loneliness was oppressive! Times when the monotony of the silence and sacrifice nearly drove you mad! Yet you turned all those temptations into greater and greater virtue. The more you were alone, the closer you were to God. You became so completely conscious of His nearness, His loving care. It became so easy for you to speak to Him. There were no distractions. Your silence wasn't empty; it was full, full of God and His love.

And how deeply you meditated on the eternal truths. In their glowing light, what peace and humility filled your heart.

DEAR LORD, the silence, prayer and self-denial combined to make John the greatest man next to St. Joseph and You that ever lived. Teach me then not to neglect these great means of grace. I so easily praise the worth of silence and spiritual reading with my lips, but so easily forget to do it. Compel me by Your grace to read and pray each day—to have that deep, internal silence of not being disturbed by little things. It is here that self-denial comes in, my Lord. I must control my feelings from going down the easy path of self-pity and resentment and even anxiety about my own faults. Teach me to be firm with my feelings and channel them into the tranquil, peaceful silence of love.

THE PREACHING OF THE BAPTIST— SORROW FOR SIN

Luke 3:1-6, Mark 1:5-6

1. *John, thin, tanned, humble but completely self-possessed, preaches to the crowd.*
2. *The grace, my Lord, of deep and abiding sorrow for my sins and abiding love for You.*

FINALLY the time came for John to begin his work. At the inspiration of the Holy Spirit, he left his desert retreat and began to preach. His message was electrifying. The long-awaited Messiah was about to come! The word passed like wildfire! There had been no prophet given to Israel for four hundred years, and now—a great prophet, the messenger of the Messiah! The crowds swelled to thousands, breathless to hear the news that would mean liberation from the Romans, a great increase in property, riches, glory! Their ideas about religion were so wrong. They thought religion was simply a matter of going through some outward rituals to placate God and in exchange they would get material riches and honors.

John stopped them in their tracks. His message was sincere but stern and uncompromising. "Repent," he said. They were heading in the wrong direction. The first step was to repent, to turn around and go back! They must confess their sins and be baptized.

DEAR ST. JOHN, how clearly you saw that religion is a matter of the heart, not of outward actions. Religion is love. If you were going to teach them this love of God, you first had to turn them away from their sins, their selfish desires for riches, their false ambition to conquer Romans rather than to conquer themselves! And so, like a masterful teacher, you have them act out their repentance to make it more vivid and strong. First you have them publicly confess that they are sinners. This helps them toward humility and it strengthens their resolve to get rid of their sinful ways and ideas. And then you had them baptized by you. It was only a sacramental, like ashes on Ash Wednesday, but vividly it impressed on their hearts that they needed to be washed from their sins.

DEAR ST. JOHN, while I do not have their false ideas about religion, still for me as well as for them the road to God is a road of repentance. I have sinned, and each sin, great or small, turned me away from Him. I must turn back! I see now that sorrow for sin isn't something gloomy or remorseful.

Sorrow for sin is just another form of love. It is turning back to God by rejecting what took me away from Him.

My God, my Father, I repent of all my sins. I reject them now and always. Let me have an abiding sorrow for my sins, that thus I may have an abiding love for You!

PHARISEES REBUKED BY THE BAPTIST—CHARACTER

Matt. 3:7-10

1. *John's eyes burning into the eyes of the Pharisees.*
2. *The grace, my King, of character, of living a life based on principles.*

THE CROWDS were so thrilled by John's sincerity and preaching that they brought their friends from all over Judea to hear him. Judea had never seen such a revival of faith and devotion. The Pharisees became disturbed about their own leadership. So they planned to pay attention to John. They figured that they would give him the flattery of coming to hear him and thus win him over to their side and make him their instrument.

The people gave place as the Pharisees walked through to the front. They were silent now, wondering what would happen. They knew that the Pharisees taught just the letter of the Law, that they were all outward show and no more. John had taught them true religion and had shown them that outward actions must proceed from love or else they are empty and vain. They wondered now what John would do. They didn't have long to wait. A scorching rebuke struck the Pharisees as they approached the man of God. "Brood of vipers!...even now the axe is laid to the root of the trees; every tree that is not bringing forth good fruit will be cut down and thrown into the fire!"

DEAR KING, what magnificent strength of character John shows us here! What a temptation for him to compromise, to ease up on his stern insistence of repentance and meet the Pharisees halfway! After all, they were the leaders of the people. Why not try to win them over to his side? But John knew that there could be no compromise between sincerity and insincerity; no common meeting ground for love and hypocrisy. Even a conference with these hypocrites would only confuse the people. So John lives and acts according to the principles he preaches. Sincerely, clearly, forcefully, his words express what his mind and heart feel. Either they are to repent and serve God with love, or be cut down like a dead tree!

MY LORD, character is life based on principles—not on moods or feelings or caprices! How ashamed then do I feel when I put my life alongside the life of St. John! It's so hard to live by what I know is right—when the people I am with are doing what is wrong! So hard to resist from joining in unkind talk or bad stories. So hard not to accept bribes when "everyone is doing it." So hard to be called a "stick-in-the-mud" by worldly people. O my King, in those moments, let me hear the strong voice of the Baptist. "Brood of vipers!" No compromise for him! That is why You loved him so much. Lord, make me strong. No compromise for me!

THE CROWDS ASK JOHN THE WAY—GOOD EXAMPLE

Luke 3:10-14

1. *The faces in the crowd alive with joy and admiration as John rebukes the Pharisees.*
2. *The grace, my Lord, to be true to my ideals.*

THE PHARISEES were white with rage at John's biting rebuke. They turned and walked away with as much composure as their anger would permit. Almost immediately, there was a murmur of admiration and approval throughout the crowd. It wasn't only what John taught that they admired, but more the fact that he lived by what he taught. He didn't back down from fear of censure, nor did he water down his teaching through expediency or human respect. Almost spontaneously, they surged forward to John, asking him what they should do—soldiers, publicans, men of all classes. What were they to do to please God? John was pleased, but he was as firm with them as he was with the Pharisees. No empty appearance of virtue would do. They must have real, living charity, practical charity, and they must live by strict justice and fairness. They took it and they loved it!

DEAR LORD, it's almost a terrifying thing to realize the influence that one person's life can have on souls. It's so clear in this scene that the crowds were inspired not so much by ideals as by a person. Fine ideals are attractive, but people who live by them are irresistible! How wonderful that John didn't disappoint the crowds that day. If he had swerved one inch from his ideals, he would have lost them. They would have been absolutely convinced that his teaching was just another version of the old hypocrisy. But

John stuck to his ideals, fought for his principles, and he set their hearts on fire!

MY KING, whether I like it or not, souls are going to be influenced by me for better or for worse. I'm somebody's hero. I can't escape it. And those who know me and watch me aren't influenced so much by what I say as by what I am. If I'm true, if I live by my ideals, they will be inspired. And if I'm a hypocrite, I will lose them—You will lose them.

Make me true! Don't let me say what I don't really mean completely. Don't let me stand for something that I'm not willing to fight for and to die for. Let my ideals be Your ideals! Let them come from the heart. Then give me the heart to live them and never back down because of human respect.

JOHN'S WITNESS TO THE CROWD: "NOT THE CHRIST"—HUMILITY

Luke 3:15-18

1. *The men in the crowd whispering to others that John must really be the Messiah.*
2. *The grace, my Lord, to know myself as I am, and to be glad to be that and no more!*

THE REACTION of the people after John rebuked the Pharisees continued to spread. His name was on everyone's lips. Discussions about his teaching went on all day in the market place, at the well where the women drew the water, and in the courtyard of the Temple. The crowds swelled into thousands to listen to him preach. Gradually the word began to spread that he himself must be the Messiah. Who else but the great Expected One could draw such crowds? Who else could move hardened sinners to repentance and bring such hope and peace? Finally, some were urged to ask him directly. They put it in a positive way; they wanted him to know that they really believed it already. "Surely you must be the Anointed One," they told him. All listened anxiously. John shook his head: "One mightier than I is coming, the strap of whose sandals I am not worthy to loose."

O MY KING, how truly admirable is St. John in this scene. If he had been any less great, he would have forgotten his place. He would have been so flattered by the great crowds and their wonderful opinion of him that he would have imagined himself more than he was. Anyone less grounded in humility would have been so impressed with his own importance when the Pharisees came to hear him—and would have been so afraid to offend them. But not John! The years of silence and prayer in the desert had taught him true humility. He never forgot his role; never forgot who he was.

MY LORD, I need so much a humility like John's! How easily flattery goes to my head! It makes me imagine myself to be so much better than I am. And to keep up the false illusion, to have those who praise me keep praising, I shade my opinions — I say what I think they'd like to hear. It's like living a lie. And it certainly brings me no peace. For I know deep in my soul that some day the bubble must burst and the illusion fade—and then all will see me as I really am.

DEAR LORD, teach me to know what I am —with my talents and my limitations. And then let me be glad to be that and nothing more! No airs, no sham, no hypocrisy. Don't let me forget my place. When praised, let me accept it graciously, but know in my heart how much is true and how much false. And when I am blamed, let me realize how much I am wrong and apologize to that extent—and no more. Make me true, honest with myself, honest with others, honest with You!

JESUS IS BAPTIZED BY JOHN— PERFECTION

Matt. 3:13-17

1. *The Dove above the Head of Jesus.*
2. *The grace, my Lord, to do my work perfectly.*

ONE DAY as John was baptizing, he noticed a tall, lone Figure Who waited on the shore. When all the others were finished, He drew near and adjusted His garments to be baptized. John recognized Him then. It was his cousin Jesus. John did not yet know that Jesus was divine, but he did know His great holiness and sinlessness. "I ought to be baptized by Thee," he said, trying to stop Jesus; "and dost Thou come to me?" Jesus reassured him. He wanted "to fulfill all justice." John obeyed. And as the water flowed over His Sacred Head, the heavens were opened. The Holy Ghost descended in the form of a Dove upon Jesus. And the voice of the Father resounded about them: "This is My Beloved Son, in Whom I am well pleased."

MY KING, how perfectly God does His work! When man fell into sin, the Father could have forgiven him right away—without Your becoming a Man and dying for our sins. He didn't have to demand strict justice. But He did demand it—because only then could we see the beautiful example of Your life and see how God acts in human form. Only then could we realize the enormity of sin, when its forgiveness in justice required such a price! And only then, my King, could we understand how great is God's love for us. God's work is perfect.

Perfect also is Your work as the God-man, my King. You were going to take on Yourself all our sins—so You went through the baptism of John which symbolized the need to be washed from sin. And when John wanted to prevent You, as sincere as his intentions were, You didn't let him interfere with the perfection of Your work. With that beautiful humility which knew how to command as well as to obey, You insisted on the baptism of repentance. Thus, humbly and perfectly, You began Your role as Saviour. It was no wonder that the heavens burst asunder: "My Beloved Son, in Whom I am well pleased."

DEAR LORD, You teach me so clearly that if a job is worth doing, it is worth doing perfectly! Not that You want me to be a perfectionist, the sort who can't distinguish between unnecessary details and essentials.

Such a person misses the big picture, the whole work, and "fails to see the forest for the trees"! No, Lord, You want me to do my work perfectly in the sense of seeing its purpose in the light of faith, and then doing it with perfect love. Faith will let me see the essentials—the heart of the work. It will make me see that details are fine only if they can be done without neglecting the essentials. And love will make the whole work pure gold in Your sight. My Lord, Your work was perfect. Let mine be perfect too!

JESUS FASTS IN THE DESERT—SELF-DISCIPLINE

Matt. 4:1-11

1. *Jesus, kneeling beside a large rock, His Face lifted to Heaven.*
2. *The grace, my Lord, to die to my lower self.*

ONLY THE Baptist and Jesus heard the voice of the Father. The crowd was dispersing. Jesus left the water and readjusted His garments. Before John knew it, He was gone. He wandered into the barren and mountainous wasteland not too far away. And there the Son, just exalted by the Father and the Holy Spirit, manifested His human nature by suffering hunger and loneliness as any other human being would suffer. For forty days and nights He kept His lonely vigil without any food or drink. His throat became parched and ached for water. His whole body became weak and rigid with pangs of hunger. His heart longed for the comfort of human companionship. Yet there was nothing but silence. For long weary hours, He prayed—prayed for souls, the confused, the lonely, the suffering. He told His Father again and again how much He loved Him, how greatly He desired to lead all men to praise Him forever. The beatific vision flooded His soul with light and warmth. Gradually the joy of that vision poured over into His pain-wracked Body and lonely human Heart. And even in His pain He had peace.

MY KING, You never did anything without having a good reason and a noble motive. In this long vigil of fast and prayer, Your motive was not to suffer for suffering's sake. You were not a sadist or a stoic. You acted thus to show us a very great lesson—that if we are going to accomplish anything great for God, we must begin by conquering ourselves. If we are going to grow in prayer, if we expect to live the Christ-life and win souls, we have to go through the agony of dying to our lower selves. We have to pay the price!

O MY LORD, how I fail to see this! I imagine that my prayers must be lofty ecstacy. And when dryness takes hold of me, I'm ready to give up. Teach me, my Lord, that I'll never learn to pray well until I've gone through the desert of dryness and confusion and my heart is as cold as stone. I imagine that to win souls I have to be the center of attraction. And when I am overlooked or ignored, I'm despondent—as though somehow I am a failure. And yet, my Lord, no one can lead others graciously until he knows what it means to be ignored and set aside. You know all this and that's why You give me the opportunities to die to self. Let me not waste them, my King. Let me pay the price! Lead me into the desert with You that I may conquer myself.

JESUS TEMPTED BY THE DEVIL (1)— SIMPLICITY

Matt. 4:1-11

1. *The devil offering Jesus a stone.*
2. *The grace, my Lord, of true simplicity.*

THE LONG, gruelling ordeal in the desert finally came to an end. Jesus was very

thin and painfully weak. But in His soul there was peace and light and warmth. For the devil who had watched the fast, it was all very disturbing. First, the Father's witness, "My Beloved Son"; then, the magnificent self-discipline of the fast, and the soaring heights of prayer and contemplation. Surely this was the greatest Adversary he ever had to face. He determined to find out what "Beloved Son" implied. He would test Him to discover His weak spot.

"If thou art the Son of God, command that these stones become loaves of bread." A subtle temptation not to trust the Father, as though the Father in His Providence would not provide bread once Jesus left the desert area. Just as subtly, Jesus replied, recalling how the Father had fed the Jews with manna even in the desert. He wanted the Jews and all men to realize that "not by bread alone does man live, but by every word that comes forth from the mouth of God." It was magnificent! Jesus saw through the temptation and yet did not reveal His divinity. He answered as any human being might do.

O MY LORD, how I admire Your beautiful simplicity in this struggle with the prince of liars and deceivers! Satan is never direct or open in his temptations. He covers the tracks of his evil designs by presenting temptations in another form—often under the guise of something good. But deceit and craftiness are no match for true prudence and simplicity. You were single-minded, my Jesus. You had one goal—to honor the Father. The time would come when working miracles would honor the Father and inspire souls—and then You would work them. But turning stones to bread here would be an unnecessary use of Divine Power and a lack of trust in Your Father. Your simplicity brought you to the heart of the matter, past all the side-roads of deceit.

DEAR MASTER, how much I need that beautiful virtue if I am to avoid the snares of Satan! How often I have fallen for "holy temptations"! The temptation of good works—running around in a maze of work, letting my spiritual life run down until my motives were just shot through and through with conceit and human respect and self-pity! And all the time I thought I was doing so well! The devil covered up the tracks! Not to speak of all his other deceits—making me think that being timid was being truly humble; that avoiding people I dislike was charity; that certain bad books and plays were necessary adult interests because everybody was discussing them; the temptation to read the writings of the mystics, before I am spiritually mature for them! How I need Your simplicity, my Jesus! Help me to have one goal—love—love and service to You. Let that goal be my scale, my ruler, my measure of every other action. Let my question always be: "Does this help me, my God, to love You better?"

JESUS TEMPTED BY THE DEVIL (2)— SERENE TRUST

Matt. 4:1-11

1. *The glittering kingdoms of the world presented in a vision to Jesus by the devil.*
2. *The grace, my Lord, of serenity and trust in all the darkness and sin of the world.*

THE FIRST failure didn't discourage the devil. With his preternatural power, he transported Jesus to the pinnacle of the Temple. "If Thou art the Son of God, throw Thyself down," he suggested. Surely the angels would carry Him safely to the ground. And what a grand entrance into His public life to descend so dramatically, like a prophet from Heaven! Again Jesus saw through the subtle temptation. To throw Himself down when He could walk down would be the sin of tempting God—expecting divine intervention when His ordinary human powers were sufficient. "Thou shalt not tempt the Lord Thy God." With one sentence from Sacred Scripture, Jesus showed the devil that He saw through his treachery. And again He answered as any human being could do.

The devil didn't have to be told now that Jesus was more than human. His worst fears were confirmed. Unspeakable hatred tore at him. With that same abandonment and blind pride which led him to defy God in the beginning, he made his most foolish and spiteful temptation. Showing Jesus all the alluring things of the world, he said: "All these will I give Thee if Thou wilt fall down and worship me!" All the irreverence and hate of hell were in his words. The beautiful soul of Jesus revolted in disgust. With sweeping power of command, He dismissed him: "Begone, Satan . . . The Lord Thy God shalt thou worship and Him only shalt thou serve." Weak then from exhaustion, He fell to the ground, and angels came to strengthen His emaciated Body.

DEAR LORD, what a titanic struggle this was! We are liable to think that the great battles in history have been military battles. And we look upon victories like Thermopylae, Lepanto and Waterloo as turning points of history. But, my King, they were like mock battles and toy soldiers compared to Your struggle with Satan. Never since the fall of Adam and Eve did so much depend on an encounter as depended on this one. And You won! You began the victory here; You finished it with such a terrible cost on Calvary. And with You we won! Heaven was opened and grace poured out on all of us.

DEAR MASTER, so often I am tempted to be discouraged when I see the flood of evil in the world—the appalling amount of indecent books and pictures, the injustice, the impurity, the atheistic philosophies. It all looks so hopeless—until I picture this scene and realize that the ultimate victory is assured. We have to fight the battle, dear Lord, but the war has already been won! When I stop to think of it, my King, Satan's power has already been broken. How very few are possessed by the devil today as compared to ancient times. See how many millions love You deeply and lead lives of spotless virtue and burning charity. And even the apparent evil—even that can be turned to good through tears and sincere repentance and reparation. I must do my part, Lord—fight like You to conquer evil and win souls. But thrill me always with this vision that the ultimate victory has already been won!

JOHN POINTS OUT JESUS TO THE DISCIPLES (1) —DOCILITY OF HEART

John 1 : 29-40

1. *John, his hand extended toward Jesus, saying, "Behold the Lamb of God!"*
2. *The grace, my Lord, to wait for Your light with docility of heart.*

DURING the forty days of Our Lord's fast, John continued preaching and baptizing, preparing men's hearts for Jesus. He didn't know where Jesus was, or why He delayed. He just knew that in His own time, He would again appear. Meantime, John kept doing his own work. Then on the day after the temptation by the devil, Jesus did appear again at the Jordan. John was taken back at first by His emaciated appearance. In a flash he realized the whole story. Jesus had prepared for His public life with a long vigil of fast and prayer—in very much the same manner as John himself had done under the inspiration of the Holy Spirit. Jesus must be ready now to announce Himself to Israel! So John pointed to Him with reverence and deep feeling: "Behold the Lamb of God, Who takes away the sins of the world!"

DEAR KING, there are so many admirable traits in John the Baptist. One of the most attractive is this docility of heart, this willingness to wait patiently in the darkness until You manifest Yourself in Your own time and in Your own way. Once You came to him at the Jordan, he naturally would have supposed You were ready to begin Your work. But then, as suddenly as You had come, You disappeared. John didn't know where You went or why, or when You would return. Another man would have been tempted to be annoyed at being kept in the dark. After all, he was the messenger to announce Your coming! Why shouldn't he know the whole plan? But such thoughts or feelings never occurred to John. He let You work in Your own way and in Your own time. He was content to keep doing his work in the dark until You chose to send him the light.

O MY LORD, how I need this wonderful docility of the Baptist. I'm so tempted to be resentful if I'm not taken into the confidence of others—if they don't explain to me every reason for their actions. Teach me that confidence cannot be forced. I must wait and let others tell me their plans in their own time and in their own way.

WHAT IS even worse, my Lord, is the way I lack this docility with You! I want to see clearly Your whole plan for me. I grow impatient with my spiritual progress—can't understand why You don't hurry it along. I resent temptations and obstacles and failures. And because I can't see the reasons for them, I grow despondent and weak in faith. O my King, teach me to be like the Baptist. Let me know that You have a plan for my life, even though I don't see it. In Your own time, You will open it all to my eyes. Meantime, let me love the darkness as a chance to trust You with complete docility. Like John, I will keep up my work, my efforts toward perfection, without resentment. And some day You will come with Your light and Your peace.

JOHN POINTS OUT JESUS TO HIS DISCIPLES (2) —DETACHMENT

John 1 : 29-40

1. *The Baptist watching John and Andrew follow Jesus along the bank of the river.*
2. *The grace, my Lord, to be detached even from my friends and loved ones.*

JOHN THE BAPTIST was disappointed when he pointed to Jesus that first day and no one seemed to notice Him. So he gathered his close friends about him after the crowds had dispersed, and told them all about Jesus and the wondrous voice of the Father from Heaven. On the following day, Jesus appeared again on the bank of the Jordan. "Behold the Lamb of God!" the Baptist called out clearly, proudly. His disciples were ready then. John and Andrew left their place by his side and followed Jesus. "Master, where dwellest Thou?" they asked. "Come and see!" Side by side they walked with Him along the bank of the river. Above the heads of the crowd the Baptist watched them leave and follow Jesus. He was surrounded by the crowd, but the man of the desert was lonely once again.

DEAR JOHN THE BAPTIST, what beautiful detachment you showed at that moment when you directed your friends to Jesus! Your life had been so terribly lonely in the desert—without human companionship, without friends to share your hopes, your lofty thoughts and ideals. And then the Holy Spirit called you out of your lonely retreat and gave you wonderful friends—sincere patriots like John and James, impetuous, lovable men like Peter and Andrew, guileless, gentle Philip. They were men with whom you could discuss spiritual ideals, men who were generous with their time and energy in helping you with the crowds. How you had learned to love them! And yet, now that Jesus came on the scene, you didn't hold them back one minute. Any lesser man would have kept some of them with him, would have made the excuse that he needed experienced helpers to continue his work. Not you! God needed them elsewhere. Their spiritual advancement depended on their being with Jesus. So to Jesus you sent them, even though you knew you would miss them so much.

MY LORD, how admirable is that detachment of John the Baptist! How clearly he realized that friends and loved ones are loaned to us by God—are not outright possessions. I fail here so easily, my King. I forget that my loved ones are only loaned, and I strive to hold onto them, no matter what may be Your plan or their own spiritual needs. I spend all my time with them to the neglect of others who need me. I hold them back from serving You better when their new task will take them away from me. And like flowers that are held too tightly and crushed, I crush and ruin Your beautiful gifts of friendship by overindulgence and exclusiveness.

DEAR LORD, loving my friends is good, but only if I love them rightly. I must love like John, with detachment. Keep me from indulgence, my Jesus, and from exclusiveness. Teach me to love them with open hands—ready to let You take them whenever You wish.

JESUS CALLS HIS FIRST APOSTLES— VOCATION

John 1 : 41-51

1. *The startled look on Peter's face as Jesus shows that He knows him.*
2. *The grace, my Lord, to know my vocation and generously to follow it.*

IT WAS about four o'clock when John and Andrew started to speak with Jesus. For the two or three hours until sunset, they listened and asked questions. When they finally left to find their brothers and friends, it was with hearts that were inflamed. "We have found the Messiah!" Andrew called out to his brother Simon. But Simon was one who would judge for himself. How amazed he was then on the following day when Jesus looked at him for the first time and seemed to see right through to the depths of his soul. "Thou art Simon, the son of John," Jesus said; "thou shalt be called Cephas (which interpreted is Peter)"—the Rock!

Philip had the same feeling as Simon. Too timid to approach Jesus on his own, he discovered that Jesus saw into his heart and knew his desire. Suddenly Jesus was saying to him what he so wanted to hear, "Follow Me!" Nathaniel also. Before Philip told him the good news, Jesus had already chosen him.

DEAR LORD, this scene gives us so much comfort because it makes us realize how completely we are loved and cared for by Divine Providence. Peter and Nathaniel thought that they were coming to judge You—and if they approved, then to choose to follow You. With bold easy strokes You showed them that You had chosen them. From all eternity it was decreed that Simon would be the Rock, that Philip and Nathaniel, James and John would be Apostles. Their hearts and minds and souls were fashioned with the qualities You wanted them to have—in order best to do the work You wanted each one of them to do. No detail lay outside the care and plan of Your loving Providence.

DEAR FATHER in Heaven, like the Apostles and indeed like all other persons on earth, I am called by You to a special vocation—to do a work for You that no one else can do. For this work You fitted me with the right talents, the distinct personality, the proper disposition. How important, my Father, that I find my true vocation and have the courage to follow it cheerfully! The vocation You want for me is for me the path to happiness and true greatness. To be the living fulfillment of Your Holy Will — what greater peace — what greater way to accomplish the work You have destined me to do.

Let me listen for Your call, my Lord. With the help of a spiritual director, let me analyze my abilities and limitations — and above all, my deepest desires—to find which path You wish me to walk as You say "Follow Me!"

THE WEDDING FEAST AT CANA (1)— CALMNESS AND PEACE

John 2:1-12

1. *The sad look on the face of Mary as she sees Jesus so thin and worn.*
2. *The grace to be calm and peaceful under tension.*

MARY LOOKED forward so anxiously to the wedding at Cana. It had been three months now since Jesus had left her to begin His work. How she longed to see Him again. The longest time that they had been separated before was the three days He was lost in the Temple as a Boy. But all those years she had Him to herself. What intimate and lovable conversations they had shared! What joys in talking about the Father and the life of virtue! And then the three lonely months, three months almost unbelievably empty. And now! Now she would see Him again!

Mary worked hard at the feast. She got there early and helped in all the preparations. She knew how much was on hand for food and drink; she tried to make everything pleasant for the couple and the guests. And then someone came in and told her that Jesus was coming. He had five or six friends with Him. Mary folded her apron and went out to meet Him. She almost lost her breath when she saw Him! He was so painfully thin from the fast; His skin so dark and weather-beaten! But she said no word, gave no sign. She welcomed Him; she greeted His friends. She couldn't help but be attracted to the youthful, sincere, enthusiastic John. She little suspected that some day soon Jesus would give her into John's keeping.

MY MOTHER, you were so wonderful and strong in this scene. Another woman would have burst into tears at the sight of Jesus. Not you! You had such complete mastery over your feelings. Any other woman would have gotten excited at meeting all His friends, would have been nervous and fidgety and anxious. You were so different. You were calm as you welcomed them, gracious as you talked, thoughtful as you guided them to their places and began to serve them. You were always Yourself!

MARY, MY MOTHER, teach me the secret of your calmness and peace. When the unexpected happens to me—as it did to you that day—I tend to get so excited and worried. And when emergencies arise, I trip all over myself, I make others nervous, and I get nothing done. Teach me to be humble, my Mother, to accept myself as I am, and to be perfectly resigned that others see me as I am. Then I will not be nervous about how I do things, will not be overanxious to impress others! I will do what I can calmly and peacefully, and leave the rest in God's Hands!

THE WEDDING FEAST AT CANA (2)— CHARITY

John 2:1-12

1. *Mary noticing the worried looks on the faces of the waiters.*
2. *The grace to make myself be interested—really interested—in the needs and plans of others.*

ONCE JESUS and His new friends were reclining at table, Mary served them and did all to make them feel at home. She was graciousness itself as she anticipated their needs in the most gentle and unobtrusive way. But suddenly she began to notice the furtive glances and the worried looks of the waiters, the whispered advice to be more sparing with the wine. Gently she excused herself from the little group and went to the kitchen. Just as she suspected, there was very little wine left. She felt so badly for the young couple and for the embarrassment that they would soon have to face. But wait! Maybe Jesus . . . She went back to her Son and got His attention. She spoke simply, gently. She told Him the facts: "They have no wine." Jesus almost seemed to resent it. He knew His Mother so well. She never wasted words.

A statement of someone's need made by Mary was really a plea for help. And yet the hour of the miracles had not yet come. He had planned to wait for John to finish his work. Jesus told this to Mary, but it was in a way that she knew He was not refusing. She smiled her thanks. She called the waiters and, nodding towards her Son, she said: "Do whatever He tells you."

MY MOTHER, yours was a truly great heart and a charitable heart! You truly felt for others. There were so many worries on your mind that day—worries about Jesus and how thin He was, anxiety to please His friends and make them at home. And yet you made yourself think of others. Another woman would have said, "It's none of my affair; I should mind my own business." Not you, my Mother. Everyone's suffering was your business.

O MY MOTHER and Queen, how I need that beautiful virtue of kind, unselfish interest in others. I get tired of listening to their stories and I start talking about myself instead. I get annoyed at the moods and changes of others and I show it. And thus I miss opportunities for humility and charity. And I fail to be like you and like Jesus!

Teach me to adopt the mood of those I'm with! Make me be interested in others and in their plans and stories and ideas. Let me be more enthused about their plans than about any ideas of my own. Let me feel for their sorrows or embarrassment more keenly than for my own. Let me be like You, my Lord, and my Mother!

JESUS CLEANSES THE TEMPLE (1)— CHRISTIAN FORTITUDE

John 2:13-25

1. *The mob surprised and frightened before the angry look of Jesus.*
2. *The grace, my Lord, of courage to fight for what is right.*

AFTER A FEW DAYS' stay at Capharnaum, Jesus and Mary and the first five Apostles made the journey to Jerusalem for the Passover. When they entered the Temple, they heard its usual peace broken by a great uproar. Men were shouting and bargaining, oxen and sheep were bleating. Jesus stiffened. His Father's house made into a market place! A fierce, set look came over His features. His hands seized some cords and tied them into a whip. His eyes never left the scene before

Him. He walked forward then, arms outstretched. "Take these things away!" He cried out. His voice was strong, yet trembling with anger. An uneasy fear came over the crowd, as His eyes burned into theirs. They hurried away their oxen and sheep, those in back urging on those in front. The money-changers alone held their ground. Jesus seized the end of their tables and sent them flying end over end. They became panic-stricken then. They grasped what coins they could and ran. Jesus stood alone in the courtyard. Peace settled again over the Temple.

MY LORD, how I admire You in this scene! We are so liable to think that being a Christian means being a weakling and a "mouse"! How wonderful to see that distorted notion so firmly dispelled by the example of Your magnificent courage! Your Father's house was being desecrated; there was reason for the fighting—so You fought! You didn't care what they thought or what they would say. His glory was primary! Nor did it matter to You that You were alone against them all. Your courage was so great and Your cause so just that the entire crowd fled before You.

DEAR MASTER, it is so easy for me to get confused on this important point. I'm so liable to think that Your command "to turn the other cheek" means to take any insult and never fight back! And so I become afraid to fight—or if I do fight, I feel very badly, as though somehow I had let You down. Teach me the real meaning of Your words. Turning the other cheek means being willing to forgive and forget when the injustice is over. It does not mean giving in to the injustice, or being a weakling.

Give me Your courage then, Lord, to fight for justice and fairness. Give me the backbone to say what I know is right, even though others oppose me. Courage, Lord! Magnificent courage like Yours!

JESUS CLEANSES THE TEMPLE (2)—JUST ANGER

John 2:13-25

1. *The rulers of the Temple rushing towards Jesus.*
2. *The grace, my Lord, to fight only for a worthy cause.*

THE TEMPLE authorities rushed out from the Priests' Court very much annoyed that someone had usurped their authority.

A delegation of some five or six of them walked quickly to where Jesus stood, determined to put Him in His place. Suddenly Jesus turned to face them. Anger burned in His glance. This was the group most responsible for the disrespect to His Father's house! The fierce look in His Face made them all halt in their headlong rush. Fear began to seize them. Forgotten then was their determination to put Him out forcefully. Instead they stammered out a question: "What sign dost Thou show us, seeing that Thou dost these things?" Their change of attitude and the timidity of their question showed Jesus that He had already won His point. They didn't question what He had done! They just asked for a proof of His authority. This was reasonable, so Jesus gave them a sign—the coming miracle of His resurrection from the dead. Pointing to Himself, He said: "Destroy this Temple and in three days I will raise it up."

MY KING, Your magnificent example shows me so well the conditions for just anger. First of all, You had a good cause for Your anger—God's glory. Secondly, Your anger was only as strong as was necessary, and no stronger. You overturned the tables of the money-changers because they wouldn't move. But You didn't touch the cages of the dove-sellers because they listened, and left the Temple. And finally, Your anger subsided when You achieved Your goal. There was no pouting or stony silence before the rulers of the Temple. You faced them and answered their question reasonably and fairly.

O MY KING, how often I ignore each of these conditions in turn, thus making my anger unjust. I get irritable and cranky over little things, and thus prove myself as small as the things that irritate me. My King, teach me not to fight until I have a cause worth fighting for.

So often also I lose my temper completely when I get angry. I become unreasonable and denounce everything about the opposition. Teach me Your marvellous self-restraint, my King, so that I may have self-control even when I'm angry.

And, dear Lord, once the dispute is over, teach me to "turn the other cheek." Don't let me assume that cold, aloof air that I have taken so often. Help me to be big, to forgive and forget.

JESUS CLEANSES THE TEMPLE (3)— BENEFITS OF JUST ANGER

John 2:13-25

1. *John's look of admiration for Jesus as Jesus leaves the Temple.*
2. *The grace, my Lord, to realize the benefits of taking a stand and fighting for justice.*

THE RULERS of the Temple pretended not to know what Jesus meant when He gave them the sign of His resurrection. But they did know. And after His death, they showed that they understood by asking Pilate to guard the tomb. The money-changers and merchants also understood clearly that they were wrong. Those among them who were sincere would never violate the holiness of the Temple again. The Temple was a peaceful and prayerful place once again. And all the issues were clear.

MY MASTER, one of the big advantages of just anger is that it "clears the air" of all misunderstandings and sets issues and ideals in bold relief. Persons can go on for years being guilty of selfishness, injustice and all kinds of harm to others, without ever clearly realizing what they are doing. It is only when someone has the courage to fight for what is right, that the wrongdoing is sharply defined. And then the path is cleared for the guilty one to correct his abuses. This "clearing of the air" is so much better for him, my King, than allowing him to continue in his selfishness and injustice. "Clearing the air" is good for the one offended also. It enables him to get the rancor and hurt out of his heart so he can start again to feel kindly toward the offender.

O MY KING, how often I have been too timid to make clear some unjust matter to the offender. I just got more and more angry inside, felt so sorry for myself, and got to the point where I couldn't stomach the guilty party. How wrong this was, my King. And how bitter the feeling became! If only I had fought, "cleared the air," had said what was wrong—it would all be out of me. I'd relax in my feelings toward him because I would know that he was conscious of his fault.

Help me to have courage, Lord! If the injustice is too small to fight over, then let me be big enough to forget it—to take it as one of those necessary annoyances that have to come in every life. But if it is big and worth fighting for, then, my King, teach me to fight—bravely and with restraint, with forgiveness at the end!

NICODEMUS COMES TO JESUS (1)— NEW LIFE OF GRACE

John 3:1-21

1. *The light of the oil lamp reflected on the earnest faces of Jesus and Nicodemus and the young Apostle John.*
2. *The grace, my Lord, to appreciate sanctifying grace and avoid what would take it away.*

NICODEMUS watched in amazement when Jesus cleansed the Temple. Our Lord's sincerity and air of authority struck him. This was the stuff of which prophets were made! He called one of the Apostles aside and asked where Jesus would stay overnight. And that night he came. It was an exciting moment for the Apostles, for Nicodemus was a member of the Sanhedrin.

Nicodemus was generous in his compliments to Jesus and they were sincere compliments because his was a sincere heart. He felt that there was very little lacking to himself. He would find out just what little remained for perfection. Jesus left him under no illusion. The Old Law was just a shadow and a preparation. He must take on an entire new life; he must be "born again." By natural birth he took on human life, became the child of his parents. Before he could begin to please God, he would have to take on the divine life of grace, become a child of God.

DEAR LORD, You made clear to Nicodemus that life in Your kingdom was not an external thing, not something that we put on on Sunday—like a new suit—and then take off the rest of the week. It wasn't even just a strong effort on our part to be good—fine as that is—because with our purely human life we could do nothing to gain heaven. For that we needed a new life, an interior life—grace. Grace would dwell in our soul and raise our soul to a new level of living, a created sharing of the very life which God Himself has in an uncreated way. Thus grace would give us the ability to share God's happiness in heaven.

The powers of our soul would be elevated also. Our mind would now be able to think with supernatural faith; our will, trust and love with supernatural hope and charity. And every good action we now performed would not be a mere human action—it would be the action of a child of God, and hence very pleasing to God.

DEAR MASTER, I see now that true greatness lies not in doing great things, but in being something great—being alive with grace and charity. I feel ashamed that up till now I valued grace so little; that I was unconscious of the unspeakable dignity it conferred upon me! And when I think of the times that I endangered it so—by entering the occasions of sin!

O my Lord, let me be great in grace and charity. Let me die rather than lose my supernatural dignity by mortal sin!

NICODEMUS COMES TO JESUS (2)—SACRAMENTAL SYSTEM

John 3:1-21

1. *The Apostles and Nicodemus listening attentively to Jesus.*
2. *The grace, my Lord, to love the Sacraments as my way to holiness.*

THIS DOCTRINE of rebirth was hard for Nicodemus to understand. He took Our Lord's expression, "born again," in the literal, physical sense. So Jesus explained that membership in His kingdom was accomplished by a spiritual rebirth, by the coming of a new life—sanctifying grace. He compared grace

to the gentle, cool breeze that was blowing about them. They couldn't see where it came from or where it went, but it was real, and it was refreshing. So also with grace. One could not see it, but it was real and it was a new life. A man would know that he was receiving it, because it would be given to him by means of an outward sign. "Unless a man be born again of water and the Spirit, he cannot enter the kingdom of God."

DEAR MASTER, You were a perfect Teacher and a most gracious Redeemer to accommodate Yourself thus to our limitations! You knew that we had to see, that we needed to be assured that we were pleasing to You. So with these words You began the wonderful Sacramental system—that series of seven visible signs, through which You would give us Your invisible grace. Like the radio waves that fill the air, Your grace is real, but it cannot be perceived by our human senses. So You give it to us through signs that we can see, to assure us that we are receiving it.

Here You tell us about Baptism, the beginning of the new life. Later You will tell us about the others: Confirmation, which makes us grown-up Christians and soldiers;

Holy Eucharist, Your Own Body and Blood to nourish our spiritual life; Penance, like a second Baptism, when we lose Your grace through mortal sin; Matrimony, to propagate the Mystical Body; Holy Orders, to bring supernatural life to souls; and Extreme Unction, to strengthen us in our last great struggle at death. Each Sacrament increases our interior life of grace, and each gives special helps according to the individual purpose of the Sacrament.

DEAR LORD, Nicodemus must have looked surprised at this lavish outpouring of supernatural gifts. So You told him how they would be won for us. They would be purchased at the frightful price of Your Passion and Death! Through Your death we would come to life!

Lord, how I should prize this priceless inheritance—the Sacraments! When I receive them, I can know that I am receiving Your grace and sharing in Your life. Let me love them—especially Penance and Holy Eucharist—and let me receive them often and devoutly. Let me value them according to the price that was paid for them.

NICODEMUS COMES TO JESUS (3)— INTERIOR LIFE

John 3:1-21

1. *Two children: one in a coma, hardly breathing; the other, full of life, running, playing.*
2. *The grace, my Lord, to cultivate the interior life of grace.*

JESUS MADE CLEAR to Nicodemus that the life in His kingdom was the new, interior life of grace, which made a man a son of God. He also explained that though grace was invisible, we could know we were receiving it because He would give it to us through outward signs, called Sacraments. Once we received the first Sacrament, of Baptism, then we were living with the Christ-life in our soul.

Up to this point, the transformation in us is God's work. But, as Jesus will tell us later on in the parable of the sower, once the seed of grace enters the soil of our soul, from then on it is our work! All growth then depends upon our cooperation, our prayer, our self-discipline and generosity.

TO BE A CHRISTIAN then, my Lord, means to nourish this Christ-life of grace and charity until it infuses everything we are and think, everything we say and do. By sincere meditation on the Gospel, our minds must absorb Your outlook and ideals. By self-discipline and devotion to our duties, our wills must be forged with the steel of Your magnificent virtues. Then the seed of Your grace will find fertile soil—soil that is ready to give of itself in order that the seed might grow to Your full image and likeness.

DEAR MASTER, how badly I have neglected this inward life! As though the Sacraments were magic tricks or secret formulas that could make me a saint in spite of myself! As though the seed could grow without the soil!

DEAR LORD, help me to prize Your Sacraments so much that I won't abuse them again by careless preparation or sloppy, thoughtless reception. Teach me to make the soil of my soul ready for Your grace. Let me prepare remotely by regular spiritual reading and by an earnest, sincere prayer life. And as I approach the Confessional or Holy Communion, let me stir up true sorrow for sin, ardent desire for Your presence, and gratitude, my King. Let gratitude be the most notable mark of all!

LAST WITNESS OF JOHN—CONSENT TO BE HUMAN

John 3:22-36

1. *The anxiety and hurt look on the face of John's disciple; on the face of John the look of joy and peace.*
2. *The grace, my Jesus, to accept to be what I am, to be human, with all its limitations.*

AFTER THE evening with Nicodemus, Jesus and His new band of followers left Jerusalem and headed for Jericho and the Jordan. There crowds came to them as they had come to John. John had moved up the river nearer to Galilee, busy as usual preparing men for Jesus. Jesus and the Apostles preached—but it was still the preaching of John, the preaching of repentance to prepare for the kingdom. And like John, they baptized and had men confess and acknowledge that they were sinners.

One day one of John's followers saw the crowd and felt a pang of jealousy for his master, John. He got into a heated discussion with one of the Apostles and then left to tell John about Jesus. There was indignation in his words: "He to whom thou hast borne witness, behold He baptizes and all are coming to Him!" It wasn't fair; he was hurt for his master. But as he looked at John, he detected a wonderful light of peace and joy come over his face—as though somehow his work had borne fruit. John explained that it was precisely that men might know and love Jesus that he, John, had come. This was his work and his mission. And he added: "This my joy, therefore, is made full. He must increase, but I must decrease."

DEAR LORD, what exquisite humility John had. He is the very essence of contentment with his mission, his work, with the love of some and the hatred of others, with the praise of some and the biting criticism of others; content with his life of silence and with his hectic life of preaching—and eventually even with prison and death. What beautiful humility, to know one's place and to accept it graciously! How big it made him, my Jesus; how joyful when others were envious; how content when others rebelled!

DEAR MASTER, so much of my trouble comes from forgetting my place—from not accepting to be human. I get despondent with my faults, I resent temptations, I get annoyed at criticism and correction and fight strongly against opposition! And all because I don't accept to be human—for all these are the common lot of all human beings. In my pride I want to be above all these things. And so, instead of taking them all in stride with joy and contentment, I resent them and they get me down.

Teach me, Lord, the humility of this very great man, St. John! Let his shining character and manliness in this scene so thrill me that it will form a burning ideal in my soul.

THE SAMARITAN WOMAN (1)—ZEAL

John 4:4-26

1. *Jesus, weary, seated at the well.*
2. *The grace so to love souls that I will work for them even when I'm weary, and be content to sow what seeds I can.*

IT WAS about twelve miles from the banks of the Jordan to the little town of Sichem in Samaria, and uphill all the way. Jesus and the Apostles made the journey in May. They arrived in Sichem about noon, weary from the walk, hot and thirsty. Jesus sat at the well to rest. But when the Samaritan woman came for water, He engaged her in conversation and asked her for the favor of a drink. Like a perfect teacher, He led her from the known to the unknown; from water in the well to sanctifying grace—a continuous fountain of life-giving water.

He knew how to reverse His methods, too. For when she became a little flippant and said: "Sir, Thou hast nothing to draw with," and later, sarcastically, "Sir, give me this water that I may not thirst, or come here to draw," Jesus parried and changed His attack to show her that He saw right through her. "Go, call thy husband and come here," He said. He knew it would sting a bit, but it was only for her ultimate cure. He was the Divine Physician, and so strong in His love that He could cut in order to cure.

I ADMIRE You there at the well, good Master! I marvel at Your untiring zeal, Your concern for a single soul. I love the patience, care and wisdom with which You worked for her conversion. Nothing stopped You in Your work, neither weariness or hunger or embarrassment, nor even the flippancy on the part of the woman.

O MY LORD, I do love souls, too, and want so much to win them for You. But so many things can stop me and discourage me. Shyness for one! I'm afraid to speak about religion to strangers, fearful to make the approach—and Your work is left undone. Weariness is another! When I am tired, I get irritable and don't want to bother with people—instead of making myself be pleasant and trying to plant some good seed. The same is true of opposition or surliness or sarcasm from people. Either I get angry in return, thus driving them further away, or else I give them up as hopeless. All this instead of following Your magnificent example of calm, majestic patience, planting some good seed, speaking the truth calmly and leaving the person on good terms, hoping that the truth will sink in. I must plant as well as reap, and I must be willing to plant even the seeds which take a long time to grow!

THE SAMARITAN WOMAN (2)—TRUE WORSHIP

John 4:4-26

1. *The woman listening to Jesus.*
2. *The grace, my Lord, to offer Holy Mass "in spirit and in truth".*

ONCE JESUS revealed to the Samaritan woman that He knew about her sinful life, she grew panicky and quickly changed the subject. Jesus was patient with her. The Good Shepherd was content to explain and to wait—and in the end He won her soul. She asked why the Jews considered the Samaritans as heretics and did not recognize the worship which had been offered in the Samaritan temple on Mt. Gerazim (at that time destroyed). Jesus explained that the Jews were God's chosen people, and so in their Temple at Jerusalem the sacrifices which God commanded were offered. These were the ones which were acceptable to God.

She looked downcast, feeling that religion was something only for the Jews. Then Jesus told her the Old Law was only a preparation for the true kingdom of God, to which all men would be called. In the New Law men would give God the worship most pleasing to Him—"worship in spirit and in truth."

LORD, this was such an important point that You were making here. All sacrifices are symbols; they are outward signs of our internal love and praise and gratitude. The important element in every sacrifice is this internal element—our sentiments of esteem and praise, our feelings of gratitude and love and sorrow for sin. Without this interior love, the outward symbol would be as empty and meaningless and as hypocritical as the kiss of Judas when he betrayed You! Whenever we offer a gift to God, it is the love which prompts it that pleases God, not the gift itself.

My King, this was true even of that perfect gift which You offered on Calvary. It wasn't Your death that pleased the Father; it was Your love which accepted death to reconcile all men to Him. "True worshippers will worship the Father in spirit and in truth."

DEAR MASTER, what a lesson for me! Even though Holy Mass is a reoffering of the sacrifice of the Cross, for me to please You at Mass I must offer it "in spirit and in truth." The Mass must be my gift, my outward way of telling You of my love, my sorrow for sin, my esteem and praise. Otherwise I'm just a bystander at Mass—like those people at Calvary who just watched it all out of curiosity. They stood there, my King, at that supreme moment in history and yet came away unaffected, unchanged, because they were only bystanders, not offerers! They didn't "worship in spirit and in truth."

Lord, Holy Mass is a beautiful act of love on Your part to Your Father. Let me make it my act of love too!

JESUS CURES THE OFFICIAL'S SON (1)— SPIRITUAL VALUES

John 4 : 43-53

1. *The desperate look in the eyes of the official whose son was near death.*
2. *The grace, my Lord, to avoid worldly values and natural likes and dislikes.*

JESUS and His first few Apostles continued their journey to Galilee after the stay at Sichem. As they came near to Cana, Peter, James and John headed back towards Bethsaida. On their way they passed through Capharnaum. One of Herod's officials recognized them as associates of Jesus. He recalled the wonderful cleansing of the Temple and the story of the water made wine. New hope began to build up in his heart. Perhaps his dying son could still be saved. He spoke to the Apostles, discovered that Jesus was heading for Cana. Perhaps if he could bring back Jesus quickly, on horseback! Summoning some of his soldiers and bringing an extra horse, he raced to Cana. Finding Jesus, the official asked Him to mount the extra horse immediately. Time was so short and his son so sick! Jesus seemed unimpressed by the urgency of the situation; nor was He impressed that this man held an official position and quite some authority. He looked at the man and spoke slowly: "Unless you see signs and wonders, you do not believe." The man's manner and tone of voice changed. Humbly, he pleaded: "Sir, come down before my child dies." Jesus was moved. "Go thy way; thy son lives."

DEAR MASTER, You certainly knew how upset this poor man was. And You above all would be sympathetic and kind. Yet You deliberately seemed to wait. Is it not because You wished to cure the father as well as the son? A politician and a worldly man, he was impressed with a sense of his own importance and his power to command. He had to realize that there were some things before which he was hopeless and helpless. Used to Herod's court and worldly splendor, he valued material things too much—riches and physical power and force of arms. You had to show him the power of the spiritual. So, in a masterful way, You brought him to the point where he became humble, and with humility pleaded his cause. It was then that You cured his son. His humility succeeded where his arrogance had failed. By curing the boy at a distance, You impressed upon his worldly mind the pre-eminence of God's power over all material forces.

MY SAVIOUR, there are many times that I need this cure. I can easily be impressed by beautiful worldly possessions—a nice home and car, nice clothes. I can be awed by political power and those who possess it. Cure me, my King! Don't let me be ruled ever by natural likes and dislikes! Let me see all people as souls made to Your image and likeness—whether they are physically attractive or plain, rich or poor, influential or simple. Let me see them as souls, and work for them out of love for You and just strive that they become better spiritually for our having met each other.

JESUS CURES THE OFFICIAL'S SON (2)— GRATITUDE

John 4 : 43-53

1. *The royal official embracing his young son who is now completely well.*
2. *The grace, my Lord, of deep, abiding gratitude.*

AFTER he left Jesus, the official and his servants rode back a way towards Capharnaum. Thoughts rushed in on him as he rode along. He had never met a man like Jesus before. Other men had been glad to do him favors, realizing his power and influence. Other men feared him and bowed to him. But not Jesus. Humble and gentle as Jesus seemed, He was the strong one; it was He Who gave the commands. The official felt a little ashamed now of his pride, and so glad that Jesus had taught him humility. His thoughts went then to his son. Somehow or other he knew now that the boy would be all right. There was a great deal of peace in his heart.

As they neared Capharnaum, some horsemen came riding out in their direction—his servants. They seemed joyous. No need to trouble the master, the boy is well again, they shouted. The official wasn't surprised. He asked them what time the boy grew well. It was the exact hour that Jesus had assured him! A surge of love and gratitude welled up in his heart. He was afraid to talk lest they detect the emotion in his voice. He rode home and entered the house and embraced his little boy.

DEAR LORD, there was no stronger bond You could put on his heart than that gift of life to one he loved. As they sat at table that night, the official told the whole story to his wife and children. He invited the servants in also, that they might hear. They noticed the change in him; they were breathless as they heard him tell of Jesus with a sincerity they had never seen before. And then when he told them of the cure—a cure at such a distance—they, too, found faith.

DEAR MASTER, gratitude is a beautiful form of love. It turned this whole family into Christians. Should I not be ashamed then that I have had so little gratitude myself for Your goodness to me? What You have done for me far outshines a cure from sickness. You cured me of the disease of sin; You restrained my wild feelings and passions from plunging me into untold depths of shame and sorrow. You made me a Christian and let my eyes see "what prophets and kings desired to see and have not seen" — the ineffable truths of Christianity and the incomparable beauty of Your life and words and deeds. I should live on gratitude! It should suffuse my whole life! Teach me to be grateful and let my gratitude be love.

THE MIRACULOUS DRAUGHT OF FISHES— GOD'S LOVE FOR ME

Matt. 4:18; Luke 5:1-11

1. *Peter kneeling before Jesus.*
2. *The grace, my Lord, to realize that You love me personally and individually.*

JESUS was now going about Galilee, preaching in the synagogues on the Sabbath or teaching a group here and there by the lake. One day as He preached at the shore by Bethsaida, the crowd pressed on Him so much that He sought Peter's fishing boat and drew away from the shore. After He preached and the crowd left, He asked Peter to sail out into the deep water and lower his nets. Peter and Andrew were weary. They had labored all through the night without any success and they had just cleaned their nets. But they had learned to love Jesus in their short acquaintance—so they would do it to please Him.

And then a remarkable thing happened. Hardly was their net down than the tug of fish on it strained it nearly to breaking. They shouted to their partners, James and John, to help them. Sweating and pulling, they dragged in the great catch until the boat nearly sank with the weight. They were overjoyed as they nudged the prows against the sand. Then suddenly Peter remembered how it all happened. Jesus was out of the boat now and on the shore. Peter ran over to Him and fell on his knees before Him. "Depart from me, for I am a sinful man, O Lord!" Jesus was pleased. He put out His Hand on Peter's shoulder. "Do not be afraid," He said, "henceforth thou shalt catch men."

DEAR MASTER, we are surprised at first when we see Peter's reaction to the miraculous draught of fishes. He had seen You change water into wine at Cana. He knew how You cured the official's son even at a distance of twenty miles. Yet here he was so overcome by the miracle and so conscious of his unworthiness, because here the miracle was done for him personally. He was so impressed by Your goodness, my King, once he realized how good You were to him. It was the same as the vivid appreciation St. Paul had later on, when he realized that You had died for him. He sounded as though he could hardly believe it when he spoke about Your death: "He loved me, and delivered Himself up for me!"

MY LORD, what unction and sincerity would be added to my love for You if I began to realize like Peter and Paul how much You love me and do for me personally! I tend to get myself lost in the crowd. I know that You are good to all of us, that You died for all of us and give Your grace to all, but I get in the rut of thinking that all Your goodness is for this big group—is for mankind in general—and that I'm just a little grain of sand on the vast seashore of mankind.

Dear King, let me see that my life wasn't given to mankind; it was given to me. And my eyesight, dear Lord, is mine to use—and You gave it to me. And grace and heaven at the end You purchased with Your Blood that I might have it. O Lord, let me realize! Let me love You as You deserve!

JESUS DRIVES OUT AN EVIL SPIRIT—"HOLY TEMPTATIONS"

Mark 1:21-31

1. *The devil throwing his victim into a convulsion.*
2. *The grace, my Jesus, of true spiritual growth—slow, gentle, steady.*

AFTER the miraculous draught of fishes, the fishermen Apostles were with Jesus continually. He now made Capharnaum the base of operations for His ministry in Galilee. There He preached in the synagogue. The people liked Him; they noticed how sincere He was, how direct and to the point—not like the Scribes and Pharisees.

Suddenly a man possessed by the devil let out an unmerciful shriek. "What have we to do with Thee, Jesus of Nazareth? Hast Thou come to destroy us? I know Who Thou art, the Holy One of God!" A terrible fear came over all. For a moment there was silence. Then came the firm, forceful command of Jesus: "Hold thy peace, and go out of the man!" The devil convulsed the man in a fit of rage; again the horrible scream, and he fell on the ground, still. Jesus raised him up. He was well and at peace.

MY KING, at first sight we might think that the devil was helping Your cause by making the possessed man openly profess Who You were—"the Holy One of God." But it was just another clever, insidious attack. It would hurt Your work if too much were revealed too soon. You were the perfect teacher, the master spiritual guide. You knew that children who needed milk would choke on meat; that they had to know and love You first as man so they wouldn't be afraid of Your Divinity when they discovered it. You knew that their spiritual growth must be slow and steady and silent, not abrupt. And so You met the devil head on, rebuked him and drove him out.

DEAR LORD, the devil still uses the same trick in the form of "holy temptations." How often have I been ensnared by them—the temptation to do too much too soon. How often have I taken on too much work while enjoying great fervor, and then in moments of dryness become cranky and complaining! How often I have been imprudent about mortifications! How many times have I become so engrossed in order and neatness, plan and efficiency, that I have made them a fetish and a goal in themselves—and almost completely forgotten charity! "Holy temptations"—the devil's work! Open my mind and heart to the gentle guidance of the Holy Spirit, my King. Let my growth be steady and gentle and true.

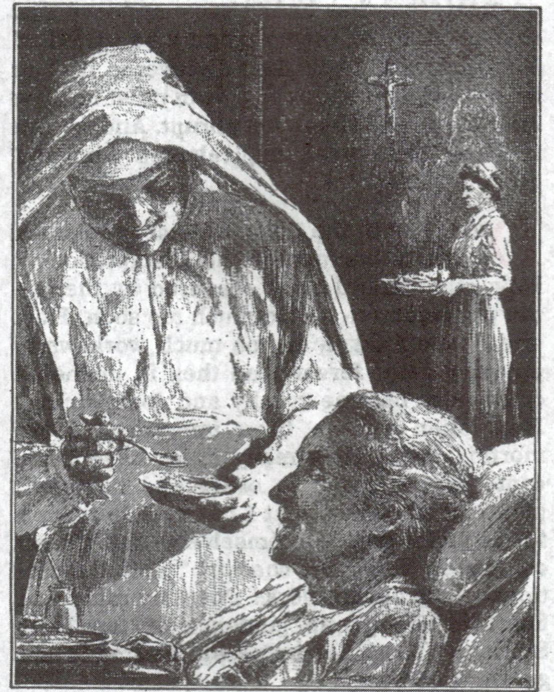

AN EVENING OF CURES—LOVE FOR THE NEEDY

Mark 1:29-33; Luke 4:40-41

1. *Jesus resting His Hands on each sick person.*
2. *The grace, my Jesus, of positive charity for every suffering person.*

WHEN JESUS left the synagogue with His Apostles, many of the men in the crowd followed along, anxious to be near Him. At the home of Peter's mother-in-law, they learned the news of her cure by Jesus. The reaction was immediate! Perhaps their own sick and possessed! They couldn't bring them to Jesus now because of the Sabbath rest, but as soon as the evening came! The word spread like wildfire. And when it was six o'clock, they came from all over the town, bringing their crippled and sick, the blind and the lame! Jesus came to the doorway of the little home. What a pitiable picture as He looked out! How He loved them! Slowly, gently, He went from person to person. He spoke to each one, consoling, resting His Hand on their heads, healing. They grabbed His Hand and held It close to their cheek and cried. Some fell at His feet and kissed the hem of His garment. He smiled gently; He waited for each one to show his feelings in his own way. Only the possessed ones tried to dispel the quiet mood of charity and gratitude. They screamed out their untimely revelation: "Thou art the Son of God." But just one look from Jesus, one word of command, and the awful frenzy left them, and they, too, knelt in quiet, peaceful gratitude.

DEAR LORD, it is no wonder that the Apostles were reminded then of the prophecy of Isaias: "He Himself took up our infirmities, and bore the burden of our ills." They realized that You actually felt every suffering and sorrow with each one of those poor people at the door that evening. This is true sympathy, my Lord, to suffer with the sufferer, to fathom the depth of his grief, to feel the sting of his pain. Suffering is insistent! It makes us act quickly to find relief. When we feel another's suffering as though it were our very own, then we will work so quickly and sincerely to ease their pain.

O MY KING, few virtues will make me so like You as this beautiful fraternal charity—this sympathy for the suffering. There are so many who are suffering all around me! Not only the sick but the lonely, the confused, the depressed! O Lord, I must not go on unconcerned—as though it wasn't any of my business. I must be keen to observe who is in pain or sorrow. I must be anxious to share it with them—to listen, to show them I know what they are suffering, to offer my help and, above all, to pray for them with all my heart. Never let me turn away or be cold. Never let me pass by unconcerned!

JESUS CURES A LEPER—DETACHMENT

Mark 1:35-45

1. *Jesus resting His hand on the bowed head of the leper.*
2. *The grace, my Lord, not to desire anything too much.*

ON THE morning following the cures, the Apostles were surprised to find that Jesus had gone. They found Him on a hill nearby, absorbed in prayer. It was to preach the kingdom and save all men that He had come, He told them, so He must go on to the other towns. It was on this missionary tour to the lake towns that a leper came up to Jesus. When the Apostles saw what he was,

they drew away from him in fear. But Jesus didn't move. The man knelt before Him, looking up into His Sacred Face. "Lord," he whispered, "if Thou wilt, Thou canst make me clean." Jesus waited for a short time. The leper didn't move or say another word. Then Jesus stretched forth His hand and rested it on the leper's shoulder. "I will," He said, "be thou made clean!" Immediately a change came over the withered body! Feeling came back into the man's stiff fingers. The sores dried up and vanished; the thrilling glow of life surged through his whole body. He rose to his feet so happy he couldn't speak.

DEAR LORD, I admire so much this poor man's spirit of detachment. There was no demanding note in his petition, no excessive pleading. He just knelt before You, and as simply as he could he expressed his faith in Your power. The rest he would leave to You. "Lord, if Thou wilt, Thou canst . . . " What beautiful detachment! And what peace he had, because even about his cure from leprosy he had no excessive desire. We can't be hurt when we don't desire too much.

MY KING, how many of my anxieties come from attachment. I want my own way, my own plan. I want so much to have this person think highly of me. I want to be with this friend rather than with that one, in this certain place rather than some place else. And so when I ask, I'm nervous, fearful, just can't stand to be refused! How this poor leper puts me to shame! What could I possibly desire as much as he would have desired to have his health and the chance to return to his family. Yet he knew what God wanted was best—so even this he left in Your hands.

O my Lord, show me that I can never be hurt if I set my heart on nothing but Your Holy Will. Teach me to be detached that I may walk in Your peace and joy!

JESUS CURES THE PARALYTIC (1)— SACRAMENT OF PENANCE

Mark 2:1-12; Luke 5:17-26

1. *Jesus looking into the eyes and soul of the paralytic.*
2. *The grace, my Lord, of most sincere, devout confessions.*

JESUS returned again to Capharnaum. He was really a hero there now. He couldn't enter the city without being surrounded by crowds. But this time there was a difference.

This time the Pharisees were there also, gathered from all over Galilee and Judea to hear Him and watch Him. During His talk, a group of men brought to Him a paralyzed man who hadn't been cured with the others. When they couldn't get through the crowd, they carried the man to the roof and removed the tiles. They knew they would make some noise and raise a lot of dust. It would interrupt the Master in His speech. But somehow they felt sure that He wouldn't mind. They had seen the look of unspeakable tenderness in His eyes the evening He cured all the sick. He seemed to have a special love for the suffering. He would want them to bring this sick man, too. So, carefully, they lowered the poor man by a mat and ropes until he lay before the feet of Jesus. They had guessed rightly. Jesus stopped His talk. He bent down to the sick man and looked into his eyes. "Take courage, son," He said, "thy sins are forgiven thee."

DEAR MASTER, they guessed rightly about Your tender care for sick bodies. But they certainly never expected this greater mercy—this healing of sick souls. You thus began a work of mercy that would mean more to the world than any physical cure. Our deepest wounds are our sins, my Saviour. It is our sins that destroy the life of grace in our soul and make us worthy of hell. It is our sins that make us suffer most even in this life—torturing us with guilt feelings, with complexes and anxieties. How wonderfully good that You should come to free us from all these wounds! For this healing, more than for the cures, You were called "Jesus—Saviour."

MY KING, I know how peaceful and happy the paralytic felt when he heard Your word, because I, too, have felt the great relief of peace in the Sacrament of Penance. Not once or twice but again and again You have spoken through Your priests: "Take courage, son, thy sins are forgiven thee." And my sins were gone; I was Your friend once more.

And yet, Lord, how often I have abused this most gracious Sacrament of Your mercy—rushing into Confession with hardly any examination of conscience, making a mechanical recitation of "usual" sins, scarcely giving a thought to sorrow or purpose of amendment. Lord, let me realize what a treasure Confession is! Let me approach it with reverence and true contrition!

JESUS CURES THE PARALYTIC (2)— DIVINITY OF JESUS

Mark 2:1-12; Luke 5:17-26

1. *The Pharisees whispering to each other.*
2. *The grace, my Jesus, to realize Who You are!*

JESUS' words of forgiveness to the paralytic made the Pharisees stiffen in anger. They looked at each other with looks that betrayed their outraged feelings. Some expressed in a whisper what all felt in their hearts: "Who is this man who speaks blasphemies? Who can forgive sins but God only?" It was exactly the reaction that Jesus expected and wanted. No one else but God could forgive sins on his own authority. They themselves professed it. Jesus looked up then from the paralytic and faced them. Nothing is hard for God, He explained to them, whether it be curing a body or a soul. But that they might know He had power to heal the soul, which they couldn't see, He would heal the body, which they could see. "Arise, take up thy pallet, and go to thy house." The Pharisees gasped! The stiffened limbs were moving; the man was cured!

MY LORD, this is Your first claim to be divine. They weren't ready for it before, so You didn't reveal it. Now You claimed a power which belonged only to God. Sin is an offense against God; it is for God alone to forgive it. You even let them make that point themselves and make it with great indignation. And then You proved by a miracle that You were really speaking the truth, that You had the power in Your own name to forgive sin. Not just delegated power, as You gave later to your priests, but power to forgive on Your own authority! You proved that You were the eternal Son of God!

DEAR MASTER, if only I realized what I believe and know — that You are Almighty God Himself in a human nature! How I would love the Gospels then, my King! How carefully I would search them for every word You said and every thing You did. And, my King, with what great effort would I strive to be like You!

Yet I am so cold and careless. Mohammedans probably know the Koran better than I know the Gospels. Business men are much more attentive to their accounts than I am to Your Real Presence in the Blessed Sacrament!

Forgive my carelessness, dear Lord! Open my eyes to see that You are God Himself Who walked this earth. Let me love to pore over what You said and did. Let me take great delight just to sit in Your presence with the Gospel story before me—until I think and love and act like You!

THE CALL OF MATTHEW—PERSONAL LOVE FOR JESUS CHRIST

Luke 5 : 27-32

1. *The Eyes of Jesus looking into the eyes of Matthew.*
2. *The grace, my Lord, of deep, personal love for You.*

JESUS had just cured the man whose sins He forgave. The people were amazed, the Pharisees rebuffed. Jesus left the house with His Apostles and headed toward the lake, just a little south of Capharnaum at Tabgha. There, on the wharf, sat Matthew in the tax-collector's box. Jesus saw him, caught his eye, and said, "Follow Me." Matthew "arose from his place, and left all behind and followed Him."

DEAR LORD, what a deeply personal thing religion is! It is a relationship of love between You and a soul—and not just a set of meaningless and disconnected laws or outward observance. We don't see it right at all unless we see it as personal devotion and love for You and the Father and the Holy Spirit. It was a Person that Matthew followed, not a set of laws or a system of ideas. It was for a Person Whom he valued more that he left his riches that he then valued less.

St. Matthew, teach me to see Jesus as you saw Him that day, that I, too, may love Him that much and leave all to follow Him. You had noticed, hadn't you, for weeks before the perfect manliness and dignity of His manner—His humility, which showed itself in absolute disregard for human respect. You had been so impressed by His perfect peace and calmness. The discipline of His life, the ideal of living for others, of bringing the truth to those in darkness—how these ideals began to fire your heart and inflame your imagination until all worldly values seemed pale next to them!

And then, suddenly, Jesus was looking into your eyes, your soul. He spoke, He invited you to what you wanted so much. You mustn't hesitate, mustn't stop to collect your belongings or delay in any way. He must not think you didn't want to be with Him. It was an absolute response, right away. And you were never sorry.

MY KING, call me like this. Look into my eyes; pierce deeply into my soul. Let my desire for virtue, my sufferings, my joys, my work—all be a personal service of love for You!

THE SUPPER GIVEN BY MATTHEW—LOVE FOR SOULS

Mark 2:15-17; Luke 5:30-32

1. *The angry looks on the faces of the Pharisees.*
2. *The grace, my Lord, of loving souls for whom You died.*

IN GRATITUDE for his calling by Jesus, and to say good bye to his friends, St. Matthew had a supper party. The crowd, composed of tax-collectors and their friends, didn't take too much care about fulfilling the requirements of the Pharisees and were therefore legally unclean or "sinners." It was a group composed of all kinds, from grave sinners right down to those who did their best to be good. Jesus loved them, loved them the way a doctor loves those who are sick and need him, the way a good nurse loves the patients in her ward. The part He liked most about them was that they were for real; they were not hypocrites, like the Pharisees. They knew their faults and acknowledged themselves for what they were. Jesus could do something with souls like that.

MY LORD, when the hypocritical Pharisees came and complained about Your eating with these men, You felt nothing but disgust for them. The Father wanted souls, You told them. And it was precisely sick souls that were in danger of being lost that needed Your attention. You must be all things to all men in order to gain all men. They were the leaders; they should know this; they themselves should be trying to win these very souls instead of glorying in their outward show of piety. Mercy and zeal are what count with God, and not the outward works of sacrifice that proceed from pride.

O MY KING, I love You very much in this role of merciful Redeemer and Shepherd of souls! What a consolation to me to know how forgiving You are to me. I must love souls very much. I must see beyond the rough exterior, their uncouth ways, the fresh manner which so often is just a defense mechanism of their guilty conscience. I must see the soul and love the soul and work tirelessly like You to win it. Teach me, Lord, to be "all things to all men." The big obstacle is the terrible self-centeredness caused by pride: thinking of self, my comfort, my ideas, fearing what people will think of me. O my Divine Master, help me to get rid of self and self-love that I may seek souls for You!

THE QUESTION OF FASTING—ADAPTING OURSELVES TO OTHERS

Luke 5:33-39

1. *A festive banquet for a wedding.*
2. *The grace, my Lord, to "rejoice with those who rejoice and weep with those who weep."*

SHORTLY after the dispute about eating with publicans and sinners, the Pharisees were observing a day of fast. Some of them noticed that the Apostles were not fasting, so they approached Jesus. If He were really teaching a holy doctrine, why did His Apostles eat and drink, while the followers of the Baptist and the Pharisees fasted? Jesus explained to them that there are times for rejoicing and feasting, as well as times for fasting. No one would think of fasting or doing penance on the joyous occasion of a wedding banquet, would they? They had to agree to that; that made sense. Well then, He was the Bridegroom, coming to claim His Bride, the people of Israel and the New Israel, the universal Church He would establish. This was an occasion for joy, then, not for sorrow or fasting. The time would come later on when His followers would fast.

MY MASTER, You are so perfectly human as well as divine. How well did You understand the charity of "rejoicing with those who rejoice and weeping with those who weep." Nothing can so jar a festive occasion as someone who remains aloof and refuses to participate in the fun, who is gloomy when everyone else is happy, who makes it evident that he is fasting when everyone else is feasting. He throws a damper over the bright joy everyone should have. To take on the mood of those around us, to share in the occasion and give of ourselves—this is charity after Your pattern, my Jesus, and true humility as well.

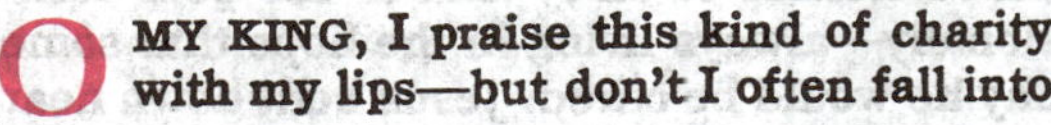

O MY KING, I praise this kind of charity with my lips—but don't I often fall into the selfishness of remaining aloof and being ultra-serious! I must get out of self and feel what the others are feeling. "A little nonsense now and then is relished by the wisest men!" If they are pensive and thoughtful, let me keep quiet. If they are enthused about a pet idea, let me be enthused and listen and listen and listen! This is the humility of the hidden life and the charity of the public life wrapped up into one.

JESUS CURES A HELPLESS INVALID—ZEAL FOR THE TRUTH

John 5:1-15

1. *Jesus taking the sick man by the hand.*
2. *The grace, my Lord, to teach Your truth and Your ideals, even if it means a fight.*

SHORTLY after the question about fasting, Jesus and the Apostles made a visit to the Temple, probably for the feast of Pentecost. At the pool of Bethsaida Jesus saw a very sad victim of sickness—a man who was practically a helpless invalid for thirty-eight years. He begged for his meagre living. He asked friends to carry him to the pool occasionally—always living in the hope that some day he would be cured. Jesus bent down near him. "Dost thou want to get well?" and then, "Rise, take up thy pallet and walk." The poor man felt life come back into his withered, atrophied limbs. They felt strong, they responded to his will—he was standing and moving! He couldn't believe it—but he was not asleep! It was true! He was cured! He looked to thank Jesus, but He was gone. He must do what the Master told him. He rolled up his pallet and started for his home.

MY LORD, You knew what would happen when the Pharisees saw this man carrying his pallet on the Sabbath. He had waited thirty-eight years; he could certainly wait another day! We can't miss the fact that You were really looking for a head-on clash with the Pharisees. You cured on the Sabbath, You told him to carry his pallet and You met him again in the Temple so he'd be able to tell the Pharisees Who You were. Why, Lord? Surely it was that You knew the fight was on between their ideas of religion as a mere outward observance and Your idea of inward love. The clash had begun in Galilee; it had to be finished. Their false notions made religion a body without a soul, and they just had to be corrected. So You didn't run away from the fight or dodge Your obligation to teach. You loved peace, like the rest of us, but not at any price!

DEAR MASTER, I admire You so much in Your refusal to take the easy way out of difficulties! What splendid courage and zeal! It makes me feel ashamed of my own tendency to run from trouble, to neglect correcting others when I know it will mean unpleasantness, to be too timid to say a word in defense of the person everyone is criticizing; ashamed, too, of my reluctance to defend high ideals, when they are being scorned. I tell myself that peace is best. But, O my King, to sacrifice justice or zeal or ideals for peace is too high a price to pay! I love Your courage. Let me imitate it!

JESUS DEFENDS HIS DIVINITY—LIVING FAITH

John 5:16-47

1. *Jesus in earnest discussion with the Pharisees.*
2. *The grace, my Lord, to live by what I believe; to seek perfection.*

ONCE the Pharisees knew that it was Jesus Who commanded the cured man to "violate" the Sabbath, they sent a delegation to Jesus to rebuke Him. These were the learned men in Jewry, so it gave Jesus a chance to talk to them in theological language about His divinity. Just as He claimed a divine prerogative before the Pharisees of Galilee—the power to forgive sins in His own name—so now He claimed two divine attributes before this delegation: the right to "judge" all men, and the possession of "life in Himself" (independent life). Like a perfect teacher, He was preparing their minds for the revelation of the Blessed Trinity. They objected strenuously to these claims which would "make Him equal to God." And they ridiculed Him as a braggard—pointing out that He had no proof or witnesses, except His own words. Jesus listened. Then, with magnificent strokes, He outlined a presentation of proofs that no sincere theologian could resist. It was witnesses they wanted? He would give them more than the two required by the Law. First, there was John the Baptist, whom everyone recognized as a prophet. Then there were the numerous miracles of Jesus, which could be done only through divine power. Would the Father give Jesus this power, if Jesus were lying? Third, there were the inspired books of the Old Testament, which foretold the main details of His life.

And, lastly, Moses! Moses, who "wrote of Jesus," would stand up to condemn them to the Father for not believing Him.

MY MASTER, from this moment onwards, no one with intellectual honesty could ever ignore You or Your teaching. With clear sanity and calmness, You claimed to be God —and You proved it with incontestable proofs. Those who don't accept You, my King, are those who refuse to face facts or live by logic. They are among those unfortunate souls who let their feelings and their prejudices dictate to their mind. But facts are stubborn things, and they remain despite blindness and prejudice. The moon is a heavenly body and a satellite of the earth, no matter how many dreamers say that it's green cheese. And You remain God, my Jesus, eternal, almighty, all-loving and good—even if some men just won't face the truth!

DEAR LORD, while I condemn them, do I myself truly realize what Your divinity means? Since You are God, everything You taught is absolutely true—as God is true! Heaven is real, more real than earth—and not just wishful thinking. And grace is real—a sharing in God's own life. Growing in grace and love are the only real treasures which never fade or rust. If my heart isn't set on these treasures, my Lord, if perfection isn't my big ambition, if I still chase after worldly possessions and honors—then I'm really an atheist in action, if not in belief. And I'm as big a dreamer as those who don't accept Your claims at all!

THE DISCIPLES PLUCK CORN ON THE SABBATH—PURE INTENTION

Mark 2:23-28

1. *The Pharisees shouting at the Apostles.*
2. *The grace, my Lord, of a pure intention in all that I do.*

IT WAS the Sabbath day. Jesus probably preached in the Synagogue a good part of the morning. The Pharisees could find nothing to contradict in His talk. But they followed Him and the Apostles as they left and strolled along together. Being hungry, the Apostles took some of the corn, rubbed it in their hands, and ate it. Immediately the Pharisees burst in on them with their supposed righteous indignation. They screamed at Jesus, "Thy disciples are doing what is not lawful for them to do on the Sabbath!" Again Jesus stressed the primacy of charity and kindness. He cited David's example. He told how the priests violated the Sabbath rest in the Temple and rightly so. And then He concluded: "If you knew what this means, 'I desire mercy and not sacrifice,' you would never have condemned the innocent! The Sabbath was made for man, and not man for the Sabbath."

DEAR MASTER, these men considered themselves holy and very upright and pleasing to God. They felt that they were much more virtuous than You or the Apostles. And if asked why they felt this way, they would have pointed to their prayers, their fasting and abstemiousness, their obedience to the Commandments and study of Scripture. Outwardly they really looked good. And yet, my Saviour, You show them that they missed the point completely. Not that their works of piety weren't good. But their works of themselves were outward and empty. The works needed a soul, and the soul of every virtue must be love. You expressed it here in terms of "mercy" because mercy is love in action.

I HAVE such a fear, dear Lord, that I will be a Pharisee. Meditation, devotion to duty, spiritual reading, etc.—all this is good only as a body. It needs a soul, and the soul is love. Sacrifice and works done from pride and complacency disgust You. Love is the only coin You value.

Haven't I done so much just to be considered good by others? Don't I glory in others having a high opinion of me? Do I not resent correction and criticism very much? My King, probably I have never done a single thing out of love alone.

The enemy is self in all its insidious forms, my Master: thoughts of self, plans for my own advantage, talk of self, self-pity, looking for sympathy. I detest them, my Lord. Help me overcome them.

THE MAN WITH THE WITHERED HAND— HUMILITY OF HEART

Luke 6 : 6-9; Matt. 12 : 10-12

1. *The anger in the Face of Jesus at the blindness and pride of the Pharisees.*
2. *The grace, my Jesus, to hate the Pharisaic spirit, and to grow in humility of heart.*

JESUS was again teaching in the Synagogue on the Sabbath day. Near the front, where Jesus could see him, there sat a man with a withered hand. Whether or not he was put there deliberately by the Pharisees, they still saw in his presence an opportunity to ensnare Jesus and bring charges against Him. They were still smarting from the sting of their previous defeats. Hypocritically, they asked Him: "Is it lawful to cure on the Sabbath?" Jesus recognized the trap and would have answered them directly, but He was anxious to prepare the ground and to win them over. So He asked the poor man to stand up so the Pharisees could see his pitiable condition and how much he needed help. Then Jesus spoke with gentleness, appealing to them: "I ask you, is it lawful on the Sabbath to do good or to do evil?" He wanted them to see that not doing the good we can do is really the same as doing harm. They didn't budge an inch. Just silence. No words, because He could wither them with logic; yet no giving in. Anger began to flash from the Face of Jesus. They would draw out an ox from a pit on the Sabbath, but they wouldn't cure a human being! Then Jesus looked with pity on the man. "Stretch forth thy hand!"—and it was well!

DEAR LORD, from all these conflicts with the Pharisees, we can see the basic

difference between their spirit and Yours. Both sides professed to be serving God and seeking for holiness. But they placed holiness in outward things—fasting, dietary laws, ritual washings and Sabbath observance. These are all good as means to an end; they are not the goal or end itself! And when they are performed with pride and self-satisfaction, they actually hinder one from becoming holy rather than help.

You told us, my Lord, what holiness really is—that it is love. Love is to be the soul, or else the actions are dead bodies. Holiness is internal; it is a pure intention to do all for love of Thee—without any taint of self-love or glory. And O my King, how beautiful then do all our actions become! Then they are expressions of love, outward proofs of love; they are means to make love grow more pure and to make selfishness decrease.

O MY KING, this pharisaic spirit is the greatest danger in my spiritual life — the most insidious snare, the most awful cancer. I love to be looked up to and praised and thought well of. I constantly wonder about what people think of me, and consequently, much of my outward actions, explanations, excuses and talk is to throw myself into the best possible light. Save me from self, dear Lord! Your power alone can do it. Jesus, humble Jesus, enemy of pharisaic hypocrisy, make me like Thyself!

JESUS PREACHES AND CURES—THE GOSPEL OF CHARITY

Luke 6 : 11-13; Matt. 3 : 6-14

1. *The throngs pressing upon Jesus.*
2. *The grace, my Lord, to live and teach the Gospel of Charity.*

THE CURE of the man with the withered hand convinced the Pharisees that they could never win Jesus to their way of thinking. They wouldn't even let themselves think that His way was right, that the miracle had proved it. Not one of them mentioned this as they conferred with the influential men of Herod's court about capturing Jesus and putting Him to death. When Jesus realized this He withdrew from Capharnaum and travelled south along the shore of the lake. He had come into the world to die, but not then, not until His work of teaching and healing was done.

Much to the wonder of the Apostles, thousands of people followed Him—Jews from

Galilee, from Judea and Perea. Even people in Tyre and Sidon heard of His works and came to listen and to see. The crowds were so large and enthusiastic that sometimes He had to sit in a boat a little off the shore in order to be heard by all. Then after preaching, He would go through the crowd, talking to each of the sick, healing them; encouraging those in sorrow, trying patiently to convince those who were sceptical; bringing a welcome peace to those who were possessed. They were so deeply moved! Many fell down at His Feet sobbing with gratitude, only to be raised by a gentle Hand and a reassuring smile, a smile that told them that He knew they were grateful, that He was happy for them.

MY LORD, there is just absolutely nothing that so spreads Your teaching and so wins hearts as this Gospel of Charity in action. When the people heard Your words, so sincere and to the point, they were very moved. But when they experienced Your charity in action, Your care for them, Your gentleness—they were absolutely captivated! No wonder St. Matthew saw here the fulfillment of Isaias' prophecy: "He will not wrangle, nor cry aloud, neither will anyone hear His voice in the streets." It was not by contentious arguments that You would win souls, not by hysterical emotional appeals or loud shouting that could be heard all over, but by the sincere and soft appeal of charity and patience. It would extend even to the spiritually dead, who seemed hopeless. "A bruised reed" You would not break, a "smoking wick" You would not quench.

MY LORD, let me never lose this vision of the Gospel of Charity! I'm so liable to get into arguments when I try to convince others of Christian ideals, or else overemphasize my point with unrestrained emotions. It is true that I mean well, but I miss the mark. Souls aren't won by arguments, my Lord; hearts aren't inspired by shouting or hysterics. I'll convince others of Your teachings only when they experience in me the attractive warmth of Your charity. My King, let me love and live and teach the Gospel of Charity.

"BLESSED ARE THE POOR IN SPIRIT"— TRUE POVERTY

Matt. 5:3

1. *Peaceful setting on the gentle slope above the lake at Tabgha, as the crowds anxiously await Jesus' message.*
2. *The grace, my Lord, of true poverty — poverty of spirit.*

JESUS had spent the whole night in prayer in preparation for this day when He would choose His Apostles and deliver His great sermon on the mount. This morning, as the crowd assembled, He had called out twelve of His followers, the Apostles, to stand close beside Him. Then, moving from the lakeside, He went to the little mound above Tabgha and there He sat to await the crowd. They were anxious and eager to learn, their human hearts thirsting for happiness, longing for the great key that would unlock the mysteries of life and suffering. Suddenly His lips began to move, and He told them His teaching, His way to peace and joy. All the beatitudes were a surprise to these worldly-minded people, but none so much as the first: "Blessed are the poor in spirit, for theirs is the kingdom of heaven."

DEAR LORD, You emphasized being "poor in spirit" as the first step towards that true happiness which is holiness. It is not just the poor, then, who are holy—not just those who have little or nothing. Apparently they could still be rich in spirit—greedy, desirous, envious, jealous—and, as such, they would hardly be Christians and hardly happy! You stress that it is not so much a question of how much we have, but a question of our dispositions about the things of the world—money, fame, honors. Desire is the root of the evil. The true Christian must be detached, must be at peace with reference to all worldly things. If they come his way, fine! He can take them and use them for God. He may even seek them for that purpose. But there must be no craving for them, no anxiety, no terrible letdown if we don't get them. We must be more desirous to need little than to have much.

O MY MASTER, help me not to deceive myself in this important matter. The snare of the world is so insidious and the lure of nice things so strong that I have to fight for true poverty of spirit. On the other hand, self-deceit is so subtle that I am liable to think myself poor in spirit, just because I don't possess certain things — and all the while I may crave them or use the possessions of others.

Help me to realize, my Saviour, that it is mainly my will, my desires and convictions that really count. Help my will to be set upon You, not on possessions or honors or praise. Let me love You so much that I shall be detached from all else.

"BLESSED ARE THE MEEK"— PATIENCE

Matt. 5:4

1. *Jesus standing silent before the false accusers in the Sanhedrin.*
2. *The grace of strength to be meek and patient.*

ONE OF the great things Jesus taught us was to hold ourselves aloof from riches and the things of the world. The man who can do that has a great deal of real freedom and peace. He is poor in spirit; he is rich. Now Jesus goes a step further and teaches us to be aloof from all excess in our feelings and emotions, especially in anger and pride. He tells us of the joy and peace in being meek. The meek man is the man who learns to react calmly in trying and difficult circumstances. He has feelings, but he has trained those feelings not to get out of control or be set off by pride or self-pity. He has made himself see that it is foolish and childish and small to pout, to be upset by small insults, to imagine wrongs, to exaggerate slights or to feel sorry for himself. He realizes he is a bigger man for ignoring and overlooking these things than he would be if he let them get him excited and upset.

MY KING, sometimes worldlings will confuse meekness with weakness, and laugh at the man who strives for it as though he were unmanly. Nothing could be more wrong! The exact opposite is the truth! How foolish it is to give way to childish pouting, irritability and smallness! How foolish to be hurt by little things and then snub the person who offended us! It takes bigness and manliness to treat these things for what they are —little things, unworthy of our notice. It takes great strength of soul to remain at peace at such times.

SOMETIMES, my Lord, I can be big and ignore slights and insults. And when I do so, how wonderfully peaceful and joyful I am and how much more a man. But at other times, I am so small I am ashamed! I get annoyed and hurt at some stupid little insult or remark. I complain. I tell the story again and again with great feeling so others will join me in my self-pity. And at such times, I am a child and not a man at all.

O my Lord, teach me to have the serenity of perfect patience and meekness. Help me to take people as I find them and life as You send it. Help me to be as big and manly as You!

"BLESSED ARE THEY THAT MOURN"— SORROW, A FRIEND

Matt. 5 : 5

1. *The face of Mary as she watched Jesus on the road to Calvary.*
2. *The grace to see the good that suffering can do.*

JESUS in the first two beatitudes taught the absolute necessity of detachment from worldly things and from our own feelings if we were to achieve holiness and greatness. In this third beatitude He lets us know that He realizes what a price we must pay for such detachment. We will have to suffer the loss of worldly things; we will suffer humiliation and insult and have to be big about it all. And we shall probably have to suffer ridicule for striving for perfection. All this suffering doesn't rest easy on us; sorrow is hard to bear. But Jesus tells us that we are blessed when we suffer it. And He assures us that it will end; that after the suffering will come comfort and peace.

MY MASTER, this third beatitude isn't just a kindly warning to us that suffering will come; it isn't even just an assurance that after suffering peace shall come again. Your "blessed" says more. It implies that there is something very good about sorrow, something very enriching about suffering. And that is so true, my Lord. Sorrow makes us thoughtful and deep, makes us kind and sympathetic; makes us realize the emptiness of the things of the world and the true beauty of Heaven. That's why You gave so much sorrow to Your Mother, my King. By it, You made her the Queen of Angels and men.

AND YET, though I know all this, still how childish I am when sorrow comes. I tend to get sorry for myself, instead of having it make me sorry for others. I fail to see how great and recollected sorrow can make me. Help me to change, my King. Let me realize at the moment of sorrow what greatness of soul sorrow can produce in me, as it did in Your saints. And let the joy of this vision bring me peace and serenity even in sorrow. As Mother Rose Hawthorne wrote of it:

"Sorrow my friend, I owe my soul to you.
And if my life with any glory end,
And if the words are true,
Said, sorrowing, when I am dead,
Sorrow, to you the praise,
To you the funeral wreaths are due."

There are some traits of holiness—bigness, understanding, greatness of soul and depth of feeling—that only sorrow can produce. That is why You send it, my Lord. Let me see it that way!

"BLESSED ARE THEY THAT HUNGER AND THIRST FOR HOLINESS"—DESIRE FOR PERFECTION

Matt. 5:6

1. *Earnest, sincere faces of the Apostles as they listened to Jesus.*
2. *The grace, my Lord, to be haunted by the vision of Christian perfection and never to rest without attaining it.*

JESUS had just given some of the most important qualities of holiness—poverty of spirit; the self-control of meekness; the vision and faith to let suffering do its work. A hard task, this business of holiness! And yet the end result so unspeakably beautiful and worthwhile, so ennobling and peaceful. And to encourage us in the work of holiness, Jesus gives a new beatitude: "Blessed are they who hunger and thirst for this holiness." He assures us that we are blessed and happy even before we attain it, as long as we want it so very much.

MY MASTER, what beautiful encouragement You give me in this beatitude. You know how holiness seems so far away from me, and so You draw me on by showing me that You are pleased with me even when I am trying. You don't seem to mind how far away I may be at any particular time from the ideal, so long as I have the thirst for it, so long as I am not content to be mediocre. The very striving brings a happiness and joy all its own.

O MY LORD, how little I have thirsted for perfection! Strongly at first, but now so seldom and so spasmodically! I seem content not to be doing spiritual reading or thorough examens! All I give is a nodding acquaintance to the realization that I should do better. I speak and think uncharitably, and it gets so that I hardly even notice it. O my King, help me to change! Not in the sense of fretting, but in the sense of really desiring so much to be better. Let the imitation of You, the beauty of Your life, be a burning and shining light that haunts me and gives me no rest until I am like You. And each day, let me strive to bridge the awful gap! My joy shall be in Your promise that when I hunger and thirst enough, I "shall be filled"!

"BLESSED ARE THE MERCIFUL"— CHARITY IN ACTION

Matt. 5:7

1. *Jesus curing the man with the withered hand on the Sabbath in spite of the Pharisees.*
2. *The grace always "to bear the cup" of charity.*

JESUS has brought us up the mountain of perfection in the first four beatitudes: detachment from the things of the world and from unruly feelings, the true use of sorrow and suffering, and then the all-important thirst for holiness, which keeps us struggling up the mountain. Now, in the last four beatitudes, Jesus gives us the view from the mountain: He lets us see the various aspects of the charity of those who are perfect. The first is charity towards our neighbor, charity in action, called mercy. "Blessed are the merciful, for they shall obtain mercy." Shortly before His sermon on the mount, Jesus had vividly demonstrated what mercy entailed. He went to the dinner given by Matthew, even though there was a rough crowd there—publicans, sinners, men and women of questionable morals, people who were coarse and vulgar and given to excess in eating and drinking. Still Jesus went. And when the Pharisees were scandalized, He quoted His Father's words given through Osee: "I desire mercy, and not sacrifice."

MERCY in this case, my Lord, meant love in action. It meant that You took these people as You found them. They had a great many faults, right! No one knew that better than You! But You chose not to concentrate on their faults, but rather on their good points and on their needs. You made Yourself think of how very honest and open they were, how very real and true. And they made You warm up to them despite their vulgarity. And You thought about how much they needed You and how good they could be and would be when they listened to You. There was Your mercy. And how beautiful it was! And how pleasing to the Father of all, Who wants all to be saved from their sins and be holy!

MY LORD, how easy it is for me to see only the surface of a person's character. How easy for me to be repelled by their vulgarity or sourness, or worse, by any deceit or disloyalty. And I turn away from them. I write them off my books and act as though they didn't exist. Or else I think about their faults so much that I get more and more angry. How uncharitable! How lacking in mercy!

Teach me, my Lord, this mercy of discounting people's faults and just seeing their virtues and their good possibilities. Teach me to start right now to be merciful. Make me keen in discovering what is good in them and let me love the good qualities until I love the person.

"BLESSED ARE THE CLEAN OF HEART"—LOVE FOR GOD

Matt. 5:8

1. *Jesus stretching forth His Hand toward the woman of Magdala and saying, "Much is forgiven her because she has loved much."*
2. *The grace, my Lord, to love strongly and constantly my Father in Heaven.*

JESUS was describing what perfection really means: loving. In the last beatitude, He showed one aspect of love He wants in us, i.e., love of our neighbor. This was to be not merely a nice feeling, but real love, love in action. And so He described it in terms of mercy. Now Jesus describes the essential element of this love which is perfection—love of God. And here also, He would not have us think of love as being a nice glow, a mere feeling and nothing else. And so He speaks of this love for God in terms of our everyday living. If we have the love of God which is perfection, then in everything we do God is the One we will be trying to please. There will be no selfish intentions; we will be "clean of heart"—with just one dominating, overpowering motive: all for love of Him.

IT IS SO EASY, MY LORD, for our motives to get all mixed up, so easy to think that we are acting for love of God when in reality we are seeking some selfish goal or advancement —wanting to be considered holy, looking for approval or praise, etc. Not that the praise and approval of others is a bad thing in itself. If we love God first and others are inspired by it, praise us for our love and imitate us in our love—then the praise is very good. But the right order is to love You first, my Father, Who art all lovable and good. This is what is just and right and fair, and this is what truly enriches our whole being, that we love above all things You Who are the Infinite Beauty and Goodness and Source of all other good things. "Clean of heart" are those who observe this right order at all times, who are so fortunate as to have fallen in love with Love Itself!

AND YET, MY LORD, while I know this in theory, how little and how weak has been the force of this dynamic love on my actions. Nothing is difficult for one in love. The fact that temptations are so difficult to fight, that I grow weary with routine and with good works, the fact that prayer can become so routine rather than a wonderful, joyful opportunity to talk to my Beloved—does not all this prove that I am not "clean of heart"! I'm losing out on all the vital powerful force that personal love for my Father could bring to my daily living. And I'm failing in the most essential element of Christian perfection.

Teach me then, my Lord, to love. Let all that is beautiful inspire me to see You! Let Your life thrill me with its goodness. Let me love, and as a reward, let me love more!

"BLESSED ARE THE PEACEMAKERS"— RESULTS OF LOVE

Matt. 5:9

1. *Mary Magdalene at the Feet of Jesus, absorbed in Him.*
2. *The grace, my Jesus, to love purely and thus have Your peace.*

JESUS has just described for us in the last two beatitudes the essential element of Christian perfection—charity, love for neighbor and love for God. Now He tells us two beautiful attributes of those who have this true charity. They will be peacemakers and they will be courageous fighters for justice. "Blessed are the peacemakers," He tells us. Once we are clean of heart and just seek to please our Beloved in every action, then a wonderful serenity suffuses our whole being. It is partly peace, partly joy, partly the radiance of one in love. But it is there, and like all goodness and warmth, it is diffusive of itself, it radiates from us to all around us. And they, too, experience the effect of this serenity. We become "peacemakers."

MY MASTER, the real cause of tension and anxiety is conflict—the conflict of opposing emotions. Lack of peace comes from wanting to be right with God and yet wanting our own way—the satisfaction of our own desires and the fulfillment of our own will. From this conflict comes anxiety, tension, sin, guilt feelings. But when a man is "clean of heart," when he so loves God that he just wants to please God in all things, then there is no conflict and no tension. Because pleasing God becomes his own will and desire, his own fulfillment and God's Will are identical. And there comes the tranquility of order—peace, Your peace which the world cannot give or take away.

This peace would radiate to our neighbor, my King, just of itself. But when we love our neighbor also, then we make a conscious effort to see that he enjoys that peace too. We soothe all conflicts, we teach the gospel of peace, we feel for others, we pray for them and hope that they will feel this same unspeakable warmth and serenity. Love is a healing force; love makes us peacemakers.

MY KING, I fail to be a peacemaker precisely at those times that I fail to love You rightly. I grow tense and anxious when my plans don't go right, when I go unnoticed, when my idea of success isn't accomplished.

Lack of love is the cause. If I become "clean of heart" and do all things for You and do the best I can, then I can forget about results—absolutely forget about them, because results are in Your Hands! You are pleased by love, not by results. Teach me to love then. And from love let me have peace. And let peace go from me to do its healing work. Amen.

"BLESSED ARE THEY WHO SUFFER FOR JUSTICE"—COURAGE

Matt. 5:10

1. *The Apostles being beaten for preaching the Gospel.*
2. *The grace, my Jesus, to love You so strongly that I'll be glad to suffer and fight for You.*

JESUS gives us in this beatitude the second quality possessed by those who have this love which is Christian perfection—courage of heart in the face of all opposition. These perfect souls are not only peacemakers, but they are strong, courageous champions of holiness. They meet great opposition from the world and the devil, and from those people who feel that their holiness shows up their own mediocrity. And so these perfect souls are called fools, or scorned as pious

hypocrites. Often worldlings try openly to provoke them by impure stories or vile language, or taunt them by calling them weaklings. But throughout all these persecutions, the perfect souls are patient, peaceful and strong.

MY MASTER, teach me to realize that the source of their strength is in their great love. They love holiness because they know that holiness is the Father's great work in the world. And they know that if something is worth loving, it is worth fighting for. And so, like first-line disciplined soldiers, they will struggle, fight and suffer any persecution for the sake of holiness in themselves or others. They steel their hearts against the fire of temptation; they bear the monotony of doing good with genuine cheerfulness and perseverence. They will make any sacrifice to win souls—patient with their weaknesses, fighting to shake them from lethargy. And above all, they have that beautiful moral courage not to care what others think of them, as long as they are pleasing to You! They are truly blessed, because they have found a love worth fighting for.

O MY KING, as much as I desire the grace to suffer persecution bravely, so much do I dread having a "persecution complex." The first is a quality of holiness; the second, a mark of weakness. Those who really love You know that like You they are "set for the rise and fall of many," that like You they will be loved and hated. It's all a necessary consequence of "setting fire on the earth." So they take it bravely, without any bitterness or self-pity. They are miles apart from the weaklings who imagine that everyone is against them and trying to hurt them.

Dear Master, never let me feel that I am persecuted! Never! Let me love holiness and fight for it — and with a brave and cheerful heart, be willing to pay the price of any opposition!

"SALT OF THE EARTH . . . LIGHT OF THE WORLD"—MAKING VIRTUE ATTRACTIVE

Matt. 5:13-16

1. *The earnest Face of Jesus as He calls on the Apostles to spread the good news.*
2. *The grace to be joyful and cheerful, to radiate Christ.*

HAVING shown the crowd His formula for true happiness and peace in the beatitudes, Jesus now urged them to spread the good news to others. They were to be "salt of the earth and light of the world"—to shine so brightly before men that they might see the good works and glorify the Father in Heaven. He makes it clear to us that we dare not be shy. We dare not hold back and let others do the work. Precious souls are in danger and time is running out!

DEAR MASTER, You not only remind us of what we should do, but also show us how to do it. Your words are chosen so carefully so we will surely understand. Salt preserves, salt gives taste and zest to food. And once it ceases to give taste, it is no good. Once a light burns only for itself under a bushel, it is of no worth. It's worthwhile only when it shines out to others and leads them through the darkness. Teach me this lesson, my King. I must make virtue attractive by being both virtuous and attractive myself.

IN THE light of this realization, O my King, how greatly I have failed at times. So often I am grouchy and irritable. How can that attract? I often wallow in self-pity—complaining, telling my grievances and showing how I'm neglected. What can that do, my King, except draw disgust for religion? O teach me to be big, manly; let me absolutely

refuse to be hurt or grieved, to complain or feel sorry for myself. Let me be cheerful, friendly, approachable, charitable. I don't have to go against my nature. I don't have to be an extrovert if I'm not one, or clown around if this is not my temperament. My joy can be a quiet kind of joy—but joy it must be! And the joy must shine out! Teach me to smile often, as often as I can.

"UNLESS YOUR JUSTICE EXCEEDS"— RESPECT FOR OTHERS

Matt. 5:20-26

1. *A person laughing hard at the mistakes of another.*
2. *The grace, my King, to respect every human being so much that I'll never laugh at or ridicule anyone.*

JESUS in the sermon was now answering one of the real problems in their minds: "What about the Mosaic Law?" He explained that He had not come to destroy it, but to bring it to completion and perfection. His law of the Gospel would demand an even greater holiness. "Unless your justice abounds more than that of the Scribes and Pharisees, you shall not enter the kingdom of heaven."

The first example then that Jesus gave concerned charity towards our neighbor. Of old, murder was forbidden — the complete hatred. But for Christians even the slightest infractions against charity are wrong. Getting angry (unnecessarily, of course) or ridiculing our neighbor, laughing at him or scorning him —all such offenses are intolerable for Christians.

MY MASTER, I can see so readily why You included such offenses in Your prohibitions. The physical harm of murder or any lesser physical injury is only one way in which we can seriously hurt our neighbor. In a very real sense, we can hurt him more by our sharp tongue and razor-edge sarcasm. The knife of ridicule plunges more deeply than steel, and wounds frightfully the sensibilities of our neighbor. And quite often the injury is not simply of the moment. In many, many cases our ridicule eats deeply into a person's consciousness, helps to give him an inferior feeling about himself. The ultimate results can be so far-reaching. He can become shy, timorous, nervous—or else, become resentful and hateful as his personality rallies its forces to fight back. And it all began with our ridicule and laughter.

O MY KING, I know from experience that being laughed at and ridiculed can hurt so much! And yet, although I am careful never to ridicule a person to his face, do I not indulge in laughter at the expense of others? Do I not poke fun at others' faults and idiosyncrasies and foibles? It could get back to them and hurt them so much. And even if it doesn't, I am still hurting and ridiculing another human being—a precious soul for whom You died! Don't let me do it again, my King! Humor—yes! Good fun and laughing with another—fine! But no ridicule! No laughing at another! Not ever, my King!

SIMPLICITY (1)— ALMSGIVING

Matt. 6:1

1. *A Pharisee boasting about his charity to the poor.*
2. *The grace, my Lord, of true simplicity in my motives.*

JESUS had explained in detail how their holiness had to exceed that of the Scribes and Pharisees—especially that it had to be holiness of heart and not just outward show. One beautiful expression of this interior love was to be their fraternal charity—their living

of the golden rule. Now Jesus went on to give them two characteristics of this true holiness: the virtue of simplicity and the virtue of trust.

He told them "not to do their good works in order to be seen" and honored by men. For if they did, they would be victims of duplicity, torn between two motives: wanting to please God and yet wanting to be honored by men. They would have mixed emotions, confused loyalties, terrible conflicts and anxieties. And they wouldn't please God. The love which is holiness must be simple. It must dominate all lesser loves. It must be a wonderful, peaceful, unmixed giving to God.

DEAR SAVIOUR, it should be clear to us why You want a heart that is single. When we go to a hotel, people serve us, carry our bags, prepare our bed and bring food—all fine acts of service! And yet, we are unmoved emotionally, because all this service is done for a gratuity and not out of love. How different when we are invited to the home of a friend! We are welcomed, we are shown the same services, we are entertained—but it is so different; it is so beautiful and warm, because it is done out of love. Love ennobles every act of service. Like a Midas touch, it turns even the smallest deed into gold. And so with You, my King, it is love that matters. The almsgiving out of pride doesn't please You at all. Anything that divides our heart automatically lessens our love and so just mars the beauty of our service.

DEAR MASTER, I need this lesson so very much. I profess to do all things out of love for You—and yet in reality how mixed my motives are! I do carefully the duties that can be seen by others, but how careless I am about those that can't be seen. I do acts of service for others, and when they don't appear to be grateful, how annoyed I get. "That's the last time I help him!" I mutter, proving that love was not my motive! And how ready I am to discuss all the work I do and the good I've accomplished—using all sorts of clever devices so that people will notice what I've done. How far from that beautiful simplicity, that love which cares not about praise, but only about You! Lord, teach me to love the hidden work and do it perfectly. Let me check my motives each day in my examination of conscience—until my love is simple and true!

SIMPLICITY (2)— PRAYER

Matt. 6:5-21

1. *The Pharisee and the Publican praying in the Temple.*
2. *The grace, my Lord, to honor my Father with my heart, not with my lips.*

JESUS had shown them the necessity for simplicity in their almsgiving. As wonderful a means as it was to achieve holiness, it could be ruined by pride. Their giving had to be motivated by love, or it was nothing! Now Jesus went on to show that the same was true of prayer and fasting. The Pharisees prayed at great length, but their prayers were riddled with duplicity and pride. They only prayed in public places where they could be seen and admired by others. They used long, high-sounding phrases so that others would be impressed by their holiness. It was almost unbelievable that they should pray and never think of God! Yet that's exactly what they did! And so their prayers meant nothing to God, nor to themselves. Neither their hearts nor their lives were changed one bit—"as sounding brass and tinkling cymbals."

DEAR LORD, teach me to understand that real prayer is the work not of our lips but of our mind and our heart. Of our mind and heart—because love is the work of our mind and our heart—thinking about our Father's Goodness and Loveliness in our mind, and feeling for Him, wishing Him well in our heart. We have no need, therefore, for long, beautiful cadences or striking figures of speech. Love is measured by the intensity and sincerity of our words, not by their number or beauty. Our prayer may be short. But if it tells of our love for our Father, or expresses our wonder at His Goodness, our delight in His Beauty, our gratitude for His gifts, our sorrow for offending Him by sin—then it is most sincere and pleasing to Him and helps us to love Him more.

DEAR LORD, help me to have true simplicity in my prayer life. Many times I have to pray in public, because our Father deserves public honor as well as private devotion. But even in public worship, I must worship "in spirit and in truth," I must still "close the door and pray to my Father in secret." Not just physical presence, then, my King! Let me pray the Mass, not just attend.

You know, too, how I must repeat prayers again and again, as in the Holy Rosary. Teach me to realize that the real prayer of the Rosary is not the repeated Hail Mary's, but loving, thoughtful meditation on the mysteries. The Hail Mary's must be simply a childlike lisping to my Mother to mark the time of my contemplation and affection. Don't let me stop at words, my King, but let my prayer be the outpouring of my heart!

SIMPLICITY (3)— MORTIFICATION

Matt. 6:16-23

1. *The Pharisees with sad, long faces.*
2. *The grace, my Lord, of sincere, daily examinations of conscience.*

JESUS was still talking about simplicity and the importance of a pure intention. He had shown that almsgiving and prayer were worthless without it! Now He discussed fasting and mortification in the light of that same truth. He told them not to be like the Pharisees who fasted only to appear to be holy before men. They disfigured their faces and looked gloomy so others would think they were making great sacrifices, and conclude that they were deeply spiritual. The whole thing was an act of religion without any religion in it! It was merely a human bargain. They suffered this amount of discomfort in order to gain this amount of praise and esteem. A purely natural contract—like purchasing a dozen eggs! And Jesus made it clear that they only got what they bargained for—human praise, nothing else! Their hearts were not changed over, nor their lives made beautiful, nor was there any praise from God!

DEAR MASTER, let me see the tremendous importance of faithful, sincere examination of conscience, if I am going to attain the self-discipline of holiness. The Pharisees were half right. They knew that our unruly passions would dash us to spiritual destruction unless they were checked and ruled by mortification and self-discipline. But they had no self-knowledge. They mortified one of their weak passions, not their strong ones. They fasted from food only to wallow in uncontrolled pride and conceit. And their very act of mortification made their last state worse than their first.

DEAR LORD, teach me that I must have a target before I can aim and shoot. I must know my dominant passion, my big faults, the faults that are interfering with perfect charity, before fasting or any mortification can do me any spiritual good. If I am proud, then it isn't fasting I need. It's the mortification of welcoming corrections and humiliations. If I'm lazy, it isn't playing second fiddle that mortifies me; it's the sacrifice of doing the hard things first and energetically that I most need. And if my big temptation is sensuality, then physical mortifications can make me strong. But I must see the target! I must face myself honestly, ruthlessly, by sincere, daily examination of conscience. Only then will I be true.

"DO NOT BE ANXIOUS"— TRUST IN DIVINE PROVIDENCE

Matt. 6:25-34

1. *The pure white lilies of the field.*
2. *The grace, my Lord, to do my best and leave results to my Father.*

JESUS had finished His instruction on simplicity. They saw clearly now that no amount of outward activity—no matter how good it was in itself—could replace inward sincerity and simplicity of heart. They knew now that God wanted love.

Jesus therefore went on to stress that love must be marked by loyalty and trust, especially the love that should exist between God and His creatures. "Do not be anxious for your life, what you shall eat; nor yet for your body, what you shall put on." He didn't tell them that they shouldn't work for their food and clothing. God expected them to do their part. Not to do their part would be the sin of tempting God. His key words were, "Do not be anxious." Once they had done their part, their Father would surely do the rest. "Your Father knows that you need all these things."

DEAR KING, in reassuring them of the Father's loving care, You used three solid proofs, which give certainty and peace to all of us. First, You reminded them that God gave them the greater gifts of existence and life. Wouldn't He naturally give them the lesser gifts of food and clothing? Secondly, You showed the Father's minute and painstaking care of the birds of the air and the lilies of the field. Could they possibly doubt that He would take even greater care of them, who were of such greater value? And, finally, what if they did choose to be anxious and fret —what good would it do them? How could they completely guard against misfortune and accidents? Which of them could "add to his stature a single cubit"? If they didn't trust in God, they were miserable, because then they couldn't trust in anyone.

O MY LORD, the trouble with me is that I do get anxious and worry about so many things—just as though I didn't have a Father Who watches over me. Failure especially makes me anxious and nervous. Dear Master, show me that all this fretting is disloyalty. Show me that once I act with a pure intention, and do my best, then I should put aside all worry; my Father will do the rest. Even if I seem to fail, the failure is only apparent. It is sent by my Father only to produce some greater success—to make me more humble or patient, to teach me lessons that can only be learned in failure and sorrow.

Teach me then, my Lord, not to be anxious. Let me realize that I have a Father!

THE CENTURION'S SERVANT (1)— COURTESY

Matt. 8 : 6-13; Luke 7 : 1-10

1. *The Centurion seated by the bedside of his sick servant.*
2. *The grace, my Lord, of thoughtfulness and courtesy.*

AS JESUS came back to Capharnaum after delivering His sermon on the mount, He was met by a delegation of Jewish officials. They appealed to Him to cure the servant of a Roman officer. They explained how good the Centurion had always been to the Jews, how he was actually the one most responsible for the building of their synagogue at Capharnaum. Jesus agreed to accompany them to his house. Delighted, the Jewish elders sent two messengers ahead to tell the Centurion. As they neared the house, the messengers returned. The Centurion knew that he was only a pagan, they told Jesus. Jesus therefore would be legally defiled under Jewish law for entering his home. He wasn't worthy that the Master should go through all that. Let Jesus only say the word and his servant could be healed.

O MY KING, what an example of Christlike charity and courtesy we have in this Roman officer! For a Roman to be concerned about his servant at all was unusual, since most Romans treated their slaves little better than animals. But that he should put himself out to ask a favor for him, thus putting himself under obligation to a subjugated people—that was the highest charity! A man in authority never likes to ask favors, for he knows he will be asked many more in return. Yet this Centurion asked a favor for his slave.

And, my Lord, what exquisite tact and courtesy. He didn't ask You directly, for the elders might have been hurt, so he asked them to ask You. And when he discovered that You were going to enter his house and thus suffer legal defilement, he acted quickly to prevent You from suffering that embarrassment. If ever a man was the living fulfillment of Your golden rule! He constantly saw the point of view of others and felt for them.

DEAR MASTER, this pagan soldier puts me to shame. How often others are sick and I fail to realize their pain, fail to visit them and offer my help! How often I am tactless and careless. I don't mean any harm, but I bypass certain people, not thinking . . . and they are hurt, sometimes badly. And Lord, how many times I could have saved others embarrassment, discomfort, chagrin just by anticipating how they would feel and by acting to avoid the embarrassing situation. Let the Centurion's splendid example teach me to be thoughtful and courteous.

THE CENTURION'S SERVANT (2)— FAITH

Matt. 8 : 6-13; Luke 7 : 1-10

1. *The Face of Jesus so pleased as He hears the message from the Centurion.*
2. *The grace, my Lord, of strong, living faith.*

THE MESSENGERS from the Centurion reached Jesus as He neared the house. The report they brought was a most beautiful act of courtesy and faith. The Centurion knew that Jesus didn't have to enter his house in order to cure his servant. He firmly believed that Jesus only had to say a word of command and the sickness would be dispelled. Just as an officer commands his men and they must obey, so he believed that Jesus could command all the forces of nature and they must listen. "Jesus marvelled" at his faith. He couldn't help but contrast it with the scepticism and unbelief of so many of the Jews. And He told those near Him that the Centurion was only the forerunner of untold millions of Gentiles who would find faith in Him and then salvation.

DEAR LORD, undoubtedly this Centurion was friend of the official whose son You had cured at a distance a short time before. He had seen that miracle and from that time on he didn't have to see again—he believed! You had proven that You spoke and acted with divine authority—that was enough for him! He believed in You. Whatever You said or did from then on, he would accept. He didn't have to see any more.

O MY LORD, faith is a lovely compliment to You and the Father! It means that we accept You on Your word with absolute certainty. Once You show us Your credentials—the miracles which only God could perform—then we firmly profess that we don't have to see any more. God is all-knowing and all-good. God cannot lie or deceive. Once You have shown me that You are God, I believe! I don't ask to see anything else. You founded Your Church on the Apostles —I believe and I love Your Church. You told me that You are present in the Holy Eucharist —I believe with all my heart and reverence You there! You told me that the Father watches over me with tender care, that He lets all things happen for good — I believe, I believe! And no matter what sufferings come, I don't ask to see the reasons, I don't ask You to enter my house and explain. I believe that You only have to say the word and all things work together unto good. I believe, my King. "Say only the word and my soul shall be healed."

JESUS RAISES A WIDOW'S SON— DIVINITY OF JESUS

Luke 7:11-18

1. *The astonished, fearful looks on the faces of the crowd.*
2. *The grace, my Jesus, to contemplate Your divinity with awe and wonder.*

ON HIS next missionary journey from Capharnaum, Jesus travelled thirty miles to the little town of Naim. A large crowd went with Him. As they stopped occasionally on the journey, He talked to them about spiritual truths. They never met anyone like Him before. He seemed to speak right to their hearts.

It was late in the day when they arrived at Naim. A funeral procession was coming out of the town gates. The crowd from Capharnaum stood aside respectfully as it passed. There seemed to be only one close relative of the young man who was dead—his mother. The sadness of it struck them. Before they realized it, Jesus was approaching the bereaved mother. "Do not weep," He said, and then He took the young man's hand. Everyone was spellbound. They hardly knew what to expect. "Young man, I say to thee, arise!" Color came back into the pallid cheeks, his eyelids moved and opened. Some women in the crowd screamed. His mother rushed to him. He sat up. Jesus gave him into her tearful embrace. And then He turned and slipped through the crowd that gathered around them.

MY MASTER, up to this time You had performed many different miracles and wondrous works, but now You showed that You were the Lord and Master even of life and death. Life is such a tremendous thing, my Saviour, so precious, yet so elusive. Medical science can do so much to cure sickness and help nature prolong life. But once the precious gift of life itself is gone, medical science has to close its books and put away its instruments. It can never call life back. But You did! No diagnosis, no medication or injections; no high voltage shock—just a word, and the departed soul obeyed and returned to the dead body. How can anyone honestly doubt Who You are, or question what a blessing Your coming has been to the world! As You brought human life back to this boy, You brought the supernatural life of grace back to the world.

MY KING AND LORD, never let me get accustomed to the idea of Your divinity. As I wonder again and again at the exquisite beauty of a country scene, as I love to sit and watch the mountains and streams and never grow tired—so let me be filled with wonder and joy that God has become man and walked among us. Let me be filled with joy to know that You have opened heaven for us and given us Your life as a model. Just as You took this young man's hand, You take mine and say, "Young man, ... arise" to new life, to perfection; arise and come after Me and share My Friendship. Let me never lose the wonder of it—never!

JOHN THE BAPTIST IN PRISON— SERENITY IN TRIAL

Matt. 11 : 2; Mark 6 : 17

1. *The serene, peaceful face of John as he sits in the dungeon at Machaerus.*
2. *The grace of serenity in all unnerving trials and problems.*

TEN months before John's death, Herod Antipas, at the prompting of Herodias, had John imprisoned at the fortress Machaerus. It was an abrupt change for the Baptist to be taken so suddenly from his active life of preaching and preparing men for Jesus. It was as sudden and complete as that other change when he was first summoned by the Holy Spirit to leave the quiet and solitude of the desert and begin the busy, hectic life of a prophet. Both times John made the change calmly and graciously. There was no nervous anxiety, no fidgeting, no desire to hold on to what he had before. Whether he was in prison or with the crowds, he radiated an air of serenity and peace.

DEAR ST. JOHN, you were peaceful in all situations because for you religion was no stereotyped outward activity. You understood the great value of seclusion and silence and prayer in bringing a soul close to God. And so no one was as prayerful and as silent as you in the desert. But you never made this life of retreat an end in itself. So, when asked to give it up for the hectic activity and noise of the ministry of a prophet, there was no heart-rending sacrifice or lack of peace. God can be served by talking as well as by silence; by work as well as by prayer. And what a prophet you became! Thousands came to hear you and were won. You really made men ready for their King.

And now that you were seized by an empty-headed tyrant in the midst of your glorious ministry, and imprisoned, you still show the same peace and resignation to God's Holy Will. No anxiety about the souls you couldn't reach now; no fretting about Herod interfering with God! God could be served even in prison. God could use instruments even as mixed-up as Herod. You knew that true religion was loving God and cheerfully doing His Will. And so you had joy even in your prison dungeon.

DEAR KING, how I need this vision of what holiness means! How often do I not fret when my plans fail or go astray! How anxious and nervous even when things go right—for fear that they might not continue so. I'm so shortsighted. My plans are not important. No set way of acting is sacrosanct—not even pious and good acts. Only loving and peaceful acceptance of Your Will.

THE BAPTIST SENDS A DELEGATION TO JESUS (1)—ZEAL

Matt. 11 : 3-15

1. *John talking earnestly to his close followers in his prison cell.*
2. *The grace, my Lord, to thirst for souls.*

IN THE eyes of Herod Antipas, John the Baptist was not an ordinary prisoner. Herod had a secret admiration for this man of the desert, who had the marvellous self-discipline and courage that he himself lacked. So, as the weeks went by and it became clear that there would be no popular uprising over John's imprisonment, he allowed some of John's followers to visit him. These wonderful friends were a great comfort to John. Their loyalty, their goodness, their thirst for spiritual things brightened up his prison cell. And yet their very loyalty was a trial to him. He wanted so much for them to meet Jesus and follow Him—even though he would miss their visits. But when he tried to explain that Jesus was the Saviour, they wouldn't listen—they would just talk about making plans for his escape.

Finally John conceived a plan. If only they could see Jesus for themselves and observe first-hand His charity and goodness, then they would be won to Him and make splendid disciples. So John pretended that he had a question for Jesus. They were to go and ask Jesus whether He was the Promised One or not. It was a clever ruse, just another way of "bearing witness to the Light." His zeal made him inventive.

DEAR MASTER, it's no wonder that You then delivered Your beautiful eulogy about John. In unselfishness and zeal for souls, he was the greatest prophet who ever lived. He was no "reed shaken by the wind"; rather he was unbending in the face of human respect and criticism. Not a worldling "clothed in soft garments" of worldly pleasures and adornments—but a man of self-discipline and simplicity. But most of all, he was a prophet—a man whose every thought and word and desire was to bring souls to You!

DEAR MASTER, it is said that a man is really educated when he knows something about everything and everything about one thing. It is somewhat the same with a great apostle. He must have an interest in everything human—and therefore be warm, interested, approachable. And he must have an overwhelming interest in one thing human—precious human souls! The light in which he sees all things, his sense of values and proportion, his measure of success and failure—all are dominated by the one big goal that dominated John—bringing souls to You!

DEAR KING, let that be my ideal! Make me a great apostle. By Confirmation, I have an obligation to be Your soldier and fight for souls. Let all that I do and think and say help to edify and draw souls to You. With Cardinal Merry del Val, I pray: "Give me souls, take all else!"

THE BAPTIST SENDS A DELEGATION TO JESUS (2)—CHARITY

Matt. 11 : 2-15

1. *The friends of John listening to Jesus.*
2. *The grace, my Lord, to love all men sincerely.*

THE FRIENDS of John made their way up the Jordan valley. It wasn't hard to find Jesus. The people were all so interested now in the great Wonder-Worker that they were able to direct them to the place where Jesus was teaching. They came and stood with the crowd to hear Jesus. They watched wide-eyed as people brought to Him the lame, the blind, the sick, and He cured them. It pleased them that One so busy and rushed by the crowd took time with each sick person. He seemed to soothe their troubled hearts and souls as well as their sick bodies.

When the last of the sick were gone, they approached Jesus themselves. They almost felt a little ashamed to ask their question now. So they mentioned how John the Baptist had sent them to ask Jesus whether or not He was the One Who was to come. Jesus was kind in His answer. His actions spoke for Him. "Go and report to John what you have heard and seen: the blind see, the lame walk, the lepers are cleansed, the deaf hear, the dead rise, the poor have the Gospel preached to them."

MY KING, it is interesting to notice what You pointed to as proof, when they asked You whether or not You were sent by God. You pointed to Your works of charity—the spiritual and corporal works of mercy! That's such an important lesson for us who are Catholics, my King. We have the true Church, founded by You to bring truth and grace to all men. But we will prove to our Protestant and Jewish neighbors that we are sent by God only when we can point to our spiritual and corporal works of mercy! It isn't arguments that win souls; it's charity. They will recognize that we have Your true teaching only when they see in us Your true love!

DEAR MASTER, how often I have been proud and unkind, especially towards my Protestant and Jewish brethren! I've forgotten that my faith has been a gift to me, not something that I've earned. And I've looked down on those who don't have it. I've questioned their sincerity. I've argued with them, but I haven't listened to them. I haven't explained in a gentle, kind way. And how often I have actually scandalized them by unkind talk and bad example!

Dear Master, because I can't agree with a person's religion doesn't mean I mustn't love the person. Teach me to love, to love sincerely all men, to be kind in my thoughts, kind in whatever I say, kind in the way I act! Let me preach Your Gospel by living it!

BANQUET AT HOME OF SIMON THE PHARISEE (1)—GREATNESS OF SOUL

Luke 7:36-50

1. *Simon and his servants ignoring Jesus.*
2. *The grace to be big in heart and soul.*

SIMON and his friends were anxious to meet and talk to the new prophet. And yet they recalled only too well the five conflicts between Jesus and the Pharisees of Capharnaum a short time before, and how bitterly the Pharisees had been defeated. So Simon and his friends at Magdala effected a compromise. They invited Jesus, but did not show Him the ordinary courtesies given to guests—the "shalom," or kiss of peace, the washing of His Feet and anointing of His

Head. Jesus noticed the rudeness and was hurt. A lesser man would have turned around and walked out right then and there—or else have pouted. Not Jesus! He was too big! He went in and took His place just as though nothing had happened.

DEAR MASTER, what greatness of soul marked Your every action! Discourtesy hurts everyone, even big men. Downright rudeness makes one terribly angry, if one is the fighting type; it makes one pout and look hurt, if one is the weak type. It is only a man who is strong and well-balanced emotionally who can take all slights and insults in stride. "A man is as big as the things that get him mad!" It takes a big man not to mind little things. This bigness is also the result of Your perfect humility, my King. You had proper self-respect; You knew Your dignity, so You didn't have to be reassured of it by any marks of courtesy from Simon.

DEAR LORD, in view of this truth, am I not so small? I notice slights and neglect so quickly! I often bring them to the attention of others in order to get sympathy. Or else I get very angry or look very hurt. O my King, teach me to be big! Absolutely no insult can hurt me if I refuse to let it. The only one it hurts is the person who gives it; it makes him less a Christian! It can also hurt the person who lets it annoy him. But it absolutely cannot touch the person who has proper self-respect, who is big in heart and soul. Make me big, dear Lord! Don't let anything less than sin upset me!

BANQUET AT THE HOME OF SIMON (2)—COURAGE

Luke 7:36-50

1. *The woman kneeling at the Feet of Jesus.*
2. *The grace of courage to disregard human respect.*

JESUS and His disciples took their places at table, reclining on the couches. The tone of conversation was a bit stiff and forced as the Pharisees awaited their opening and tried to get into position to catch Jesus in speech or action. And then something surprising happened—something they had not planned or foreseen. A woman entered. She carried a jar of ointment and made her way straight to Jesus; she didn't seem to notice anyone else. She wasn't disturbed by the reproving glances of the Pharisees or their air of appearing shocked. She didn't even notice them.

She knelt before the Feet of Jesus—His Sacred Feet, still covered with the dust of the road. In a second she realized what had happened and the tears poured forth from her eyes. They trickled down her cheeks and over His Feet. Pensively, tenderly, she washed away the dust. She loosened her long, beautiful hair and dried His Feet. The Pharisees showed their indignation, but Jesus let her go on. With tender eyes, He showed her that He approved. She broke the vase of ointment, and anointed His Head and Feet. She pressed her face against His Feet and kissed them.

DEAR MASTER, there are few scenes of such beautiful love and tenderness even in the Gospels. And just as beautiful as her love and repentance is her great courage. She just didn't care at all what the Pharisees said and did. She wasn't swayed one bit, my Lord, not one bit, from her purpose because of their indignation, resentment or snide remarks. You loved her for that as much as You did for her sorrow and tender love.

O MY LORD, I am so much influenced by what people will think and say. I look so much for approval and praise, and I'm so afraid of criticism and opposition. Teach me to be like her; to see absolutely nothing except You in every hard situation. And, O my King, give me the courage to do just what You want with perfect calmness. No haughtiness, but no fear either!

BANQUET AT HOUSE OF SIMON (3)—CHARITY

Luke 7:36-50

1. *The guests staring at Jesus with deep interest and the hushed silence as He explains the woman's action and defends her conduct.*
2. *The grace to love God and others with a most sincere and honest affection.*

JESUS sensed the air of opposition. He heard the whispered words of surprise and indignation. But He said nothing at first. He let Mary Magdalene show her affection. He didn't even stop her when she kissed His Feet. It was her way of showing love and sorrow. He knew that love was like that. And He knew how to receive love graciously as well as give it. But then, as she finished, He rose to her defense. And the lesson He taught as He defended her was so beautiful and so basic that it is at the very heart of religion.

DEAR MASTER, how wonderfully beautiful is Your defense of Mary. And how kind is Your approach to the Pharisees, even though they have insulted You and were treating Mary like an outcast. You tell Simon that Mary is far from an outcast, that Mary is a saint dearly beloved by You and Your Father. And You explain. The reason so much has been forgiven her, the reason she was so holy then is because "she has loved much" and she wasn't afraid to show it. She was better than they, and why? Because they "loved little." In spite of all their fasting and prayer and show of piety, they were far from God—because they lacked love. You were teaching again the doctrine of the pure motive, the necessity of the eye being single. You were stressing again that it is love alone that matters with You and Your Father.

O MY KING, I so easily get confused! I so easily mix up the means to become holy and holiness itself. If I am zealous just to be considered a good Christian, I'm wasting my time. If I pray just because it's the thing to do—as I do so constantly with my morning and night prayers and my rosary—it does me very little good, nor does it give You any honor or glory. If I'm kind to people only because I like them and avoid those I don't like, how can I fool myself that I am living by love? O my King, make me true! No more "phony" holiness like that of the Pharisees! No more appearances without the substance! Teach me to love You as Mary did — all-out and completely and unashamedly! And let me love all others for Your sake—taking them as I find them, allowing for individual differences of temperament, allowing them to be themselves!

OUR LADY AND FRIENDS MINISTER TO JESUS—HIDDEN SERVICE

Luke 8:1-3

1. *Mary and the other women preparing a meal for Jesus and the Apostles.*
2. *The grace, my Lord, to take second place graciously out of love.*

AFTER describing the remarkable scene in the house of Simon, St. Luke mentions how Mary Magdalene joined the little band of women who cared for the needs of Jesus and the Apostles. From that time onwards, Magdalene was very often the companion of Our Lady. Purity regained by sorrow and purity never lost dwelt very nicely together in the service of Jesus. Both were beautiful in His eyes!

Our Lady and the other women served Jesus and the Apostles in many ways. They bought food and prepared the meals. They helped to make the women who came with the crowds feel welcome and at ease. The beauty of their own enthusiasm for Jesus caught fire in the hearts of the others. And yet in all the missionary journeys around the lake, in all the preaching and working of miracles, they were womanly—they never intruded themselves. They were in the background, ready to serve when they were needed, but never in the way, never "taking charge."

DEAR LORD, what an attractive virtue is their lovely, self-effacing service. Like St. Joseph in the days of Your hidden life, they knew how to take second place so cheerfully and graciously. St. Paul would explain later on how there are so many different functions in Your Mystical Body, the Church. Not all can be Apostles or teachers or leaders. Some must play the lesser roles. How beautiful when one accepts his role—no matter what it is—and does it well. For as

You taught so beautifully in the parable of the talents, it isn't the importance of the role that counts with You—it's the love and devotion with which we perform it. These women played a lesser role, but they were saints, because they fulfilled it with generous, self-effacing love.

DEAR MASTER, there are times when You want me to lead—and when You do, I shouldn't be afraid to step forward and fill that role. But there are times also when You want me to take second place, to go unnoticed, to be passed by and overlooked—perhaps at work, perhaps at a party with friends. No matter! I should be as happy to serve in lesser roles as I am when leading and directing. It's a beautiful type of charity that can cheerfully give of itself, even when its service seems unimportant and unnoticed. Let me have this kind of love for You, Lord! Let me be glad to take second place anytime You want it of me. Cheerfully, Lord, graciously—like Joseph and Mary. Only then is it a service of love!

THE TRUE BRETHREN OF JESUS— SPIRITUAL BRETHREN

Mark 3 : 20-21; 31-35

1. *The crowds pressing upon Jesus.*
2. *The grace, my Lord, to love You and the Father with complete trust and resignation.*

OUR BLESSED LADY had mixed emotions as she followed Jesus and watched Him preach to the poor and heal the sick. She felt intensely happy at the way He was loved, proud of the good He was doing for others! But it hurt her as a mother to see the toll it all took on His human nature. He worked very hard during the day, and then in the evenings He spent long hours in prayer with His father. There seemed to be so little time for meals or rest. But she didn't intrude. She knew that He had to work in His own way. She was there when He needed her, but she never forced her own ideas, never nagged even when it seemed to be for His own good. Then one day the crowd pressed so much upon Jesus with questions and sick ones that He couldn't get a bite to eat all day. His relatives felt that He was overdoing it. "He has gone mad," they exclaimed and wanted to make Him leave the crowd for a while. Mary restrained their well-meaning efforts. She reassured them that she would get a message to Him to come for some food. "Behold, Thy Mother and brethren are outside, seeking Thee," the messenger said to Jesus. He waited for a moment and then said: "Who is My Mother and who are My brethren? For whoever does the will of My Father in heaven, he is My brother and sister and mother!" A warm glow filled all of them. They felt so close to Him now.

DEAR LORD, when two people love each other as much as You and Mary, there is perfect understanding and sympathy of heart—without any need of explanation. Knowing her, You understood that her message wasn't just nagging or interfering, that it was just her way of calming some over-anxious relatives. In like manner, You knew that she would understand, even though Your words seemed to minimize her place in Your life. You emphasized that doing God's Will meant more to You than any physical relationship. Only in this way would the people understand how much You loved them and how much it meant to You that they love the Father. You knew that she would understand

that she was still first in Your affections, even more for her love as a saint than for her love as a Mother.

MY LORD, love is like this—it expects and it deserves trust and understanding, even when it seems to overlook and hurt and ignore! It's a proof of Your love for me then, my King, when You send me periods of dryness, when You let me suffer misunderstandings and failures. You want me to trust and love enough to know that there are reasons—even when I can't see the reasons. And when I do understand and say, "Your Will be done," You are so pleased! Your love is reciprocated! Help me by Your grace. Teach me to love completely!

PARABLE OF THE SOWER—NATURE AND GRACE

Matt. 13 : 1-23

1. *The sower strewing his seeds across the ground.*
2. *The grace, my Lord, to receive the Sacraments with sincere preparation and reverence.*

THE CROWDS had been following Jesus for months now. They were fascinated by His personality and miracles. But many of them had no real change of heart. They still thought of Him in terms of a worldly Messiah who would conquer Rome. And they followed Jesus almost as children would follow a circus, only to see what startling miracles He would perform. In order to do His real work, therefore—to effect a change of hearts—Jesus began to speak in parables. They were attractive stories, easy to remember, but not obvious in their lesson. The listeners would have to think and ask further information. Those who were insincere would just walk away—the "circus" was over! But the sincere ones would think and ask—and then Jesus could lead them to a true understanding and a change of heart.

Jesus began with the masterful parable of the sower to show them that their efforts plus God's grace were necessary for holiness. The seed which was sown fell on four types of ground, but only on the good ground was it able to take root and bring forth fruit. The seed is God's grace, Jesus explained, and the ground the various types of souls.

O MY KING, how beautifully did You thus explain the roles played by Your grace and our efforts! The soil of our soul is absolutely helpless to bear any spiritual fruit by itself. Life must come from the seed—God's grace. Nothing else can supply this life—neither effort on our part or any human philosophy or human ingenuity. We could plant pebbles by the thousands—even in the best soil—but we'd never get a single stalk of wheat! Without the seed of grace, there is no spiritual life. Human effort alone can do nothing!

But then You show us the rest of the picture—the important truth that once the seed is in the ground, then everything depends upon the soil. The seed gives the beginning of life—but it does not produce virtue or sanctity automatically. It comes into the soil of our soul to work there. But once it is there, everything depends upon the cooperation of the soil! Unless we strive for virtue, unless we exercise the necessary self-discipline of avoiding occasions of sin, of striving for silence of heart and for a sincere prayer life—then the seed can't take root. Both must work together for sanctity.

MY LORD, I know how absolutely essential the Sacraments and the Mass are as fountains of grace. But I'm so liable to imagine that the automatic and mechanical reception of the Sacraments will make me a saint. I'm wrong! They are tremendous sources of grace—but I must do my part, by preparing well, by reverent reception and careful attention and, above all, by trying to put to use in virtue the graces the Sacraments give. Help me to receive Penance with sincere sorrow, to attend Holy Mass with great devotion and generosity, to receive Holy Communion with the reverence of a soldier preparing to receive his King!

CALMING OF THE STORM—TRUST

Mark 4:35-40

1. *The fearful look on the faces of the Apostles as the storm reaches its height.*

2. *The grace to love the dark hours and the trials as a proof of my trust and love.*

AFTER the day of preaching in parables and giving long explanations, Our Lord was tired. He was anxious to go apart from the crowds with His Apostles. So He invited them to cross with Him to the other side of the lake. The fishermen in the little band took over, Peter directing, John and James getting the boat ready. They were happy to be off by themselves where they could relax and talk with each other and with the Master. Jesus talked with them for a little while and then lay down in the stern of the boat and fell asleep. Midway across, heavy clouds appeared and then a fierce wind that swept down often between the Lebanon and Anti-Lebanon mountains to the north. It was a fearful storm. Waves nearly flooded the little fishing boat. The four fishermen bravely gave orders, lowered the sail, bailed out the water. But they could not allay their own fears or the fears of the other Apostles. Anxiously they looked to the Master. But He was asleep. Apparently He didn't know or care. They shook Him and shouted to be heard above the wind. "Lord, save us; we are perishing!" Jesus looked at them. He didn't move. "Why are you fearful, O you of little faith?" And then He arose, and raised His hand. They had never seen such majesty. "Peace, be still!" And suddenly, silence, peace, a great calm came over the waters.

DEAR LORD, Your mild rebuke to the Apostles teaches me one of the most important lessons I must learn—the absolute necessity of trust in You. Actually they were showing faith and trust in Your power to do something about the storm. Certainly they had faith in Your power and they had trust in Your willingness to help! But they lacked faith in Your goodness. They felt that they had to remind You! To trust someone with a secret and warn him not to reveal it is an act of trust. But to tell him a secret without warning him not to reveal it is perfect trust and perfect love. In this case we just know that the person will keep our secret without the necessity of being reminded.

LORD, it is this perfect trust that You want me to have—not only trust in Your power, but in Your goodness and providence as well. It becomes most pleasing to You when a problem is one very dear to me and when I cannot see the reasons why You let things happen as You do. If I trust in these cases, and refuse to admit anxiety or worry to my heart, then You are really pleased. Teach me, my King, to trust like that. If You are God at all, You are all-good, and all-loving. Let me not be anxious!

THE GERASENE DEMONIAC— THE VALUE OF SOULS

Mark 5:1-20

1. *The horrible scene of the man dashing himself against the rocks.*
2. *The grace to meet all problems face on—doing my best and trusting, and not calling them impossible.*

IT WAS a tragic scene that met the Apostles and Jesus when they landed on the eastern shore of the lake. The poor possessed man was cut terribly and bruised and bleeding. He shouted and went on as though he were crazy. Jesus spoke: "Go out of the man, thou unclean spirit." That exorcism drove him into a frenzy. "What have I to do with Thee, Jesus, Son of the Most High God? I adjure You by God do not torment me!" the devil said through the man's lips. Jesus let the devil tell that his name was Legion and gave permission to him to enter a herd of swine nearby. And then the swine became frenzied as the man had been, and rushed headlong into the sea. The herdsmen ran away in terror and told the whole story to the townspeople. They came out quickly in a group, eyeing the cured man suspiciously and anxiously, and they begged Jesus to depart from their shores.

DEAR LORD, You were the very essence of thoughtfulness. You would never have let the herdsmen lose so much (even though all things are really Yours to dispose of as You will) unless You had a very good reason. Were You not showing them and us, my King, the immeasurable value of a soul! For You to tell them the great worth of a soul was one thing, but to demonstrate it so vividly was quite another thing, and so much more real and impressive. Hundreds of animals were sacrificed to save one human soul. You acted as though there were absolutely no comparison in value between the two. How tremendous the cured man must have felt! How impressed must the Apostles have been! They were to be fishers of souls — such precious prey!

DEAR MASTER, I have inherited the work of the Apostles. Give me, then, this sense of the inestimable value of a soul. That poor man looked like such a hopeless case. Yet, my Divine Shepherd, You sought him out and found him and You carried him back to the fold. I am so liable to give up when a person seems hopeless! Don't let me. Teach me to leave something with each one—a good thought, a smile, an act of kindness and, most of all, a prayer. Teach me to fish with a long line as well as with net and hook.

JESUS CURES THE WOMAN WITH A HEMORRHAGE—FRATERNAL CHARITY

Mark 5:25-34

1. *Woman touching the cloak of Jesus.*
2. *The grace, my King, of true fraternal charity.*

WHEN JESUS and the Apostles crossed the lake again and came to Capharnaum, a large crowd was there to welcome Him. Two people in the crowd were especially anxious to see Him: Jairus, whose daughter was dying, and a woman who had been suffering for twelve years with a chronic hemorrhage. Jairus spoke to Jesus about his daughter, and Jesus agreed to go with him to cure her. As He made His way through the crowd, the woman with the hemorrhage reached out to touch His cloak. She felt so

embarrassed about her affliction that she had hesitated to come to Him openly when all the others came to be cured. But she believed in Jesus, believed so strongly that she felt only to touch His cloak would cure her. Her faith was rewarded. As soon as she touched it, she felt well. She slipped back into the crowd and was so happy. Then, suddenly, Jesus stopped. "Who touched my cloak?" He asked. A fear came over her. She waited a little, hoping that He would dismiss it and go on. But no. He was insisting: "Power has gone forth from Me!" Nervously, she made her way through the crowd and knelt before Him. Sobbing, she told her story. The gentle smile on the face of Jesus reassured her, even as she spoke. Then He praised her publicly for her faith, and resting His hand on her head, He said, "Go in peace."

DEAR MASTER, why would You make her ackowledge her cure publicly when she seemed so ashamed and so anxious to be unknown? You were the very soul of kindness and thoughtfulness. Besides, more than ever now You were telling the people you cured not to tell anyone. Why change, especially in her case? My King, it is precisely because You were kind that You acted as

You did! You knew how twelve years of embarrassing affliction had made her terribly self-conscious, had made her withdraw into herself. You wanted her to know that there was no reason for inferiority feelings just because she was sick. On the contrary, she had great faith—she should hold her head up high. Making her come forth relieved her of her anxieties that people would find out. Now everyone knew of her sickness and everyone knew of her cure! There was nothing more to fear.

DEAR MASTER, I love the way You treated each person as an individual—taking into account each person's problems, anxieties, sufferings, needs. No wonder each one You cured felt close to You! People were never "cases" for You; they were persons!

Lord, teach me to see that each person is unique and special. Teach me to listen, to listen a great deal, so I will know their individual needs and sufferings. Teach me to put myself in their place, so I will feel their problems deeply. And then let me put my knowledge and love to work!

JESUS RAISES JAIRUS' DAUGHTER FROM THE DEAD (1)—CHARITY

Mark 5 : 35-43; Luke 8 : 50-55

1. *Jesus taking the young girl by the hand.*
2. *The grace, my Lord, to radiate Your beautiful charity in my life.*

THE CURE of the woman with the hemorrhage was a source of great rejoicing to all except Jairus. He wanted to feel for her, but his only daughter, the light and joy of his life, was dying, and the Master was being delayed. Then his worst fears came true. A messenger came from his house: "Thy daughter is dead. Why dost thou trouble the Master further?" It was too much for him; he broke down and sobbed almost without control. He felt the hand of Jesus on his shoulder, and looked up. "Do not be afraid," Jesus told him; "only have faith and she shall be saved."

When they arrived at the house, Jesus put out the professional mourners who were wailing and making a din. He only allowed the three closest Apostles and the girl's parents to enter the room with Him. They knelt down beside the little cot. Jesus took her cold white hand in His, "Girl, I say to thee, arise!"

All at once color returned to her cheeks. She opened her eyes. Jesus helped her to sit up and then stand. Jairus and his wife took her in their arms; they nearly crushed her in the warmth of their affection and joy. Then, suddenly, they realized their debt to Jesus. They turned to Him. Graciously He dismissed their thanks, and told them that He was happy for them. He only asked them not to spread the story of the miracle. The little girl kept looking at Him. She would never forget Him!

DEAR MASTER, what an exquisite example of feeling for others! You were reluctant to work miracles now in Your effort to get across Your message by parables. But Your sympathy for the suffering just forced You to perform them. And, O my King, the thoughtfulness in the way You went about it! You knew that Jairus was crushed by the news of his little daughter's death, so gently You reassured him that she would be all right. You understood that in their great grief they wouldn't want a crowd around, so You dismissed the mourners. You even made most of the Apostles wait outside. And then, with magnificent graciousness, You showed them that You were as happy to bring her back to them as they were to receive her. Your charity meant as much to them as Your miracle!

DEAR LORD, there is just nothing that will make me so like You as this beautiful virtue of charity. I want so much to be like You, especially in this habitual thoughtfulness and feeling for others. Lord, I promise here and now never to speak uncharitably either to others or about them. I promise to accept to be hurt rather than to hurt others—except in those cases where the hurt is to cure, and therefore done out of a higher charity. And not only negative charity, avoiding unkindness, I also promise to do the good that I can — to listen, to be interested in the plans and ideas of others, to be enthused about their projects, to smile, to be cheerful. Help me, my King, help me to radiate Your charity.

JESUS RAISES JAIRUS' DAUGHTER FROM THE DEAD (2)—SCORN

Mark 5 : 35-43; Luke 8 : 50-55

1. *The professional mourners scorning Jesus.*
2. *The grace, my Lord, never to ridicule another person.*

WHEN JESUS arrived at the home of Jairus, He heard the terrible wailing and din caused by the professional mourners. The hypocrisy of it disgusted His sincere soul. They had no real feeling for the girl who died, certainly no understanding of the great depth of sorrow that Jairus and his wife were suffering. Their noise and wailing only made that suffering more intense. So Jesus dismissed them. He did it with as much kindness as He could. This wasn't the time to talk to them about the difference between hypocrisy and sincerity. He would send them away in an unobtrusive way by saying that there was no cause for weeping. The girl was "asleep, not dead." But to such superficial people His kindness meant nothing. They openly laughed at Him; they derided Him—making jokes about that rare kind of stupidity that couldn't tell the difference between death and life. Their quick change from mourning to derision showed how right Jesus was. He didn't say another word. It was themselves they were hurting, not Him!

DEAR LORD, just as charity is the most beautiful adornment of a human being, so there is probably nothing more ugly than that special unkindness of "laughing others to scorn." The attempt to make others look ridiculous, to portray them as fools, as worthy of derision and scorn—there is just no greater injury to the dignity of a human person (with the exception of leading another into sin). We would rather be hurt physically, or even considered evil and guilty of sin, than to be laughed at as a fool! Even if the person doing it is just covering up his own deficiencies, as is so often the case, it is still a terrible sin, my King. It is the direct opposite to charity, an attack upon the proper self-respect a person needs to maintain proper emotional stability and a balanced personality.

DEAR MASTER, even though I don't go as far as deriding a person to his face, still have I not laughed at people and poked fun at their mistakes when talking to others? It's not as bad as it would be if they were present, but it is still laughing at another human being. It is still terribly unkind. And there is always the danger that they will hear of it, and be awfully hurt. My Jesus, by what You suffered when they "laughed You to scorn," I promise with all my heart never again to laugh at any person's idiosyncrasies or mistakes! Never!

THE BLIND MEN CURED—GRATITUDE

Matt. 9:27-31

1. *The blind men, cured, rejoicing wildly in their new-found gift of sight.*

2. *The grace to live in a spirit of gratitude.*

THE STORY of the raising of Jairus' daughter caused quite a stir. Everyone was talking about it. Two blind beggars by the wayside caught the drift of the conversations and could sense the air of excitement and awe and wonderment at such power. They began to talk. Could not such a Man Who restored life also give back sight? They stopped people and asked questions. Men tried to hurry on, but they held them and pleaded for news and asked which way the

Man from Nazareth went and where He might be now. They were told about the house Jesus used at Capharnaum; perhaps they could wait there for him. They went their way, asking directions, anxious, almost nervous with hope. They suddenly heard a great excitement—the Saviour was coming! They must profess their belief. "Have pity on us, Son of David!" He seemed not to notice or else didn't hear. They followed the noise of the crowd. They edged their way into the house. Peter or John spoke to the Master as they entered. "Master, these men beg mercy." And then, for the first time, they heard His voice. "Do you believe that I can do this to you?" The voice was so kind, with a tone that hoped they would say "Yes." They replied so quickly: "Yes, Lord!" And then they sensed Someone standing near them; they felt a light touch on their eyes. He spoke again: "Let it be done to you according to your faith." Tremblingly, they opened their eyes. And they looked into the Face of the Master!

DEAR LORD, what a beautiful scene! What a generous and glorious gift to the poor men. No wonder they went away delirious with joy! Even when You asked them to try to keep it all quiet, they couldn't repress their feelings. Seeing was so good! It gave them great draughts of happiness and joy just to sit outside and watch the people pass by, and see the children play in the street. They would walk through the countryside just to drink in the flowers and trees and sunlight. And their lips just trembled with emotion at the name of Jesus.

O MY LORD, is Your gift of sight to me any less beautiful and glorious! Just because I have never lost it, should I be any less grateful for having it! Just seeing should give me great joy, should make my lips quiver with praise and my heart be warm with joy and gratitude. O my Saviour, wake me up to see how very much I owe You. You have opened the eyes of my body; open now the eyes of my soul. Let gratitude be my way of life! Let it surround me like the air, as I just rejoice always and praise You always for Your wonderful gifts.

JESUS TEACHES AT NAZARETH—GLORIOUS ADVENTURE OF HOLINESS

Luke 4:16-22

1. *Jesus, "the carpenter's Son," standing before the lectern in the Synagogue at Nazareth.*
2. *The grace, my Lord, to see the pursuit of holiness as a glorious adventure.*

AFTER MANY long months of teaching in the lake cities, Jesus now returned to His native Nazareth. He was something of a mystery to the Nazarenes. They had known Him only as the carpenter's Son, an earnest, sincere Person, but no one special. And yet, since He left their town, He seemed to make quite a name for Himself. Rumors had it that He was a renowned preacher and prophet. Visitors claimed that they saw Him work all kinds of miracles—that His name was on everyone's lips.

Excitement ran high then, when it was reported that He was returning to Nazareth. They crowded the Synagogue to hear Him. They listened intently as He read from Isaias: "The Spirit of the Lord is upon me . . . to bring good news to the poor He has sent me; to proclaim to the captives release and sight

MEDITATION

to the blind . . ." Those words referred to the Messianic era when there would be political freedom and great riches! Jesus was explaining: the blessings promised were not worldly goods, but better gifts—spiritual blessings. The "good news" was God's full revelation. The "sight to the blind" was truth for their minds and souls, truth which would free them from the blindness of self-pity and ignorance, and give them the true freedom of interior peace! And then the startling revelation: "Today this Scripture has been fulfilled in your hearing." It nearly took their breath away.

DEAR LORD, this initial impression You made on the Nazarenes was so fine that for a little while they grasped a beautiful spiritual message. You raised their minds from the desire for worldly goods to the vision of the beauty of holiness. For a short time they caught the excitement and the adventure of striving for virtue; they had a glimpse of the truth that their hearts' true hunger was for God!

MY LORD, this must be my work also — to show others the thrill and adventure of seeking perfection, thus giving sight to the spiritually blind and peace to the emotionally disturbed. But, Lord, I cannot give what I don't have, and have continually. Those times that I do perceive holiness as an adventure—then how wonderful are spiritual conversations, how easy to put myself out for others, how simple to be big, to overlook injuries and slights! How easy to edify, encourage and help! In those moments I'm enthused about virtue and the enthusiasm seems to catch.

But, my Lord, these moments are all too few! And even when I have them, they come often simply from being in high spirits emotionally—rather than from solid, basic conviction and spiritual insight. Make me grow spiritually, my King; make me strong and stable in Your love. Teach me to bolster a real spiritual life by regular spiritual reading, examination of conscience and earnest meditation! Then the vision won't fade. Holiness will always be an exciting adventure!

THE NAZARENES ATTEMPT TO KILL JESUS (1) —JEALOUSY

Luke 4:22-30; Mark 6:2-6

1. *Surging, angry mob trying to kill Jesus.*
2. *The grace, my Lord, to be happy to be just what You made me to be.*

THE INITIAL touch of enthusiasm which Jesus inspired by His explanation of Isaias ended all too soon. Many of the men in the group had grown up with Jesus. They couldn't conceal their annoyance. Who did He think He was to be putting on airs? Evidently He forgot that they "knew Him when . . ." "Is He not the carpenter, the Son of Mary?" Where did He come off then to claim that He was the Messiah! They grew more indignant and their murmuring grew louder. When Jesus tried to show them that it was just their small-town thinking and jealousy that blinded them to the facts, they grew absolutely wild. The truth in His words stung them so deeply. There was no answer they could give except to give vent to their jealous, hateful feelings. They rushed upon Jesus and seized Him. The Apostles were shoved aside in a group. Those who held Jesus pushed Him along to the brink of the steep hill on which Nazareth was built. Women screamed but the men paid no attention to them. Some of them pushed the women back and told them to mind their own business. Suddenly in all the excitement they realized that Jesus wasn't there. They looked at each other with fearful, questioning looks. They began to feel foolish and evil. Silently, they made their way back to their homes.

MY LORD, jealousy is a terrible force for evil. And yet, like all the capital sins, it is only the misuse of what is basically a good emotion. To overcome its evil effects we mustn't try to kill the basic emotion, which can't be killed, but rather redirect it and use it correctly.

When Our Father created us, He put in us a strong desire to imitate what is good and beautiful. This is the virtue of holy emulation; it is the basis of our imitation of Your life and virtues, my King, and therefore something very good. The abuse of jealousy enters when we falsely imagine that another's good qualities make us look bad. Then, instead of admiring their good qualities, we minimize them and hate them as a threat to our own personality. The basic error is right here — in comparing our qualities with others. We are the ones who make the comparisons, my King, not You! Each of us has beautiful qualities of mind and soul. And not one has all the good qualities. You give to each according to his needs and according to the work You want him to do. Once we understand this, then no one's talents will seem a threat to us. They will be things to be admired and loved and imitated to the degree that we can.

DEAR MASTER, how I hate to admit that jealous feelings have crept into my heart and influenced my words and actions! But the truth is that they have! And it's all because I forget Your goodness to me, forget the qualities of heart and mind with which You have blessed me. If once I realized Your generosity to me, I'd forget my silly comparisons. I'd have the humility to be glad to be what You made me to be. And, O dear King, I'd rejoice sincerely over the good in others, and I'd have peace!

THE NAZARENES ATTEMPT TO KILL JESUS (2) —LOVE FOR THE CHURCH

Luke 4 : 22-30; Mark 6 : 2-6

1. *Our Blessed Lady watching the crowd push Jesus to the brink of the hill at Nazareth.*
2. *The grace, my Lord, to love You in Your Mystical Body, the Church.*

IT WAS a great joy to Mary when Jesus indicated that they were going to make a visit to Nazareth. The journey there was just filled with beautiful memories, especially as they came near to Nazareth and again saw the familiar surroundings and were greeted by relatives and friends. She was so proud, too, when Jesus was invited to talk in the Synagogue on the Sabbath. Somehow that meant more to her here at Nazareth than anywhere else. She couldn't help the secret wish that crept into her heart—the wish that they were back reliving those wonderful years of the hidden life, when He was hers.

She was outside the Synagogue with the other women when Jesus preached. She heard the murmuring and then the shouting. She saw Jesus being pushed to the hill at the edge of the town. She tried to go to Him, but someone blocked her way—told her it would be better if she didn't. An awful, sickly fear came over her. Simeon's words came back. Was it now? And then the great relief as someone reported that Jesus had just disappeared. He wasn't hurt! At last she was able to cry a little. She felt so relieved!

DEAR LORD, a necessary consequence of loving someone very much is that that person's life becomes intertwined very closely with our own. When You were honored, Mary was happier than if she were honored herself. And when You were rejected or hurt or in danger, she suffered, really suffered every bit of it. This is what it means to love someone.

If we love You, my King, this is how we should feel about You in Your Mystical Body, the Church. When new priests are ordained, or generous young men and women pronounce their vows in religious life, we should feel a genuine joy. When we hear about large numbers of converts in Africa and Korea, it should thrill us—much more than any personal success. And when Christians are persecuted, and souls are hurt by scandal and churches are closed by communists, we should feel the pain—and work and pray all the more that "Thy Kingdom come on earth as it is in heaven."

DEAR MASTER, if I loved You as I ought, my life would be interwoven with the life of Your Church. Yet, Lord, what have I done that she be honored and praised? Have I been careful to edify those outside the Church? Have I sacrificed—really sacrificed—until it hurt, for the Missions? Have I tried to interest non-Catholics in our instruction classes and volunteered to go with them, so they'd feel at ease? Have I studied Your teachings and Your life, so I could explain it all clearly and beautifully to others? If I haven't, Lord, then my life is not interwoven with Yours. And I just can't say that I love You!

JESUS SENDS FORTH THE APOSTLES—LAY MISSIONARIES

Matt. 9:35; Matt. 10:10

1. *The Apostles gathered about Jesus for final instructions before their first missionary journey.*
2. *The grace, my Lord, to be a missionary in my own walk of life.*

AFTER the sad incident at Nazareth Jesus continued His work—endless preaching, teaching, curing, listening to sorrows and worries. It was tiring work but He was so anxious to reach as many as He could. Seeing the crowds, He was moved with compassion for them, because they were bewildered and dejected, like "sheep without a shepherd." He realized how much more could be done if He could multiply Himself in the form of apostles and missionaries. "The harvest indeed is great, but the laborers are few."

He decided to do two things. First, He asked them to pray for more vocations; and secondly, He started the work of sending them out two by two on their first missionary journey. In His instruction to them before

they began, He summed up the great ideal of the Christian missionary: "Freely have you received, freely give!"

DEAR LORD, by Your own great labor for souls and through Your instructions to the Apostles, we know that Your Church is essentially a missionary Church. Paul realized this and exclaimed: "Woe to me, if I preach not the Gospel!" And while Your Apostles— Your bishops and priests — are the official teachers, still by Confirmation all of us have the obligation to be missionaries in our own walk of life. "Freely have you received, freely give."

Through no merit of our own, we have the true faith. Lord, we dare not keep it to ourselves! We have been given the ability to smile, to love, to be enthused about virtue and grace, the ability to listen, to be interested, to cheer, to console, to instruct, to care, to be patient, to be kind. We dare not wrap up these talents, my King! They must be used in the great harvesting of precious souls. "Freely have you received, . . ."

DEAR MASTER, how I have tended to think that my talents belonged to me alone, that my faith and the state of grace were mine by right. "Let everyone find it for himself" was my attitude. "I should mind my own business!" O my King, show me how selfish and wrong this is! Every person I come in contact with is my business! I must be interested. I know that I can't "barge" into their private life. I must be kind and prudent. But I must be interested! I must give of my smiles, my concern. I must speak about Your ideals; I must edify by showing those ideals in my life. I must help in some society in my parish—Confraternity, Legion of Mary, St. Vincent de Paul Society—wherever I can help. I must thirst for souls.

JOHN THE BAPTIST IN PRISON (1)— THIRST FOR HOLINESS

Mark 6:17-29

1. *Herod Antipas sitting on a bench in the dungeon of Machaerus, listening to John.*
2. *The grace, my Lord, to want holiness with all my heart!*

DURING the ten months that John was imprisoned at Machaerus, Herod spent most of his time at this fortress palace with his army officers and his court. Since he had divorced his true wife, the Nabatean princess, in order to marry Herodias, he feared that the King of Nabatea would soon invade his realm of Perea and Galilee. Machaerus, situated on the border, was of great strategic importance.

Even in time of danger, life at Machaerus was one of sport and revelry. Yet often enough Herod would leave his worldly and superficial courtiers to go down into the dungeon where John was kept prisoner. He would signal the guard to open the gate and then go in and sit on one of the crude benches in John's cell. And dismissing the guard, he would sit there by the hour, asking John questions, listening attentively to his answers. When he left, it was always with reluctance and determination to return. The man of the desert fascinated him.

MY LORD, it's not surprising that Herod admired John so much. John was everything that Herod would like to be himself but wasn't. John had magnificent self-control—abstemious in food and drink, unconcerned about riches and nice clothes — while Herod was completely self-indulgent. He loved comfort and nice things, couldn't resist excesses in eating and drinking. John had courage to stand for what was right, even if he had to stand alone. Herod wondered so at this, because he himself was such a victim of human respect, so fearful of what others thought of him. And John was deep, thoughtful, prayerful; he lived for eternity. Herod just lived on the surface of his soul.

Herod pictured himself with John's virtues and manliness. He loved to be with John and talk to him, wishing that somehow there were an easy way to achieve this character and strength. What a difference there is, Lord, between wishing to be a saint and willing it!

DEAR LORD, when I consider those two men sitting there in the dungeon, I grow fearful because both admired the same ideals. Yet one was a saint and the other a weakling—because only one was willing to pay the price! Teach me, dear Master, that just admiring virtue doesn't make me a saint. To be a saint, I just can't wish it; I have to want it with all my heart. I have to be willing to work and suffer for it. Give me this strong determination, my King. And let me prove my sincerity by imitating the Baptist. His greatness was forged in prayer and in sacrifice. Each day, then, faithful to meditation! Each day, the sacrifice of duty well done—done carefully, out of love! Teach me to pay the price!

JOHN THE BAPTIST IN PRISON (2)—HATEFUL THOUGHTS

Mark 6:17-29

1. *Hard, hateful face of Herodias as she thought of John the Baptist.*
2. *The grace, my Lord, to avoid hateful thoughts and feelings.*

HERODIAS was consumed with hatred for John. All other men would treat her like a queen, show her deference and respect, because they feared her power with Herod. John alone defied her. He openly and publicly denounced the scandal of her incestuous and adulterous marriage to Herod. She had not only been previously married to one who was still living, but that former husband was Herod's own brother, Philip. She knew what she was, but she couldn't bear to be told it. It galled her that John still went unpunished.

In denouncing her, John really condemned Herod also. She tried in so many ways to make Herod see that, but with no success. Herod seemed to fear John—even to admire him and protect him. She despised Herod for his weakness, but was careful to conceal it because she wouldn't overplay her hand. She'd wait for the right moment. But she vowed that John would never leave Machaerus alive.

DEAR KING, hatred is such a destructive force! It shrivelled up in Herodias everything that was left of any goodness or womanliness. Her hatred consumed her, blocking out all joy and warmth, destroying all ability to enjoy company or the beautiful things of nature. She was constantly preoccupied with schemes, continually torn with hateful feelings. There was no peace, no joy!

The final scene followed as a natural consequence to such unbridled thoughts. There are few more loathsome pictures, my King, than that of Herodias laughing shrilly as she held the bleeding head of John the Baptist. Even though she was able to move about at that moment, she was dead—more dead than John!

DEAR MASTER, how similar has been the pattern of hateful thoughts in myself! They have stirred up within me low, horrible feelings of hatred and resentment. I found myself going around and around in a whirlpool of repetitions of unhappy incidents—of what I said and what I should have said! There was no peace or joy, no ability to laugh or even see the humorous side of what was happening, no ability to enjoy Your love or Your presence or Your image in the beautiful things of the world.

How wrong I am to let hateful thoughts take such a hold on me! In effect I have put all the burden of charity on my will—striving to fight the unwholesome feelings with my will, while my mind is stoking the fires with hateful thoughts. O my Lord, help me to set up armed soldiers at the gateway of my mind. Let them challenge at bayonet point every unkind, small, mean thought. And the whirlpool will stop, and charity and peace will come to my heart.

BEHEADING OF JOHN THE BAPTIST— HUMAN RESPECT

Mark 6:17-29

1. *The startled, fearful look on the face of Herod after Salome's request.*
2. *The grace, my Lord, to stand for what is right, no matter what others may think of me.*

HERODIAS planned and waited, biding her time. And then one day her chance came. Herod gave a birthday party. All the chief men of Galilee were there, as well as the officers of his army and the women of the court. In the style of a Roman orgy, they devoured food and great quantities of wine. And then, in Herod's drunken, bleary-eyed state, when he would be most boastful, Herodias sent in Salome to dance for them. It worked. The compliments that came to Herod in praise of his stepdaughter turned his head. She would have to be rewarded. Anything—even half of his kingdom. And then the awful request: "the head of John the Baptist ... right away ... on a dish!" It was enough to sober him. There must be a way out! Fearfully, he looked around. Not a chance! All eyes were upon him. They would talk about him if he broke his word. He waved disconsolately to a guard to do what the girl said. Inside himself, he cursed his cowardice!

DEAR LORD, this was one of the chief causes of Herod's weakness and lack of manliness. He was a victim of human respect. He just couldn't oppose others, it meant that they were not going to like him. He simply had to have adulation and flattery, had to have his courtiers laugh at his jokes, say that he was a grand fellow, and tell him how well he did everything. He couldn't bear not to be praised. And so, when Salome made her request, he was trapped. Even though he bitterly regretted his drunken oath to her, even though he would miss John whom he admired, he just didn't have the courage to oppose the crowd. And the ironic part of his weakness was that the crowd despised him even as he gave in to her.

MY LORD, I also pretend to despise Herod for his fear of men's opinions. And yet, my King, how much I fear them myself! I'm afraid to be different from the crowd. I'm afraid to be charitable when others are speaking unkindly; afraid to oppose what is commonly accepted for fear that others will say

that I'm a prude or old-fashioned. I'm even afraid to have opinions and convictions of my own about politics or fashions or world problems. I hold back to see what others think, to watch the trend that most people take — and then I get on the "bandwagon" and follow like a sheep. And the sad results: I'm nervous and timid; I lose my identity as a human person; I influence no one for good.

O my Lord, grant me courage — strength of character to stand for what is right, even though I may have to stand alone!

JESUS FEEDS THE MULTITUDE— ADAPTABILITY

Mark 6:30-46; John 6:1-15

1. *Jesus explaining to the Apostles that they must change their plans.*
2. *The grace, my Lord, to be flexible and docile to God's Holy Will.*

THE APOSTLES returned to Jesus at a prearranged time and "reported all that they had done and taught." They were as excited as a newly ordained priest after his first taste of the apostolate. Jesus listened to them with joy. It pleased Him so much to see their enthusiasm for their work. He tried to take them to a desert place for a well-deserved rest, but it was no use. The crowds followed them from the shore. Since their spiritual needs were so great, He couldn't put them off. He preached to them about many things, counselled the anxious and disturbed, and cured the sick. It was late in the day when He finished. Then He Who had compassion on their spiritual needs felt sympathy for their physical hunger as well. With just five loaves and two fishes, He worked one of His greatest miracles and fed five thousand men, besides numbers of women and children. For the crowd it was the crowning of a perfect day. There was no doubt now that He was the Messiah. They wanted to proclaim Him King right then and there.

DEAR LORD, one of the tests of true charity is our willingness to change our plans in order to accommodate others. You knew that the Apostles needed a rest and a change. A retreat with You would give them a badly needed spiritual refreshment, a chance to compare notes and make plans for more fruitful missionary journeys. But the crowds followed You even to the place of retreat. So You changed Your plans to fit their convenience and their needs. What perfect docility You showed to the Will of Your Father! You always made plans, set up a schedule, so there would be order and efficiency. But You never made Your schedule an end in itself, You never made order a fetish! You had the beautiful flexibility of true charity; You could adapt Yourself and Your schedule at a moment's notice to fit the needs of others.

DEAR MASTER, how greatly I fail here. I want to serve You; my intentions are good. But I get such a narrow view of service. I imagine that I have to get an exact amount of things done each day—a certain definite schedule and pattern. And if anyone interferes with that schedule, I'm upset. Either I refuse them to keep my schedule, or I serve them and consider the day a loss. How wrong! It is You Who interrupted my day, dear Master. And really, it's no interruption at all! For this is the way You want to be served here and now. Lord, make me docile and flexible. Teach me that it is love that matters, not schedules!

THE CROWD ATTEMPTS TO MAKE JESUS KING —EYES ON THE GOAL

John 6:14-15; Mark 6:45-46

1. *Jesus halting the crowd, hand upraised in firm command.*
2. *The grace, my Lord, never to lose the big picture of life!*

IN THE EYES of those five thousand men, there was something very special about the miracle of the loaves and fishes. They were simple, practical men. They knew that any king who could do what Jesus just did could have a happy, prosperous nation and the most maneuverable and efficient army on earth. These thoughts were expressed openly. Excitement spread quickly. They had a new king! Shouts of "Long live the King" went through the crowd.

Jesus acted quickly. He told the Apostles to take the boat to Bethsaida. They didn't want to go. They were just as enthusiastic as the others. Jesus made them get into the boat. He told them that He would join them once He had dismissed the crowds. Then Jesus went back to the crowd and with that splendid power of command which characterized His leadership from the beginning, He halted their plans "to take Him by force and make Him a King." He slipped away then up into the mountain to kneel in prayer to His Father.

MY LORD, what a splendid example of clear-sighted vision! You had come to change hearts, not to lead a rebellion. And never for a moment did You lose sight of Your goal! You loved Your people and felt a natural sympathy for their longing to be free of Roman dominion. What a temptation for You to be caught up in the enthusiasm of the crowd and sweep on with them to defeat Rome! How easy to rationalize that through military and political domination, You could go on to achieve Your spiritual objectives! As sincere and good as the Apostles were, that's exactly how they felt. But not You, my King. You never lost the big picture! And once a person has that, how easy then to make all the little pieces of life's jigsaw puzzle fall into place!

DEAR MASTER, I'm like the Apostles and the crowd. I know that the big goal of life is to save my own soul and the souls of others. I know that it "profits a man" nothing "if he gain the whole world and suffer the loss of his soul"—and yet, Lord, it's so easy to forget this true goal—to think of success in terms of getting my own way; to consider prudence as "dodging" as much responsibility as I can; to measure greatness in terms of money, position, honors, praise! It happens all too easily!

O MY LORD, let me never lose the big picture—the vision of life as seen through the eyes of faith—that greatness is holiness! Make me do the necessary spiritual reading, and take time for silence and prayer. "Lord, that I may see!"

JESUS WALKS UPON THE WATERS—LOVING THE DARK HOURS

John 6 : 17-18; Matt. 14 : 21-33

1. *Jesus stretching forth His hand to Peter.*
2. *The grace, my Lord, to love the dark hours for what they can do in my soul.*

AS JESUS knelt alone in prayer, a terrible wind blew down over the lake and whipped up the water into a great fury. The Apostles, heading northwest, were facing right into the gale. They strained at the oars, but almost to no avail, as the boat bobbed up and down on the heavy swells. Then suddenly one of them yelled in fright: "A ghost!" An awful fear gripped them. Jesus reassured them. "Take courage," He called out, "it is I, do not be afraid!" Peter was the first to recover his composure. "Lord, if it is You, bid me come to Thee over the water." "Come," Jesus said. Peter got out of the boat. The water was firm beneath his feet. He walked toward Jesus. Then, suddenly, he realized he was a distance from the boat; the wind lashed at him. An awful fear came over him. He began to sink. "Lord, save me!" Immediately the hand of Jesus reached out to him. Above the howling wind, Peter heard the gentle rebuke: "O thou of little faith, why didst thou doubt?" As soon as they reached the boat, the storm stopped. There was great calm and peace. They could hear their own breathing. They felt ashamed of their fears and doubts. They knelt down before Jesus, their upraised faces dripping from the lashing spray: "Truly Thou art the Son of God!"

MY KING, I love Your way of dealing with the Apostles. You had to teach them faith and trust and courage. You realized that these virtues could not be learned except through bitter trials, dark hours, great fears. And so You arranged for such hours to come into their lives. You could have prevented this storm from starting. Or, once it started, You could have stopped it on the shore as easily as on the lake! But You didn't! Your love was such a strong love! You let them suffer when suffering would forge their souls into strong, virtuous men of God.

DEAR MASTER, when will I get to learn that You still act the same? When will I see that You are Jesus "yesterday, today and the same forever"—that, as You trained them through trial, so also do You train me. It is only because You love me and don't want me to be mediocre that You send trials into my life. In those dark hours on the lake You felt for the Apostles more than You did when You were with them! Help me to know that in every trial You are here, near me, feeling for me and anxious for me to accept it as You send it—to forge in my soul faith, trust and courage!

Let me love these dark hours, my King, the hours when people misunderstand me or overlook me, when my plans go wrong, when I fall into faults I thought were conquered and make mistakes that are so foolish and unnecessary! Let me love them and use them to grow like You.

JESUS, THE TRUE BREAD— LOVE FOR THE GOSPELS

John 6 : 22-47

1. *The Master Teacher preparing their minds for the mystery of faith!*
2. *The grace, my Lord, of faithful meditation on Your holy Gospels.*

WHEN THE crowds arrived at Capharnaum the next day, they were amazed to see Jesus there, since they knew He hadn't gotten into the boat with the Apostles. It was just what Jesus wanted! Later this day He was going to tell them about the Holy Eucharist. So He wanted them to see His absolute power over material things. If He could multiply bread to feed thousands, why couldn't He multiply His Sacred Body in the form of bread to feed millions! If the things of nature, like the waters of the lake and the storm, were obedient to His command, what could prevent Him from changing wine into His Precious Blood!

Only one thing remained now before telling about the Eucharist—letting them see the true lesson from His miracles—absolute faith in Himself. So He told them not to seek the material bread which He gave them yesterday.

Material food perishes. He only gave that as a sign of a greater food, "the true bread from heaven." Oh! just what they wanted. "Lord, give us always this bread!" Then Jesus gave them His exquisite discourse on faith. "I am the bread of life. He who comes to Me shall not hunger, and he who believes in Me shall never thirst." But they missed it! "Is this not Jesus, the son of Joseph, whose mother and father we know? How then does He say, 'I have come down from heaven'?"

LORD, what a tragedy that they should be so small-minded and so blind! The bread which they ate yesterday they could appreciate. Their stomachs were filled and they were happy. But the spiritual bread—Your teaching, Your wisdom, Your beautiful example of a perfect human life—this they couldn't see at all. If they had only given You a chance, my King, their whole lives would have been changed into something glorious, joyful. They would have "never hungered again, never thirsted." Matthew could have told them; he never longed for his coins or his old life once he had found You. Mary Magdalene could have told them. She above all had great hunger and thirst. But once she believed in You and loved You, she never thirsted again.

DEAR MASTER, no one before or since has ever thrilled the human heart as You have. Through two thousand years men and women have loved You, for what You taught, so dearly that they have given their lives to preach the "good news." And yet, Lord, I can be so cold. My work for You lacks enthusiasm, my life lacks joy and lustre. I'm so attracted to the forbidden fruit of sin, to the material bread that perishes.

My King, it's all because I don't let myself see You as You are. Your ideals and Your example will thrill the dullest heart. But I neglect the Gospels, I miss the spiritual reading, I'm careless about prayer and meditation. I imagine I can get along on half-remembered truths that lack fire. But I can't! Dear Jesus, my spiritual Bread, I promise to eat. Let me never thirst or hunger again!

JESUS PROMISES THE EUCHARIST— THE PERFECT GIFT

John 6 : 48-59

1. *The sincere, earnest Face of Jesus as He tells them about His greatest gift.*
2. *The grace, my Lord, to realize what I believe!*

JESUS had carefully set the stage to tell them about the Eucharist. He had shown them

His great power over material things, given them His fine discourse on faith in Him. If ever they were ready, it was now. So He told them: "I am the bread of life . . . If anyone eat of this bread he shall live forever, and the bread that I will give is My flesh for the life of the world." The Jews were startled! They looked at one another. It sounded like cannibalism—unless perhaps He was speaking figuratively, that the bread would represent His Body. They discussed it back and forth: "How can this Man give us His flesh to eat?" Jesus saw the surprised looks, noticed the whispered conversations. But He didn't take back a word of it. He repeated it with the strongest possible emphasis: "Amen, amen, I say to you, unless you eat the flesh of the Son of man and drink of His blood, you shall not have life in you . . . For My flesh is food indeed and My blood is drink indeed." Whatever else they might say about His words, they could never say He wasn't offering to give them His Body and Blood as real food and drink.

DEAR LORD, the answer to their doubts was contained right in Your words if they were only humble and sincere enough to inquire. You said: "the bread which I will give is My flesh." You were showing them that the substance of Your Body and Blood would be contained under the appearances (form, color, taste) of bread. At the Consecration of the Mass, the substance of bread, "bread-ness," would be destroyed and the substance of Your Body and Blood would take its place. The host would not be just a symbol of Your Body then; it would be Your Body. And there would be no question of cannibalism, because the appearances would not be the appearances of human flesh, but the form, the color and the taste of bread.

Nor should they have wondered at whether this could be done. What difficulty for God to change a thing from one substance to another — for God, Who made all substances and appearances out of nothing!

DEAR LORD AND MASTER, if only I could realize what I believe! What greater gift could even God give than the gift of Himself! You are really, truly with us in Holy Communion as our spiritual food and drink, "abiding in me," that I might "abide in You." You are present in the tabernacle all day and night, loving me, wanting me to come, interested in me. My King, never let me take You for granted in Your ineffable gift of

Yourself. Let me value Holy Communion and pour out my heart in my thanksgiving after receiving. Let me love to stop in to visit You after work. Don't let me take You for granted—not ever!!

THE DISCIPLES LEAVE JESUS—MORAL COURAGE

John 6 : 60-72

1. *Jesus, saddened, watching the crowd leave.*
2. *The grace, my Lord, to fight for what is right, even if I have to fight alone.*

OUR LORD'S offer of the Eucharist fell on deaf ears. The crowd grew restless and began to disperse. Many of them were muttering their dissatisfaction. "One-day wonder," they said with a shrug. The air was heavy with an atmosphere of disappointment. Who could possibly listen to such talk? His flesh as food!

On the Face of Jesus there was a look of sadness—and yet a look of determination. He didn't call them back. He didn't modify His claim. Quietly, He waited. And then, His Face set firm, He turned to the Apostles: "Do you also wish to go away?" He threw down the gauntlet. Either they believed in the Euchar-ist or they couldn't accept Him! Peter responded quickly, determined to show Jesus that they were loyal, anxious to take away as much of the hurt as he could. "Lord," he said, "to whom shall we go? Thou hast the words of eternal life."

DEAR LORD, You almost cannot conceal Your human disappointment. You offered them Your greatest gift—Yourself—and they ignored You! They were more interested in earthly food and power and honors. You were a great hero yesterday; today You were nothing! And yet, my King, You did not sway one inch from the truth or from Your principles. As much as You loved the Apostles, You put the very same test squarely to them. I so admire the courage of holding to principle despite the scalding trial of ridicule and coldness and being ignored, You were willing to stand by Your ideals, even when You had to stand alone!

DEAR MASTER, I can be brave and fight for ideals, when I have the crowd on my side—but how do I act when the crowd is against me and I have to fight alone? Am I not a coward then!! Why am I silent when I should speak up for virtue? Because I'm afraid—afraid of ridicule and laughter! And when I do speak or act, why do I explain my actions at great length and apologize for them —except that I just have to have the approval of the crowd!

How different from You, my King! When You took a stand for Your ideals, You didn't count how many were with You and how many were against You. Your only concern was being right! Make me like You. When the crowd is wrong, when they are vulgar or unkind or drinking excessively, give me the courage to do what is right—no matter how they laugh or criticize or ridicule! Give me Your courage to go it alone!

JESUS EXPOSES THE HYPOCRISY OF THE PHARISEES—HOLINESS IS IN THE HEART

Mark 7:1-22

1. *The Pharisees complaining to Jesus about the Apostles.*
2. *The grace, my Lord, of a good heart, a heart like Yours!*

THE FAILURE of His discourse on the Eucharist didn't discourage Jesus. He would keep working for souls. But now He concentrated on the training of the Apostles, His first bishops and priests. They had remained faithful and true. This made Him happy.

Now an incident occurred which gave Jesus the chance to instruct them on a very important truth. They were eating as the guests of a Pharisee in Capharnaum. Some of the host's friends from Jerusalem made quite a fuss because the Apostles ate without going through the ritual of washing their hands. The Apostles felt embarrassed and ashamed. Jesus rushed to their defense. In their sincerity and earnestness they were much more pleasing to God than their hypocritical critics. Jesus showed how the Pharisees stressed outward things rather than inward holiness of heart. For them the important things were the appearances—washings, special foods, rituals, human laws and traditions. Jesus tried to show that these things were all fine if they helped generate a true spirit of interior piety. But when they were considered more important than the love of God and love of neighbor—more important than sincerity and a pure intention—then that was putting the cart before the horse! Jesus summed it up nicely in the words of Isaias: "This people honors Me with their lips, but their heart is far from Me."

DEAR LORD, Your Church, like You, does not despise outward works of piety. In her laws and customs, She commands us to attend Mass each Sunday, fast each Lent, abstain each Friday. To her chosen sons and daughters in the religious life, She gives a rule of life, constitutions, spiritual exercises. But, like You, She has always stressed that these are the means to holiness, not holiness itself. Holiness is interior; it is the soul's growth in the divine life of grace and charity. And whenever there is a conflict between these means and charity, then charity must take precedence. If one has to care for the sick during the hours of Mass, then missing Mass is no sin. It is charity that counts! If a Sister nurse must break the rule of silence in order to console a patient, or misses prayers to perform an act of kindness, she commits no fault. Charity is supreme! Holiness is in the heart!

DEAR MASTER, I need this lesson so much. I'm so liable to be a Pharisee, to think of holiness in terms of appearances—a long solemn face, an overgrave manner, the recitation of many prayers, denying myself a lot of pleasures, always giving a pious answer in my conversations with a sanctimonious tone of voice, appearing shocked no end in hearing about sin! And all the time I can neatly combine such appearances with a mind that rashly judges my neighbor, and a heart that nourishes hateful, spiteful, unforgiving feelings! O my King, teach me what religion really is — that it is love! Show me that from the heart comes evil and from the heart comes goodness. Teach me that it is the heart that matters! And then make my heart like unto Thine!

THE CANAANITE WOMAN'S PRAYER—LETTING GOD WORK IN OUR SOUL

Matt. 15 : 21-28; Mark 7 : 24-30

1. *The woman in tears at the Feet of Jesus.*
2. *The grace, my Lord, of docility to the Hand of the Divine Artist.*

JESUS left Galilee for a while to be alone with His Apostles. But even in the district of Tyre and Sidon a Canaanite woman recognized Him and begged Him to heal her daughter who was possessed. Jesus didn't answer her. As they went along she followed them, pleading so much that the Apostles became embarrassed. "Send her away," they urged Jesus, "for she is crying after us." They wanted the miracle at least for peace, if not for pity. But Jesus refused. "I was not sent except to the lost sheep of the house of Israel." Then, He entered a house, but the woman followed. She knelt at His feet. Her pleading was pitiable.

The Apostles looked at Jesus. Surely now! They could hardly believe His answer: "It is not fair to take the children's bread and to cast it to the dogs." The woman was less shocked than they. "Yes, Lord," she said, "for even the dogs eat of the crumbs that fall from their masters' table." Jesus looked into her eyes; His tone of voice was changed. "O woman, great is thy faith! Let it be done to thee as thou wilt." She closed her eyes tightly, choking with deep emotion. "Go thy way," He said, "the devil has gone out of thy daughter."

O DIVINE ARTIST, how I admire Your work in souls! At first You seemed almost cruel in Your three rebuffs to this woman. You ignored her, You refused her and You almost insulted her. Why, Lord, except that You knew her tremendous possibilities—the depth her humility could reach—the darkness which her faith and perseverence could endure. Such virtues could only be perfected in sorrow and pain. You caused the suffering, not for suffering's sake but to produce a most beautiful and virtuous soul.

DEAR MASTER, it is so important that I understand this about You. You still want saints—heroic souls—beautiful souls. Your love is still that strong, virile love that will cause pain in order to save us from mediocrity and forge us into the pure, white steel of virtue. Then, Lord, don't let me complain in my sorrows. Make me disdain self-pity even when everything goes wrong and You seem to refuse every prayer. Give me something of that splendid woman's spirit and let me rise to the challenge! Work in my soul; I promise not to interfere.

JESUS HEALS THE DEAF MAN— GRACIOUSNESS OF JESUS

Mark 7 : 31-37

1. *Jesus taking the deaf man apart from the crowd.*
2. *The grace, my Lord, to be keenly aware of the sensibilities of others.*

JESUS and the Apostles stayed for some time outside of Galilee. He had them mostly to Himself there and could get them ready for the big test He would soon give about belief in His divinity. Then they made their way back to Galilee by the roundabout route through Decapolis and arrived at the lake. The people brought Jesus a man who could neither hear nor speak. The poor man was nervous and worried. Jesus took him apart from the crowd and showed him by signs what He would do for him. He put His fingers into the man's ears, and touching His own tongue, He then put His finger to the man's tongue—showing that he would soon be able to speak as Jesus Himself could. The man understood and smiled. He was calm now. Then Jesus raised His eyes to Heaven and said: "Ephpheta—Be thou opened." The man put his fingers to his ears in surprise. He tried to express his gratitude to Jesus and was startled almost to the point of fright when he heard his own voice. He was so grateful! He knelt before Jesus and for a moment was too choked by emotion to use his new power of speech.

DEAR LORD, it isn't just the greatness of Your miracle that I love and admire—it's the human touch with which You did it, the respect for His individuality, Your feeling for his sensibilities. Not being able to get all that the people said to him and frightened by so much attention and talk all at once, he was naturally nervous and fidgety. So before the cure You made signs to him so he would be relaxed and understand what You were going to do. And since You knew how sensitive he would be at someone making signs to him before a crowd. You took him apart from the crowd. There, alone with You, he wouldn't be embarrassed or ashamed of the signs. What ineffable graciousness, my King! No wonder the crowds were in admiration of You! No wonder they said: "He hath done all things well."

DEAR MASTER, I realize now that graciousness of manner is almost as important as charity and generosity. How often have I not ruined generosity by not being gracious. I did things for others—extra work or duty—but in such a reluctant and sour manner that I made them feel badly rather than happy. And how often have I not offered money to the needy or assistance to the poor, but in such an ungracious and undiplomatic way that they were too embarrassed to take it!

Teach me something of Your thoughtfulness and graciousness, my King. Let me have such a feeling for the sensibilities of others that I'll never act superior; never stare or make them feel awkward; never use words that have a sting, such as "crippled," "dumb," "insane" or "blind," instead of "handicapped," "speechless," "nervous," "sightless." Let me do every favor with evident joy; offer all help with a gracious smile. "Let them look up and see no longer me, but only Thee!"

PETER CONFESSES THE DIVINITY OF JESUS—LOYALTY TO THE HOLY FATHER

Matt. 16:14-20

1. *Jesus solemnly declaring that Simon was the Rock.*
2. *The grace, my Lord, of loyalty to Your Vicar, the Pope.*

THE TIME had come for the big test to be put to the Apostles. Jesus took them north again to a deserted place where they could be alone. Here they prayed to the Father and talked about the kingdom. Then He asked them: "Who do men say that I am?" They gave the various opinions: Elias, Jeremias, a prophet. And then the big test, the question for themselves: "But who do you say that I am?" Simon answered for all of them: "Thou art the Christ, the Son of the

living God." Jesus was pleased. At least they believed in His divinity. This was all-important, because they would be the ones to teach His doctrine to the world. They were ready now to hear about their place in the hierarchy of His Church. "Thou art Peter," He said to Simon, "and upon this rock I will build My Church . . . And I will give thee the keys of the kingdom of heaven; and whatever thou shalt bind on earth shall be bound in heaven, and whatever thou shalt loose on earth shall be loosed in heaven."

DEAR LORD, if You did not mean that Peter was to be the visible head of the Church, You could not have fooled us more thoroughly. You knew that the primacy of Peter and his successors would be attacked; that's why You made his appointment so clear. You used three different figures of speech to symbolize his supreme authority on earth: the rock, the keys and the power of binding and loosing.

Each significant stage in God's kingdom on earth was marked by a change of name: Abram to Abraham when the kingdom was started; Jacob to Israel when it passed from the stage of family to young nation; and now Simon to Peter when it passed from identity with one nation to a universal kingdom, a Catholic Church. Peter meant "rock." After that everyone called him Simon Peter—Simon the rock—on whom the visible Church would rest.

Peter also received the "keys of the kingdom." The one who has the keys is the one who opens and closes, the one who has authority. And then You used a third expression—the power of binding and loosing. In the rabbinical literature of the time, this expression always referred to the power to make laws and to teach. Lord, how could anyone express more clearly that Peter was the visible head of the Church!

DEAR MASTER, You are the true Head of the Church, Your Mystical Body. But Peter's successor, the Holy Father, is Your representative, the visible head, Your Vicar on earth. What love and devotion and loyalty should I not give to him! He stands in Your place. He is guided and protected by You from teaching any error about faith or morals—"the gates of hell shall not prevail against it." Make me loyal, dear Master. Let me think and feel with the Church. Love for the Holy Father and his position is love and loyalty to You!

THE TRUE DISCIPLE OF JESUS— CARRYING THE CROSS

Luke 9: 23-27

1. *Jesus sincerely and honestly putting before us the condition for discipleship—the Cross.*
2. *The grace, my Saviour, to carry the triple cross cheerfully.*

SHORTLY after Peter's confession of faith, Jesus began to show the Apostles that He must go to Jerusalem and be put to death. The shock of it struck them all like a blow. They looked to Peter to say something to Jesus. And Peter, who had taken the lead to confess Our Lord's divinity, now tried to chide Jesus for this "morbid" talk. But Jesus was firm with Peter. "Get behind me, Satan, for thou dost not mind the things of God, but those of men." Jesus made His point very strongly. And then, so that all would know once and for all, that the issue might be perfectly clear, He called together all the Apostles and the crowd of followers and told them that not only must He Himself carry a Cross but so must everyone who wanted to be His disciple. "Let him take up his cross daily and follow Me. The man who tries to

save his life shall lose it; it is the man who loses his life for My sake who shall save it."

DEAR KING, Your strong emphasis on this point shows so clearly that suffering is not merely an accident but an integral part of the training of a Christian. There must be something that suffering can do for us that nothing else can do. And it doesn't seem to be self-imposed suffering, but the cross that You give us to bear each day: the triple cross of resisting temptations, of duty and of bearing the circumstances of the present moment. It is in the triple cross that we do Your Will and unite with You in the tremendous work of saving the world.

DEAR MASTER, how little have I understood that doctrine of the Cross! I always imagined it as a big cross and was frightened at its mere spectre. And I thought of it as self-imposed mortifications which would be very painful, so I shrank in dread of them. Now at last I see that You are the perfect director of souls, that You know best just how much suffering I need and how much joy. You are the best judge of what sufferings can best cut down my pride, strengthen my weakness, bolster my faith

and inflame my love. Then, dear Master, teach me to delight in whatever You send me! Let me love the present moment and whatever it brings, and cheerfully, joyfully accept it as the doing of Your Holy Will!

JESUS IS TRANSFIGURED— THE SACRED HUMANITY

Mark 9:1-9; Luke 9:29-36

1. *Jesus "radiant white as snow" before the three chosen Apostles.*
2. *The grace, my Lord, to love and imitate You in Your Sacred Humanity.*

SIX DAYS after Peter's profession of faith in His divinity, Jesus took Peter and James and John to the top of Mt. Tabor. It was an exhausting climb. The Apostles were weary when they reached the top. They sat down to rest, while Jesus knelt a little distance away and prayed. Then suddenly they were aware of a great brightness. They looked toward Jesus. Almost automatically they rose to their feet in silent reverence. Jesus was transfigured before them. His Face shone with an unearthly brilliance, His garments were whiter than snow. Standing beside Him were Moses and Elias, the representatives of the Law and the Prophets, who foretold His coming. The Apostles could hardly contain their joy and their pride. Then out of nowhere a bright cloud came and overshadowed them—like the cloud that signified God's presence in the desert. From the cloud came a Voice of ineffable power and majesty: "This is My beloved Son, in Whom I am well pleased; hear Him!" Panic seized the Apostles. They fell on their faces like dead men. They were in the awesome presence of God! Then Jesus touched them. They heard the old familiar voice: "Arise and do not be afraid." They looked up and "saw no one but Jesus only."

MY KING, the real miracle wasn't that You let Your divinity shine through for a few moments in the Transfiguration—the real miracle was that You kept it hidden so long and so completely throughout Your life! We can see how the Apostles acted when they realized God's presence at the Voice of the Father. They were terrified! They would have been the same with You, my King, if You had let Your glory appear all the time. They would have been so overwhelmed by the power and majesty of Your divinity that they would never have learned the warmth, the gentleness, the inspiration of Your humanity. So You hid Your glory that they might know You as a Man, be able to imitate You in the ordinary duties of daily life, feel the warmth of Your love, and not just the fear of Your power. How remarkable that they could have professed Your divinity and yet say that they looked up and "saw no one but Jesus only"!

DEAR LORD, by assuming Your Sacred Humanity, You put within my reach the vast riches of Your divinity. Like the Apostles, my mind is overwhelmed by the notions of God as pure spirit, perfect Being, limitless power and beauty and love, changeless, unfathomable! But You, my King, human, pulsating with human feelings, knowing cold and heat, feeling gratitude and pain and joy, loving friends, fighting for principle, dying for love — You I can understand and imitate and follow. You in Your Sacred Humanity are "the way" on which I can find God!

JESUS CURES THE POSSESSED BOY (1)—DEEP FAITH

Mark 9 : 13-28

1. *The nine Apostles, anxious, confused as the Scribes jeer at them and people ridicule their inability to drive out the devil.*
2. *The grace of deep faith, of believing more strongly the greater the difficulty becomes.*

JESUS and the chosen three Apostles were up on Mount Tabor for the Transfiguration. The other nine were waiting for them in a little town dug into the mountain on the northeasterly side as it slopes down to the plain of Esdralon. A poor man who had a demoniac-possessed son brought the boy to them, having heard of their powers to exorcise and cure. The Apostles were uneasy because Jesus was not present, nor Peter, and the case seemed so horrible and pitiful (the boy was thrown into epileptic fits). Besides, a big crowd gathered, among them the jeering, sharp-eyed Scribes. They tried to command the devil and drive him out but they failed. They only succeeded in making him more wild. He tossed the boy around with horrible ferocity, making him tear at his own flesh with sharp nails.

DEAR LORD, the Apostles were anxious and afraid because their faith was still so weak. Appearances meant too much to them—the ferocity of the devil, the gathering crowd, the criticism and mockery of the Scribes. They thought more about the appearances and worried more about them than they thought about You and the power You had given them.

O MY MASTER, can I honestly say that appearances don't mean a lot to me? I have strong faith when I see all things going smoothly, but don't I get awfully nervous and anxious when difficulties come my way, when it seems impossible to accomplish what I set out to do? Am I not very upset when conflicting obligations come at the same time, making it impossible to do both? Instead of being calm, seeing Your Will in it all, knowing that all things are means and nothing an obstacle—how differently I act! I lose peace, I complain, I fret and worry, and try to get others to feel sorry for me!

Dear Lord, teach me in those moments to have faith. Teach me to love the opportunity those moments bring to show You that I believe in You and trust You.

JESUS CURES THE POSSESSED BOY (2)— SPIRIT OF FAITH

Mark 9:13-28

1. *Jesus looking with compassion on the boy's father.*
2. *Faith to see and live in the spiritual world constantly.*

AS JESUS came down from Mount Tabor, He saw the crowd and the commotion. Soon the crowd saw Him and, much to the relief of the nine Apostles, the people ran to Him. The boy's father made his way through the noisy throng and explained the pitiable case. As he did, the devil again stirred up the boy in an awful fit. Jesus asked how long this had been going on. All his life, the father answered, and often the devil tried to drown the boy or cast him into the fire. He pleaded with Jesus, "If you can help us, have pity." Jesus' eyes met his: "If you can believe, all things are possible to him who believes." The wonderful response: "Lord, I do believe; help Thou my unbelief." The cure, with power and dignity: "Go out of him and return not any more."

DEAR MASTER, what a lesson in faith You give me. If ever a case looked hopeless, this one did. Possessed all his life! (That is why You asked the father "How long?" even though You knew—You wanted all to realize how hopeless it looked!) The horrible tearing at himself, trying to destroy himself in fire and water! For the father, the weariness of those years, the gradual conviction that nothing could ever be done, the way people laughed and poked fun, the temptation to despair! And now, on top of it all, the inability of the Apostles to do anything! This seemed like the last hope. And then, dear King, You looked into his eyes and into his soul. "All things are possible to him who believes!" How You hope for a faith to overcome all these apparent proofs of hopelessness. What joy for You as this good man goes down on his knees and prays with beautiful humility, "Lord, I do believe; help Thou my unbelief."

MY LORD, has my faith been what You want it to be? Faith is the "evidence of things that appear not"—it means seeing the real world, the spiritual world, all the time. How I fail! Fail to see Your beauty in the beautiful things of nature; fail to see Your loveliness in the sweetness and gentleness of children; overlook the fact that it is Your graciousness in every beautiful action of those I admire—saint, friend, acquaintance. And if I fail in faith there, how much more do I fail to see Your Holy Will in the crosses, especially the little crosses, the humdrum and weary days, the selfishness and inconsideration of others. I forget that You are working through them for my good, and I rebel! And, oh, how I forget that You allow my mistakes and faults to teach me the greater lessons of true sorrow and humility. "O Lord, I believe. Help Thou my unbelief!"

THE APOSTLES QUESTION JESUS ABOUT THE POSSESSED BOY (3)—FAITH AND TRUST

Mark 9:13-28

1. *The nine Apostles gathered around Jesus in the house*
2. *The grace, my Lord, to love the dark hours and seemingly impossible tasks as opportunities to prove my faith and love for You.*

THE NINE Apostles watched in amazement as Jesus drove out the devil with a majestic command. They felt a great surge of peace and relief. They looked around with evident satisfaction at the Scribes who had heckled and questioned them and their

Master. And as Jesus dismissed the crowd, they went with Him to the place where He was staying. All were quiet. They knew that they had failed in some way. But how? They wanted to know, and they wanted Him to realize that they were trying, that they would do anything to become real Apostles. So, humbly, sincerely, they said: "Why could we not cast it out?" Jesus looked at each of them. He loved them; loved them especially then when they were humble enough to learn. But they still lacked that complete faith and trust in Him that He wanted so much, and without which there could be no working for Him or with Him. "Because you had no faith," He said. And He went on to explain how all great things in the spiritual life can be accomplished by faith, especially when it is accompanied by prayer and fasting.

DEAR LORD, You knew how hopeless the situation looked to them before You came down from the mountain. And You always made allowances for their weakness. Yet You didn't mention this to them because it was a chance to teach a perfect lesson: the lesson that faith is most perfect and most pleasing to You when the hour is most dark and the task seems impossible.

HOW I need this beautiful lesson, my Lord! Am I not discouraged at the amount of work there is to be done, the children to be instructed, converts to be sought, souls to be inspired and brought back to the fold, problems to be solved? Don't I often attempt to do too much and neglect my own spiritual life with the foolish notion that it all depends upon me? Dear Lord, what peace would come to me once I begin to have this true faith. No task is impossible to You. And as long as I do my part, at the right moment You will come down from the mountain and the task will be accomplished. Teach me that faith. Make me delight in impossible situations because then I can trust You all the more. Let me actually love the dark hours and walk through them in peace to prove to You my absolute faith in You and my complete trust in You.

RIVERS OF LIVING WATER—INTERIOR LIFE

John 7 : 2-49

1. *The priests encircling the altar with the bowls of pure water.*
2. *The grace, my Lord, to cherish silence and prayer.*

IT WAS autumn and time for the great Feast of Tabernacles. Faithful Jews lived a whole week in huts of boughs about the city of Jerusalem to remind themselves of the wanderings in the desert and to thank God for bringing them to the promised land. Jesus went privately to the feast. Only when it was half over did He begin to teach in the Temple. There was great discussion about Him. He had never studied at the great rabbinical schools of Hillel or Shemai; how then did He have such learning? The Pharisees and leaders opposed Him—and yet, would the Messiah be able to work more miracles than He had worked? The verbal battle raged on.

Then on the last day of the feast Jesus attended the morning sacrifice. The priest encircled the altar with the bowls of pure water—recalling how God had given them water from the rock in the desert. When the ceremony ended Jesus stood before all and called out: "If any one thirst, let him come to Me and drink. He who believes in Me as the Scripture says 'From within him there shall flow rivers of living waters.' " The crowd was captivated—even those attendants who had been sent by the Pharisees to seize Jesus. When they returned empty-handed and were asked "Why have you not brought Him?" they answered slowly and sincerely: "Never has any man spoken as this Man."

DEAR LORD, what a beautiful clear answer You thus gave to their quarrels and doubts! Water was a magic word for the Jews. It kept them alive in the desert. It changed barren, arid land into rich soil teeming with green grass, fine crops, beautiful flowers and trees. Like a splendid teacher You took them from the known to the unknown. You explained how the waters of grace given by the Holy Spirit could promise the same rich, green foliage of virtue in arid souls that water produced in the soil. It made sense. With this interior life they would be like an oasis, happy in themselves and a source of refreshment and inspiration to all around them.

DEAR MASTER, when shall I learn that to be an oasis I have to be attentive to the whispering of the Holy Spirit and docile to the living waters of His grace! I admit this as an absolute fact. I express it as a spiritual axiom to others. I say—how can a person be a channel of living water if he is all dried up with worldliness and sin, if he is superficial from hectic activity and noise! And yet, Lord, I neglect silence. I miss spiritual reading. My prayer is lip service and riddled with distractions.

Make me change, my Lord! Holy Spirit, lead me down the spacious corridors of exterior silence, away from the noise of excessive talking. Guide me into the beautiful majestic hall of interior silence, where no worry or anxiety can steal my attention from Your Presence. And there each day alone with You, speak to my heart. Refill the fountains of spiritual ideals with living water. Bring forth the rich green foliage of humility and charity and trust. And then let me go back to those who thirst!

THE WOMAN TAKEN IN ADULTERY—MERCY OF GOD

John 8 : 1-11

1. *Accusing fingers pointed at the tearful woman.*
2. *The grace, my Lord, to love You so much for being my Saviour.*

THE WOMAN who had been taken in adultery was trembling and ashamed. She knew the Pharisees were just using her for their own designs—like her cowardly companion who had run away when she was taken. She heard their annoyed remarks over yesterday's failure to seize Jesus. And now they were shaming her publicly just as bait for a trap. Weaklings all! Afraid to fight their battles openly. They pushed her now before Jesus. He would probably be the same. Public opinion would make Him give in to them. Then death would come. At least death would be merciful and take away her shame and her suffering.

There seemed to be silence. She took her hands from her face to see. Jesus was drawing idly on the ground. Then He looked up at her accusers. His eyes were angry and piercing. "Let him who is without sin among you be the first to cast a stone at her." All eyes had turned from her to her accusers. She could hear their heavy breathing. They looked terribly guilty. The stones began to drop. When the older ones left, the younger ones lost their nerve. They were gone. She saw Jesus look at her then for the first time. There was gentleness and forgiveness in His face. "Woman . . . has no one condemned thee?" "No one, Lord," she sobbed with new joy. "Neither will I condemn thee."

DEAR LORD, You did much more than win a brilliant argument that day. You won a heart—a soul! The condemned woman had been so bitter, when she considered how many of her accusers were themselves guilty of the same sin. How she had despised their self-righteousness and their hypocrisy! She felt that You must be the same. Even if You felt pity for her, You wouldn't dare resist them — no one ever did! She could hardly believe it when she heard You stand up to them and show them up for the hypocrites they were. It thrilled her when their accusing fingers had to drop with their ready stones, and they had to slink away in the very shame they attributed to her. You alone were sinless, yet You alone were kind. She had never seen such kindness; had never known such courage and manliness! Sin was no longer attractive to her. Her heart was attracted only to You!

DEAR MASTER, what a beautiful, personal thing religion is! It means falling in love with God — suddenly becoming aware of His infinite mercy and goodness, suddenly getting the big picture of what unselfish love it takes for One to care so much for His own creatures, to pursue them only that He might forgive them, only that He might give them more of Himself! We don't have to be taught to love Goodness — we just do love it, love it naturally! All we have to do is see it!

DEAR LORD, make me see it! Give me the big picture of the Mercy, the Beauty, the Goodness of God—the times You forgave me when I sinned, the times You restrained my wild emotions and foolish thoughts for which others would have loathed me and despised me! If anyone else were my judge, the accusing fingers would never turn away. But You were my Judge—and like the shamed woman in the Temple, I looked up—and You were my Saviour! Let me see. And let me be possessed with love.

THE MAN BORN BLIND (1)— DIVINE PROVIDENCE

John 9:1-41

1. *The look of ecstasy on the face of the blind man as he washed in the pool and then opened his eyes to see for the first time.*
2. *The grace of complete abandonment to Divine Providence.*

A WEEK had passed since the great theological battle in which Jesus clearly claimed His Divinity. Jesus and the Apostles spent every night outside the city. As they came into the Temple this day, the Apostles noticed a blind beggar. Surely he or his parents must have committed some great sin that he would be so afflicted. So they asked Jesus. And Jesus explained that affliction is not a punishment for sin, but an act of Divine Providence. God's fatherly care for the blind man and for the world had so arranged all the circumstances of his life that Jesus would come and cure him at the time that was best for the man and best suited to prove the mission of Jesus. Then Jesus assured them of the tremendous truth that God never slumbers in His watchfulness. "My Father works even until now, and I work," He had

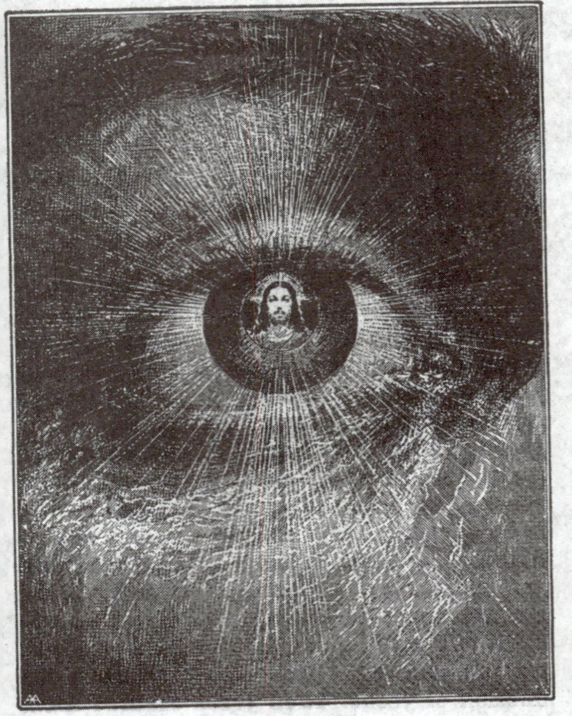

once told them. Now He told them that all this had been arranged for God's glory. Then He made clay, put it on the man's eyes, and told him to wash it away in the pool of Siloam. He thus gave the man a chance to prove his faith. Thanking Jesus, the man started out. He was so familiar with the city that he didn't need a guide. He came to the pool, knelt at its side, and scooped up the water to his eyes. Then he opened them and for the first time in his life, he could see!

DEAR LORD, what a lesson in faith and hope You teach me here. You let us know that this terrible affliction was really a blessing and not a curse or an accident as though God had forgotten this man. The whole thing was planned from all eternity—planned right down to the last detail. His blindness was to teach him humility and courage, and to engender in him deep thoughts and recollection so that he would be ready for the moment of grace—ready for his sight and courageous to be a witness to You before the entire Sanhedrin. What a warm, comforting realization to know that You love and care for us with the same carefulness and providence.

AND YET, my Lord, although I acknowledge this truth of Divine Providence with my mind, though I know You taught it, though I see logically that a dependent being must be constantly sustained by his Creator—still I live by it so little. I have anxieties and fears—just as though I didn't have a Father. I resent sufferings and trials and failure, just as though these were defects instead of instruments my Father uses to make me holy and deep and ready for the moment of grace. Lord, open my eyes! Let me see!

THE MAN BORN BLIND (2)— ADORATION OF GOD

John 9 : 1-41

1. *The cured man standing before his parents in their little home.*
2. *The grace, my Lord, of true adoration and praise for You.*

ONCE he realized that he could see, the cured man just stood still for a few minutes and looked around him. He stared at the water and the people; he looked down at his own hands and his clothing. It was almost too good to be true! His lips moved in prayer to Jahweh. His heart swelled with joy.

It was almost harder finding his way home now that he could see. He watched people as they passed by and almost expected them to stop him and question him. Then he entered his little house. He looked at his mother, mending. So this is what she looked like! And the little one-room house! "Mother," he called, "look at me!" She gasped when she saw the eyes that were once blank looking with loving care into hers. Then he told her the whole story. She embraced him and cried for joy. He must show his neighbors, too, he thought. It made him so happy to see their quizzical look, and then the shy retreat as though he were some strange creature, and then his recognition of their voices when they spoke and he called them by name. Soon a big crowd surrounded him questioning, wondering, congratulating. He was so happy that the tears came to his eyes. And it pleased him so much to tell them about Jesus. It was Jesus Who did all this for him. He wanted to shout His Name from the rooftops.

MY KING, the cured man was performing a beautiful act of adoration at that moment. Adoration is recognizing Your Beauty and Goodness and rejoicing in it in our hearts. As a cook is pleased when we enjoy her dinner, so You are pleased and praised when we take delight in Your gifts and sing of Your Goodness in our hearts.

O MY gracious and bountiful Lord, how little adoration do I give—I who am surrounded by examples of Your Beauty and Goodness and Truth! I see so much loveliness in the children I see—their innocence, their laughter, their devotion in Church. Teach me to recognize Your image there and praise You. There are so many sterling and beautiful persons around me—persons who are generous, unselfish, pure as angels, thoughtful, zealous for Your glory. I cannot help but love them! Let the love be filled with recognition of You, and as I enjoy them, let my joy be praise of You. Open for me the key to the world's secrets and beauty, my King. Let all things tell me of You, and let me love and adore You in them!

THE MAN BORN BLIND (3)—DETACHMENT

John 9:1-41

1. *The cured man standing bravely before the Pharisees in their Courtroom.*
2. *The grace, my Lord, to be detached from human respect, and from all that men think and say.*

AS HIS friends and neighbors gathered around him, the man who until now had been blind realized that many of them didn't believe he was the same person they had known. "How could he be?" they asked. "He knows us all!" others answered. So they turned to him with questioning looks. "I am he," he assured them. Then the barrage of questions: "How?" "When?" "Where?" And he explained. It thrilled him to tell the story as they listened breathlessly. A man named Jesus had done it all. "Where is He now?" they asked anxiously. "I don't know," he replied.

As the group broke up, some decided that they should tell this to the spiritual leaders. When the Pharisees heard it, they were terrified. In view of the claims of Jesus just a short time ago stating that He was God and that He was eternal, such a miracle would compel belief. They must disprove the fact of the miracle. It must be proved either hearsay or some trick. So a delegation was sent immediately to the house of the blind man. Meanwhile a Council was called. The poor uneducated beggar was made to stand facing this ominous group of intellectuals. "Tell us exactly what happened," said the chief judge. Simply, humbly, the blind man told his story. "Ridiculous!" cried the spiteful group. "This man is not from God for he does not keep the Sabbath!" But Nicodemus and a few others of the group who were also more sincere and more realistic retorted, "How could He work such a miracle if He were a sinner?" Patiently, the cured man listened to the argument. He was no theologian; he must keep silent while the learned ones talked. Suddenly the debate came back to him. He was the one cured; what did he think of Jesus? Without flinching and without fear, he answered: "He must be a prophet!"

DEAR MASTER, I admire his calmness before that imposing array of "brass." His blindness had probably given him much time for reflection and thought, and he began to know that nothing or no one can hurt a man except himself. If we are truthful and sincere, no cross-examination can disturb us. If we are detached and not looking for any praise or gain, no refusal or condemnation can hurt us. Calmness and peace are from within, and not from without.

O MY LORD, when will I come to realize this great truth? I can so easily be unnerved, anxious, upset. And why? Because I'm looking for something outside that can only be found inside. Peace, calmness, courage of heart, these are the reward of the man who is detached from human respect. Teach me that detachment, my King. When I'm tempted to be nervous and anxious, let me kneel to You in my heart, choose You above all others, and then rest.

THE MAN BORN BLIND (4)— MORAL COURAGE

John 9 : 1-41

1. *The desperate looks on the faces of the Pharisees.*
2. *The grace, my Lord, of great courage to stand for You and for principle.*

WHEN the cured man spoke to the anxious court and said he thought that Jesus was a prophet, the hateful element among the Pharisees reacted violently. They sneered and shouted that the whole story was fake, trumped up. "Get his parents!" the chief judge shouted to the attendants. "We'll get to the bottom of this."

The same extensive formalities were given to the parents with the hope of impressing them with fear of the court. The judge put them under oath, warned them that they dare not lie, explained the "treason" involved in supporting subversive elements in the country. And then, with his sternest air, "Is this your son, of whom you say that he was born blind?" They nodded a "yes." "How then does he now see?" The poor people were terrified. They hadn't been there when their son was cured, so they were afraid of their lives of not giving the right story or the correct details. "We ourselves do not know," they said. "Ask him; he is of age!" The judges were disgusted. "Call back the witness!" they called to the clerk. They would try a new tactic with him.

They were kindly now when the cured man stood before them. They were glad he could see, they told him. But they must clear up the point about how it happened. "Give glory to God," they told him. "Surely God is the One Who did it!" Then, in their most gentle manner, they continued, "We ourselves know that this man is a sinner!"

The cured man was unmoved by their appeal, even though it was so tempting for him just to agree and be able to slip away from all this trouble. But he didn't. He respected them, he told them, but he had to face facts. "Whether He is a sinner, I do not know. One thing I do know, that whereas I was blind, now I see!" They were enraged and showed it. They shouted the questions all over again. "How? Why? Where?" They ridiculed his proposal that they become disciples of Jesus! That low-born, of questionable origin! And then, silence. Then that most beautiful speech by the cured man in defense of Jesus. They held their ears; they heaped abuse. "Throw him out!"

DEAR MASTER, how I admire that man's courage! It would have been so easy for him to give in, to rationalize. After all, these men were the theologians, not he! It was so tempting just to remain silent. But that would have been taken for agreement, so he had to speak! And what a speech, my

King! He stood up for You and for principle, even when he had to stand alone.

O MY LORD, I admire the virtue of humility and the courage of heart it fosters. But it is so easy for me to give ground and to make excuses. Give me that splendid, manly courage! Not stubbornness. Let me be sure I'm right first! And then, when I am, dear King, let me go ahead and fight, and if necessary, die for You, even if I have to stand alone!

THE MAN BORN BLIND (5)—SIMPLICITY

John 9 : 1-41

1. *The astonished Pharisees, listening to the cured man.*
2. *The grace, dear Lord, to be true and to seek the truth.*

THE BLIND MAN was simple and direct, outspoken and sincere. It annoyed him to hear all these so-called learned men refusing to face the facts. When they began to cross-question him again, he realized that they were just trying to find some contradiction in his story, some slip-up in the details, in order to deny the whole thing. So he parried with them, asked them why they wanted to know. Did they wish to be His disciples? It worked! The learned lawyers were outflanked by a simple, honest man. They flew into a rage. They were the disciples of Moses, but that man! They knew nothing about Him or His origin. And then, with magnificent insight and inspiring bravery and loyalty, the cured man made his speech to them. "You don't know anything about Him?" he asked. "Never has anyone cured a man born blind. How could He be anything except a prophet from God? God certainly wouldn't let a sinner work such a miracle!" It made such sense that they found themselves not interrupting. His sincerity carried them away. There was no answer. And so they had to resort to answering with the big stick, the argument of the bully. Affecting to loathe and despise him, they sneered, "You were just born in sin, and are you trying to teach us?" Calling to the guard, they cried, "Out with him. Take him away!"

DEAR LORD, simplicity can always win the victory over hypocrisy. The Pharisees were disturbed and hard put to it in the discussion because they were trying to force their point. They weren't trying to find the truth of what happened; they were trying to force the facts to fit their preconceived notions. They were hypocrites, for under the guise of seeking only the truth, they were distorting the truth. And hence their fears, their anxieties, their show of dignity to overawe, and their undignified rage. The blind man was simple. He only sought the truth. And so he had no anxieties. He was at peace. He could face the facts and actually toy with those who were afraid of the facts.

DEAR MASTER, I hate to admit it, but how often I have sought to prove my point rather than to seek the truth. Teach me by what happened in this scene that "the truth shall make me free"! Simplicity in seeking truth will keep me from anxiety and from unmanly anger and demonstrations, and especially from all cruel treatment of my opponents in discussion. Let me seek the truth and admit it when I see it, even if it hurts. Let me be simple also in my actions, like the blind man, never putting on an act; never acting different from what I am or different from what I think or feel.

THE MAN BORN BLIND (6)—A GREAT HEART

John 9:1-41

1. *The blind man kneeling in adoration before Jesus.*
2. *The grace, my King, of a great heart motivated by a pure intention of love for You.*

THE GUARDS didn't have to put the cured man out of the Council Chamber after the insulting remarks were made to him by the Pharisees. He just looked at them for a moment with the greatest pity and then he turned silently and left. He wanted to be alone; he wanted to think and to pray. He wandered off to a deserted nook. He sat there and wondered how they could be so blind, wondered what possible motives could make them so distort truth. And then, suddenly, Someone was standing near him. The Man had a kindly face and was smiling at him. A few followers of this Man stood nearby, and then came some of the Pharisees, anxious to see what transpired. The cured man's heart began to pound — perhaps this was Jesus. Then Jesus spoke and he was sure, for he recognized the voice. "Dost thou believe in the Son of God?" Jesus asked him. "Who is He, Lord," he answered, "that I may believe in Him?" He wanted Jesus to know that only His word was sufficient for him. "Thou hast both seen Him," Jesus answered, speaking joyfully of his new vision, "and He it is Who speaks with you!" The cured man sank to his knees with perfect reverence, and looked into the face of Jesus: "I believe, Lord!" Jesus Himself seemed to be so deeply touched by the beauty of his faith and adoration. He couldn't help but note the paradox that those endowed with gifts including sight, like the Pharisees, failed to believe; and the poor blind beggar, bereft of natural gifts from birth, knew Him and loved Him and adored Him!

O MY KING, how beautifully You show me that to be great in Your eyes we don't necessarily need great gifts but only a great heart. Indeed, those with the greatest gifts of intelligence and genius seem most in danger of missing You altogether. But the simple, those with true hearts, see You and believe and embrace Your Holy Will without question or murmur.

MY LORD, it is so easy for me to get mixed up about what true greatness is. Show me through the beautiful example of the cured blind man that it lies in greatness of heart and soul. Intellectual gifts are fine, but dangerous, liable to make me proud and falsely sophisticated. A sense of humor, wit, etc., can be helps when used rightly. But they can also be sharp barbs used to hurt. It is the heart that really matters, the loving, loyal heart, the pure intention of doing all for You. O my King, make me do this work of the heart. Purify my intentions. Let me never neglect my examen, so that my heart may always be Yours.

MARTHA AND MARY (1)— DUTY OF CORRECTION

Luke 10:38-42

1. *Mary at the Feet of Jesus.*
2. *The grace, my Lord, to correct the faults of others clearly and kindly.*

WHENEVER Jesus was in the vicinity of Bethany, He stopped at the home of Martha and Mary and Lazarus. That was one place where He really felt at ease and away from critical eyes. Mary, above all, loved these occasions. She welcomed Jesus effusively and did everything to make Him feel comfortable. She sat at His Feet, asked ques-

tions and listened wide-eyed while He spoke. Martha also was glad that the Master came. She would cook her best meals and fuss to make everything attractive and tasty.

On this one occasion, however, something went wrong in the kitchen. The meal was partly spoiled. It was more than Martha's pride could take. She had to blame someone. That Mary! Just sitting in there and acting the lady! It was no wonder the food got burned! How can one person be expected to do everything! Martha stormed out of the kitchen and interrupted the conversation between Jesus and Mary. "Lord, is it no concern of Thine that my sister has left me to serve alone? Tell her therefore to help me!" Jesus was silent for a moment. He looked up into the flushed face of Martha. "Martha, Martha, thou are anxious and troubled about many things; and yet only one thing is needful. Mary has chosen the best part and it shall not be taken away from her."

MY LORD, I admire so much Your wonderful way of correcting Martha. She made a fuss about trifles. And she was angry because her pride was hurt. Someone had to show her she was wrong, so You didn't dodge the task. Hard as it was to correct a close friend, You did it. And the way You did it was so gentle and gracious! You called her by name, even repeating it, to show her that You had affection for her and were acting only for her good. And then You clearly told her where she was wrong—in putting unimportant things first—and how she could change for the better. She was hurt for the moment, but she learned. When we meet her again at the supper in Simon's house, she is at peace!

O MY LORD, teach me that one of the duties of charity is to correct others, especially my friends, and those who are in my care. It is bound to hurt them a little. No correction comes easily. So I must be prepared to pay that price—the sorrow of seeing them hurt and the chance that they may reject me. If I really love them, this is a small price to help them grow in perfection.

Don't let me be cowardly about that important duty, my King! Don't let me sneak away from it under the guise of minding my own business, or under the excuse of having faults of my own. Let me be strong! True, I must act gently; I must be calm and clear and not speak when I'm angry or working off resentment! But I must act and not run away!

MARTHA AND MARY (2)— CONSTRUCTIVE CORRECTION

Luke 10:38-42

1. *Mary and Lazarus, surprised and ill at ease when Martha got angry and complained to Jesus.*
2. *The grace, my Lord, to correct rightly — with kindness and in a constructive way.*

IT WAS a very tense moment when Martha broke into the conversation and put her complaint before Jesus. She was overwrought and excited. Without realizing it, she insulted Jesus as well as Mary. "Lord, is it no concern of Thine that my sister has left me to serve alone?" She was implying that Jesus was playing favorites, that He was just concerned with being entertained and didn't care if Martha had to work alone. And she was openly accusing Mary of being selfish. Lazarus, Mary and Jesus all felt the biting sting of her words. For the few moments before Jesus answered, a fear went through Mary and Lazarus. They didn't know how such an embarrassing situation could ever be relieved without someone being hurt very badly. It was such a relief to them, then, when they heard the gentle and careful correction by Jesus.

MY KING, anyone but You would have been so tempted to react with cutting sarcasm to Martha and point out her faults and her discourtesy to everyone. Anger so easily invites an angry retort! But that was not Your way. You waited a few moments for her anger to subside. Then, gently, kindly, You pointed out where she was wrong. It was a positive, constructive correction meant to help her to be better, and not just a venting of Your displeasure in angry, negative criticism. You told her that she was complaining only because she was upset and had tried to do too much. She must take time out from all the work and rushing about in order to find peace and serenity in prayer. This was the one thing really necessary. Mary had found it; Martha must find it, too. What a wonderful correction, my King! You were kind and You were constructive. No wonder she learned so easily.

O MY LORD, even more than the temptation not to correct at all is this temptation to correct in the wrong way. How often I blurt out angry, negative criticism! I say it in a mean way and all I do is complain about what's wrong—rather than show the person how to do what is right. My Jesus, give me the self-control to hold my tongue until I can speak calmly and kindly. No one likes to be talked down to or "told off." My correction must be kind, with respect for the human dignity of the other person. And then let it be constructive! Let me point out what is right and how to do it instead of whining about what was wrong. And if the incident is closed and nothing can be done to correct it, then, Lord, let me forget it altogether!

THE OUR FATHER (1)—TRUE LOVE OF GOD

Luke 11:1-5; Matt. 6:7-15

1. *The Apostles watch Jesus as He is absorbed in prayer.*
2. *The grace to delight in God.*

ONE NIGHT, shortly after the incident in the home of Martha and Mary, Jesus was praying to His Father. The Apostles watched Him. They had felt the need of prayer for themselves and for the souls in their missionary work in Judea, but they had found prayer difficult. Jesus seemed to find it so easy. Nothing distracted Him. And His prayer seemed to bring Him such comfort and strength, seemed to be the perfect outlet for expressing His heaven-centered thoughts and love for the Father! They envied Him. And

so when He arose from prayer, like simple, humble children they said to Him: "Lord, teach us to pray!" Jesus loved them dearly when they were like this—childlike, willing to learn, conscious of their own weakness and depending upon Him. And so He taught them a magnificent prayer.

DEAR LORD, what You taught them was more than a prayer; it was a revelation of Your very Soul, Your own deepest and most ardent feelings for the Father. The "Our Father" was an expression in words of what You felt in Your great Heart, a summary of the great ideals for which You lived and died. "Our Father," You said. Not just Yours or mine, but ours. The great God is our Father, and You our Brother, and all men my brothers and sisters. Together with You and all men then we pray—and the important things come first: that the Father's Name may be loved and praised by all, that His Kingdom, the Church, spread all over the world, that His Holy Will be done perfectly and cheerfully by all. "On earth as it is in heaven" modifies all these petitions. O my King, how beautiful the world would be then! How happy! What peace and joy among men! And what proper gratitude to the Father and Benefactor of all!

DEAR MASTER, it is only occasionally that I begin to realize that true love is this love of benevolence, this wishing well for the beloved, this delight in His good fortune, this feeling for Him and His plans. If I loved the Father as You do, my King, I would never cease to feel and pray with all my heart these first three petitions. Let me feel them deeply, Lord. Let my meat, like Yours, be the honoring of the Father and the working out cheerfully of His Will. Let me take sheer joy in His being loved and praised. And let me feel the hurt and sorrow of every sin, and try to make up to Him by loving Him more!

THE OUR FATHER (2)— LIVING IN THE PRESENT

Luke 11 : 1-5; Matt. 6 : 5-13

1. *The Jews in the desert gathering up the manna.*
2. *The grace, my Lord, to live each day as it comes and not worry about tomorrow.*

THE APOSTLES were listening to Jesus teach them how to pray. They were all ears and eyes. He had shown them how to have confidence in God, calling Him "our Father." And then He showed how love is really well-wishing; and so we pray that the

Father may be loved and praised and appreciated the same on earth as He is in heaven. Now Jesus told them how to ask for things from their Father. "Give us this day our daily bread."

DEAR LORD, surely the bread You speak of here means all our material and spiritual needs. We are to ask our Father for all of them. He wants to give them to us, but He wants us to be polite and conscious of the relationship of child and father—so we are to ask humbly for our needs. What strikes me particularly, though, my King, is that You tell us to ask for them "for this day," as though we wouldn't need them tomorrow or as though tomorrow didn't count. And that's just what You want us to see, that "sufficient for the day is its own trouble." Tomorrow really doesn't count; only today does. You were recalling to their minds the fact that Your Father fed the Jews in the desert, but only one day at a time, so they would learn to trust. The God Who feeds us today will feed us tomorrow. We must learn to live without anxiety and fear and to trust in His goodness.

MY LORD, I wonder if I will ever learn this lesson of living each day as it comes. Most of my worries and tensions are about yesterday and tomorrow, and I forget to live in today. Teach me this beautiful discipline of living in the present, and leaving tomorrow to the merciful care of my Father in heaven. My Father, "give me this day my daily bread."

THE OUR FATHER (3)— FORGIVENESS OF INJURY

Luke 11 : 1-5; Matt. 6 : 5-13

1. *The unforgiving servant beating his fellow-servant.*
2. *The grace, my Lord, readily and willingly to forgive and forget, just as I hope to be forgiven.*

JESUS had just taught the eager Apostles to ask for all their spiritual and material needs—their "daily bread." Now He stresses one spiritual gift we should ask for in a special way—the grace of mercy and the bigness to forgive and forget. And He has us ask for forgiveness of our own sins, only on this basis —that we will forgive others—and only to the degree that we forgive others. "Father . . . forgive us our trespasses, as we forgive those who trespass against us."

O MY KING, we are liable to forget just how much in need of mercy we are. Our grave sins make us worthy of hell, of being cut off forever from love and joy and happiness. Our small sins deserve to be punished. Our meanness and smallness and pettiness and pride—all make us worthy to be hated and despised by all men. And yet Your mercy saves us. Again and again You forgive us in Confession. Time after time You forget our faults and let us start fresh and try again. And continually, without ceasing, You protect us from ourselves. By Your merciful grace You protect us from falling into the basest forms of sin, protect us from being despised and loathed by our fellow men. Without Your mercy, Lord, life would be unbearable.

And yet, my Lord, we tend to forget how much mercy we have received; or we act as though we deserve it, as though it were ours by right. And like the unforgiving servant in the parable, we are stern and unforgiving to others. So in this beautiful prayer You teach us to be mindful of the mercy we have received and to ask for mercy only to the degree that we grant it to others.

MY LORD, this realization terrifies me, when I think of my own shortcomings in this regard. What numbers of rash judgments, quick and unfair condemnations! How slow to see the other's point of view! How stingy in making allowances for those who have hurt me! If You treated me as I treat others, my King, I would have to despair of heaven. Help me to be big and forgiving. Self-pity is the big obstacle! It works up all the feelings that make it hard for me to say "they didn't mean it!" Help me to loathe self-pity and to love mercy. Never let me forget the beauty of Your first word from the Cross. And then let me be the same as You.

JESUS AT THE FEAST OF DEDICATION— THE ART OF DEBATE

John 10 : 22-42

1. *Jesus with His hand raised majestically to turn them from stone-throwing to sound reasoning.*
2. *The grace, my Lord, to love truth so much that I'll be firm but not stubborn.*

IT WAS December and time for the feast of the Dedication of the Temple. Jesus walked in the beautiful portico known as

Solomon's Porch, teaching a small group as He walked along. The Pharisees approached Him, anxious to get a statement they could use against Him. Was He the Christ or wasn't He? Jesus didn't use the word, "Christ," but He pointed to His miracles as proof of His divine mission—even more, as proof that He and the Father were "one." Some shouted accusations at Him; others ran into the courtyard for stones to throw at Him. Jesus was magnificent in His composure. He raised His hand in a gesture demanding silence. They stopped. Then He spoke. "Many good works (miracles) have I shown you from My Father. For which of these works do you stone Me?" Not for the good works, they answered, but for blasphemy "because Thou, being a man, makest Thyself God." They understood His words but they missed all the proofs. He didn't take back His claim. Calmly, patiently, He tried to show them the evidence for it, the logic of it. "If I do not perform the works of My Father, do not believe Me. But if I do perform them, and if you are not willing to believe Me, believe the works, that you may know and believe that the Father is in Me and I in the Father." It was a masterpiece of logic and clarity.

DEAR MASTER, I love to watch You in Your verbal clashes with the Pharisees. What an example You give us for our discussions and disagreements with others. You were firm without being stubborn; You knew how to disagree without being disagreeable or insulting. You presented Your claim to be the Saviour and to be Divine without using their words, "the Christ," because You knew that they thought of "the Christ" as a worldly king. It was truth You loved, so You used terms that would avoid confusion. When they lost their heads in violent passion, You tried to soothe their wild anger and its ensuing blindness. And then You gave clear, compelling proofs that what You had said was true. And You listened to their side of the argument, understood their point of view—that it was very difficult for them to think of You as Divine. So You tried to approach it their way. If those who did God's work of old could be called "gods," then could You not be called Divine when You were One with the Father in sanctity and power? My King, what an example to us of dedication to the truth, of firmness coupled with respect for one's opponents!

DEAR MASTER, You know how different I am. I get my point of view and I refuse to listen to others. They can hardly say a few words before I interrupt. I get loud. I bring up personalities — rather than treating the issue and keeping to the point. And why, Lord? Because I'm scared! I feel for my point —but that's about it, feeling—not thorough understanding or conviction. And so I'm afraid to face objections and other points of view. Dear Master, teach me to be intellectually honest. Let me think out my ideas completely and clearly. Let me have a love—not for any pet themes—but for truth. Then I'll listen patiently and sympathetically. Then I'll be able to pinpoint the precise area of disagreement, and re-present my case with firmness and with kindness—like You, my King!

BLASPHEMY OF THE PHARISEES (1)— HOLY EMULATION

Luke 11:14-36

1. *Jesus curing the dumb and blind man.*
2. *The grace to see and love the good in others and then to imitate them.*

JESUS and the Apostles were south of Jerusalem near Bethlehem. People from Jerusalem or nearby brought to Jesus a man possessed. The poor man was dumb and blind —almost helpless to communicate his needs or ideas to others. Besides, the devil in him had made him fight and kick and act in a terrible way. Jesus felt pity for the man and healed him. It was beautiful to see the results. He stopped the wild activity and was calm. He opened his eyes and a smile lit his face, for he could see. He moved his lips and was able to talk. Tears came to the eyes of all around as the man knelt before Jesus and spoke his gratitude. They all agreed that nothing like this was ever seen in Israel . . . Surely this must be the Son of David!

To the Pharisees and Scribes who were present this admiration for Jesus was a hateful thing. Their envy and jealousy just knew no bounds! Envy made them miss the whole point of this beautiful cure. It was almost with a hissing sound of uncontrol that they said: "By Beelzebub, the prince of devils, He casts out devils."

MY KING, envy and jealousy can make us blind and hateful, can make us overlook the most beautiful qualities in others and thus make us miss out on so much. The Pharisees in this scene could have become great Christians if once they had allowed themselves to see Your beauty and goodness!

MY MASTER, much as I hate to admit it, am I not often guilty of jealousy and envy! Do not the good qualities of others upset me because in my blindness I imagine that they make me look worse! Whereas if I only open my eyes to see the good and beauty in others, I will see You and enjoy You and enjoy them. My life will be enriched with great inspiration. And instead of being sorry at their good qualities, I will rejoice at them and try to imitate them in my own life.

O my Lord, give me this insight. Let me see and find and love goodness everywhere. Let it inspire me to imitation and joy—not envy or sorrow.

BLASPHEMY OF THE PHARISEES (2)— SELF-CONTROL IN DISCUSSION

Luke 11:14-36

1. *Jesus listening as the blasphemous Pharisees call His kind work the work of the devil.*
2. *The grace, my Lord, to be calm and self-controlled in discussion and to answer with clarity and kindness.*

THE CROWD surrounded the cured man. A wave of great joy swept over them as they reflected his wonderful happiness. And then came the sour note. The Pharisees just couldn't stand to see Jesus praised. With all the venom of a serpent, they shrieked to the enthusiastic crowd: "By Beelzebub, the prince of devils, He casts out devils." The joy and enthusiasm of the crowd died down. They could hardly believe what was said, even though it came from the great, learned Pharisees from Jerusalem. They were quiet. Then Jesus spoke. He spoke so calmly and quietly. He presented His case in the form of questions. Is Satan a fool that he would fight against himself and destroy himself? Are the Jewish priests also possessed, for they drive out devils also, do they not? Can a strong armed person like a devil be routed, except by one stronger—by God or God's messenger? His teaching made such perfect sense! He showed up the foolishness of the blasphemy of the Pharisees. The crowd was happy again; the cured man so secure now and peaceful.

O MY KING, how I admire Your calmness in this situation, when anyone would have been justified in losing his temper and blasting the Pharisees. Their accusation was so ridiculous, anyone else would have just answered them with contempt: "How ridiculous! How stupid can one get?" Yet You didn't. You knew Your side of the case so clearly that You presented Your arguments with beautiful logic and clearness. And You were so calm, You gave them a chance to be won over without feeling beaten down.

MY LORD, I need this calmness and logic so much. I get ideas in my head—many times without reasoning out clearly all the reasons. And so when I am challenged, I panic. I lose my calm and get annoyed and try to reduce the opponent's argument to the ridiculous. And it's all because of pride being hurt that I am questioned, and pride being afraid that I cannot answer clearly.

Lord, teach me to be calm when my ideas are challenged. Make me see the fairness of looking at the other's point of view. And don't let me disagree unless I can give clear, logical reasons why I disagree. And, O my King, in giving them let me imitate Your calmness and Your peace! Humility will be the key of the matter . . . humility which will lead me to admit: "Maybe I'm wrong!" There's no disgrace in being wrong. The only disgrace is in not admitting it when I see it or in being so stubborn that I won't see it. Humility will give me calmness and peace, clarity of vision and charity in speech.

BLASPHEMY OF THE PHARISEES (3)— HUMILITY OF HEART

Luke 11:14-36

1. *Jesus making an appeal to the stiff-necked Pharisees.*
2. *The grace, my Lord, of true humility, humility of heart, being true.*

JESUS had won a great victory. He had cured the poor man and won him. He then answered the jealous, hateful accusations of the Pharisees with beautiful, compelling logic. The people were simply captivated by Him; the Pharisees, humiliated and speechless.

Yet Jesus didn't leave them that way. He had come to win souls, not simply win arguments. And so He began a deep, sincere appeal to the Pharisees. Using their humiliation as an opening wedge to get into their hard hearts and past the steel shell of their pride, He explained to them their basic fault — their pride of heart which ruined everything they did, which even put them in danger of losing their souls.

DEAR LORD, the lesson You taught them then was put in strong terms. You called their sin of pride a sin against the Holy Spirit which would not be forgiven. You wanted to shock them. You didn't mean that it really would never be forgiven. You were showing that this diabolical pride, this unbridled self-love which made them jealous and blind to all Your goodness and to the manifest miracles, this pride would never let them ask for forgiveness unless they got rid of it. And for fear that they would look at the good things they did as proofs that they really weren't so bad, You told them the story of the man possessed by an evil spirit of sin. He got rid of it and he looked good, but then the evil spirit came back with seven more deadly spirits — spiritual pride, etc. And that man who still avoided the obvious and open kinds of sin was in a worse state than he was at the beginning.

MY KING, I admire with all my soul Your appeal to the Pharisees in this scene. If ever You are the Good Shepherd, it is here. You are patient when they ridicule Your beautiful work; You explain and then You try to win them. I love You for it. And I love the teaching You try to get over to them, teaching which is so important—the absolute necessity of humility of heart. Pride made them jealous and blind. O my King, isn't that what it does to me? And doesn't it make me complacent like them, self-satisfied, loving to think of the good I've done and forgetting the poor motives and my sins.

Dear Master, pride can separate me from You! It can separate me from Your work! Let me hate it! Let me love humility of heart. Let me frequently take this test about how critical I am, how annoyed, how jealous. Make me true!

THE UNJUST STEWARD—SPIRITUAL SLOTH

Luke 16:1-13

1. *The steward sitting down with his lord's debtors and changing their bills.*
2. *The grace, my Lord, never to lose the desire for perfection.*

JESUS was continuing to instruct by His ingenious method of parables. He told them now about a dishonest steward, who was caught cheating by his lord. The lord ordered him to settle all his accounts for the last time. He was fired! Immediately the steward began to plan. He would ingratiate himself with the lord's debtors by making their bills only a fraction of what they should be. Then when he was out of a job they would remember him and take care of him.

It was a story that was simple enough and true to life. The crowd listened, waiting to hear the condemnation of the steward. They could hardly believe their ears when Jesus added: "And the master commended the unjust steward in that he had acted prudently." Jesus was telling them that they had something important to learn even from worldlings. There was something about his action that they ought to imitate.

DEAR LORD, You knew that this parable would shock both Your listeners and us. That's exactly what You wanted it to do! It hurt You that worldly men and thieves would often be so much more energetic and ingenious in accomplishing their unjust ends than we are in striving for perfection and good works. We can be so tepid and lukewarm. We settle down comfortably with venial sin and deliberate faults — never dreaming of going higher, of practicing greater virtue or winning more souls. We make the easy, comfortable compromise of spiritual sloth.

So You tried to shock us out of our lethargy, my King. You praised a thief! Not for his injustice, of course—but for his practicality, his "get-up-and-go," his energy and prudence in attaining his goal. How You wished we would have this same kind of drive and prudence for accomplishing good!

DEAR MASTER, I realize now the evil of spiritual sloth. It has caused an awful erosion in my soul—an erosion so gradual that I never even noticed it. I've become tepid and careless in my prayers. They are words now—not prayers. I pay only lip service to my examination of conscience. I have been unkind, cynical, selfish—and it hasn't even bothered me. There were no mortal sins—so I was lulled to sleep, thinking I was leading an interior life.

Dear Master, thank You for jolting me! I haven't even the "get-up-and-go" of a thief! Let me start again. Let me hate this mediocrity. To lose our thirst for holiness is to lose all color and nobility! I promise, my King, to set my sights once more on the ideal — to settle for nothing less than sanctity!

JESUS CURES AN INVALID WOMAN—ZEAL OF THE HEART

Luke 13 : 10-17

1. *The woman, bent over and terribly embarrassed.*
2. *The grace, my Lord, to rejoice sincerely over all the good things that are done by others.*

JESUS was teaching in one of the synagogues of Judea on the Sabbath. His attention was caught by a woman who was terribly handicapped. For eighteen years her body was bent over and stiffened, so that she could never stand up straight or even look up. She tried not to leave the house often. She felt embarrassed, and could hardly walk without falling ... But this day the Master would be teaching in the synagogue. Maybe . . . ! She hardly let herself hope, but she came. Jesus was deeply touched by her plight. He called her to Him. She was trembling. He rested His hands on her bent shoulders. "Woman," He said, "thou art delivered from thy infirmity." Immediately she raised her bent body until she stood up straight. She was so overcome by emotion that she couldn't speak. She grasped His hand and kissed it.

The ruler of the synagogue broke in on everyone's joy for her. Angrily he shouted, "There are six days in which one ought to work; on these therefore come and be cured and not on the Sabbath!" Jesus was exasperated with them—ruler and Pharisees alike. "Hypocrites!" He called out with vehemence. Didn't they loose animals in order to feed and water them on the Sabbath? And not a human being? They couldn't answer a word. The crowd felt at ease again. They surrounded the cured woman and shouted for joy.

MY SAVIOUR, in this scene the Pharisees proved that envy can invade even the field of good works and distort the sacred virtue of zeal. They were absolutely blinded to the beauty of her cure—not so much because it was done on the Sabbath, but because they didn't do it. If they could have exercised that power themselves, they surely would have done so. But when You did it, it was different. Then it no longer seemed noble and beautiful, because in their blindness they imagined that it made them look bad by comparison. If they only realized, my King, that charity is essentially wishing well, not necessarily doing well. There are times we are not able to do good. But if we wish well to the needy person, if we rejoice over the good that others are able to do for them, then we make the good action our own. We become a part of it. The truth is, my King, that while it is wonderful zeal to do good, it is even greater zeal to rejoice in the good that others do. The Pharisees could have been a part of Your lovely act of kindness, my King—they just didn't have enough zeal!

DEAR MASTER, You know that I have the zeal of the hands—that I love to do things for others, love to lead them to You. But, Lord, how little do I rejoice over the good that others do. How little do I possess the zeal of the heart! As though the others were not serving You at all! As though true love doesn't rejoice over all the good to the loved one!

Dear Lord, if I am to love You rightly, I must love You completely. I must be so happy that You are honored and that souls are won —no matter who wins them. Like Paul, I must have the zeal of the heart: "Provided only that in every way . . . Christ is being proclaimed; in this do I rejoice, yes and I shall rejoice." Teach me this true, complete zeal, my King, this zeal of the heart. Let every act of kindness, every noble deed thrill me— no matter who does it! Let every honor to the Church make me feel good, every act of virtue, every convert won, every conquest for You delight my heart. Then I'll have the joy of loving You in every one of them, because I become a part of them all!

LAZARUS TAKEN SICK (1)—DETACHMENT

John 11 : 1-3

1. *Martha and Mary by the bedside of Lazarus.*
2. *The grace, my Lord, of holy detachment.*

WHILE JESUS was beyond the Jordan engaged in the Perean ministry, His friend Lazarus became very sick, and though Martha and Mary did everything they could for him, his fever grew higher and higher. They kept going back and forth to the well to get cold water. They dipped cloths in it and put cold compresses to his head and chest, but nothing seemed to break the fever. It hurt them so much to see him toss and turn under the burning heat of it. Neither could sleep. They prayed as they had never prayed before. How they wished that Jesus were there! But the Pharisees had tried to stone Him in Judea, so He had gone beyond the Jordan. It wouldn't be fair to ask Him to risk His life by coming back. And yet He loved Lazarus, just as they did. They would at least tell Jesus of the sickness, and leave the decision to Him. They asked one of their close friends to go beyond the Jordan and try to find Jesus to tell him, "Lord, behold, he whom Thou lovest is sick."

DEAR Martha and Mary, I love your perfect balance and detachment. Lazarus was more dear to you than life itself. You would have sacrificed anything to save him—would gladly have taken the terrible fever that inflamed his body, would gladly have sold house and possessions to pay any physician who could cure him! And yet you would not have Jesus endanger His life or force Him to cure Lazarus. You only told Him the facts and left everything else in His hands!

What magnificent detachment! What perfect trust in Jesus!

DEAR LORD, so many of my disappointments and sorrows come from lack of detachment. I have my idea of what I want, my plan of how things should proceed. And I get my heart so set on my way that I'm blind to any other possibilities—the plans of others or the plans of my Father. So when things go other than as I planned, I'm heartsick, and terribly let down. I imagine that I'm a complete failure.

Teach me, my Lord, that beautiful attitude of mind and heart that Martha and Mary had learned at Your feet. Teach me to say about all my plans, my hopes, even the needs of loved ones as dear as Lazarus, "Lord, these are the facts—You decide! Your Will be done."

LAZARUS TAKEN SICK (2)—SUFFERING

John 11 : 1-16

1. *The breathless messenger telling Jesus about Lazarus' sickness.*
2. *The grace, my Lord, to trust You and love You in every trial.*

THE MESSENGER from Martha and Mary found Jesus surrounded by His Apostles, about a day's journey from Bethany. When he announced the message, all the Apostles looked at Jesus. They knew how much He loved Lazarus; they wondered what He would do. Jesus said to the messenger in the hearing of all: "This sickness is not unto death, but for the glory of God." He knew with His divine knowledge that Lazarus was dying at that very moment. When the messenger arrived back at Bethany the next day and found that Lazarus was dead he almost felt ashamed to tell them the message. But Martha and Mary wanted so much to know what Jesus had said. Sheepishly, the messenger told them, "This sickness is not unto death," and then turned and left. Martha and Mary said nothing. Even when Jesus didn't come the next day or the next, they did not comment. They had learned to love and trust too strongly to doubt Him. They would understand His message some day—in His own time. Meantime they would wait and trust.

DEAR MASTER, there can be no doubt how much You loved Martha and Mary and Lazarus; no question of how dear the Apostles were to You. And yet You deliberately said and did things that would make them suffer, deliberately gave them trials that would be so hard for them to understand. "A sickness not unto death"—when You knew Lazarus was dying at that very moment. No use of Your divine power to heal at a distance—as You had done to people who were not close friends at all! And then deliberately staying on in Perea two more days, when Martha and Mary needed You so much! Why, Lord? Why such deliberate coldness, why such mysterious words and actions? Because faith, like muscles, becomes stronger the more it is exercised; because charity, like gold, is purified in fire! You loved them too much to spare them in making them saints!

DEAR MASTER and Friend, how good for me to get this insight into Your ways. I'm so ready to doubt You when severe trials come; so prone to wallow in self-pity and cry out "Why?" I feel so ashamed now of my weak faith and lack of trust. The very trials are marks of Your love and care, proofs of Your friendship, which refuses to let me remain mediocre and tepid! Dear Lord, forgive me! Send me what You will. Work with me in Your own way. I trust You; I love You!

LAZARUS TAKEN SICK (3)—THE GOAL OF LIFE

John 11 : 17-31

1. *Martha kneeling before Jesus.*

2. *The grace, my Lord, to realize that life ends not in death, but in resurrection.*

WHEN LAZARUS was dead three days and the tomb sealed, Jesus told the Apostles that He was returning to Bethany to raise him from the dead. They arrived near Bethany the next day. The news of His coming went on ahead of them. When Martha heard it, she ran out to meet Jesus. She burst into tears when she saw the Face of her beloved Friend. "Lord, if Thou hadst been here my brother would not have died." There wasn't the slightest note of complaint in her words, just an expression of her faith and trust. For she added, "Even now I know that whatever Thou shalt ask of God, God will give it to Thee." Jesus felt so much for her—the busy practical Martha, she could love strongly too! It made Him happy to tell her the good news: "Thy brother shall rise." Martha was startled. Her sobbing stopped as she looked up in wonder. Did Jesus mean that He would raise Lazarus from the dead then and there? But she must not presume or put Jesus in any awkward position. "I know that he will rise . . . on the last day." Then Jesus looked deeply into her eyes and soul: "I am the resurrection and the life; he who believes in Me, even if he die, shall live . . . Dost thou believe this?" She caught her breath. She knew now what He would do . . . she knew! "Yes, Lord, I believe . . ."

DEAR LORD, how beautiful are those words of Yours, "I am the resurrection and the life"; how they ring out with comfort and peace to all men! As we grow older, one by one, death steals away our close relatives and dear friends—and we experience an emptiness and a great sense of loss. We can't call them back, or say the things we left unsaid, or hear the things we long to hear. What a comfort to know that it is not all over, that they are at home waiting for us, that they and we ourselves some day will rise again from the dead to live and love each other forever!

LORD, I get so busy rushing through life, so involved with talk and noise and activity, that I lose sight of life's goal. The story of Lazarus is so very beautiful, because we see his resurrection, we see the extremely moving reunion with his sisters and friends—and it fills us with joy just to contemplate it. Let me realize, my King, that You are "the resurrection and the life" for us also, that what You did for Lazarus then You will do for us and our loved ones at the last day. Let me take time for silence and prayer to realize all this. Let me love to contemplate the goal of my life and take from it the joy and strength it can give.

LAZARUS TAKEN SICK (4)—JESUS OUR FRIEND

John 11:17-35

1. *Mary at the Feet of Jesus.*
2. *The grace, my Lord, to be Your loyal and devoted friend.*

MARTHA hurried home. It was hard for her to hold in the good news but she must. It was only right that Mary should hear it from the Master Himself. She called Mary aside from the many friends who had gathered to sympathize with them. "The Master is here," she whispered, "and calls thee." Mary jumped up and hurried out to meet Jesus. She fell at His feet and sobbed. "Lord," she said, when she looked up, "if Thou hadst been here, my brother would not have died." She had to let Him know that she believed.

The tears were streaming down her face. Jesus recalled the last time He saw those tears—at the house of Simon the Pharisee, when they came trickling down over His feet. It hurt Him to see her sorrow. "Where have you laid him?" He asked of the friends who gathered about them. He helped Mary stand up and walked with her to the tomb. And there at the tomb, tears formed in His own sacred eyes: "And Jesus wept."

O MY KING, what a lovely thing was Your friendship for this family! You knew that You would raise Lazarus from the dead very soon—that inside of a half-hour Martha and Mary and all their friends would be just deliriously happy having their loved one back again. And yet at that moment You were so deeply moved by their sorrow and agony that strong, manly tears forced their way into Your eyes. Your friendship was no cold, calculating plan that arranged what was best for them from a distance. It was a warm, human love—strong to make them suffer, but sympathetic and generous in suffering the pain with them.

MY KING, You not only sanctified human friendship by Your example, but You invite me to share what they shared. "I have not called you servants. I have called you friends." It isn't a dream, my King, it's true! You are glad to come to me in Holy Communion, as You were happy in their home at Bethany. You plan what is best for me — as You did for them. And when it is some sorrow I must undergo, You are not far away or unconcerned. You understand, You are right there beside me.

Let me be loyal, Lord — welcome You in Communion, love to sit at Your feet in daily visits! Above all, let me trust You, no matter what You may send.

JESUS RAISES LAZARUS (1)— THE VISION OF FAITH

John 11:36-46

1. *Jesus, His hand raised aloft, calling Lazarus.*
2. *The grace, my Lord, to live by faith and trust.*

THE CROWD of people who stood near Jesus at the tomb were quite taken back when they saw His tears. "See how He loved him!" they whispered. He had cured people who were strangers; they couldn't fathom why He didn't cure His friend. They didn't realize how great love can deny a lesser favor in order to grant a greater one! Jesus told them to roll back the stone from the tomb. "Lord . . ." Martha objected, "he is already decayed . . ." She knew in her heart what Jesus would do, but her old impulse for the practical asserted itself before she could stop it. Jesus was gentle with her. She was so much like Peter—so impetuous, but so very good! He reminded her that she would see great things.

Jesus raised His eyes tc heaven: "Father... that they may believe!" And then the awesome command, the call that went beyond the grave: "Lazarus, come forth!" There was a death-like stillness. Then the shrouded figure appeared at the door of the tomb. Some of the women screamed; others cried for joy; many knelt down in adoration of the divine power. Martha and Mary fell at the feet of Jesus, sobbing with unspeakable joy and gratitude.

LORD, the raising of Lazarus was a most beautiful act of kindness to Your friends, a lovely proof of that tender care by which You arrange all things for our good. Who would have thought in those past few days that You really loved them? You had shown more concern for complete strangers on many occasions than You seemed to be showing for them, Your dear friends. Yet once we see the whole story, my King, once we see their growth in faith and trust, the increase in their appreciation of one another, their untold joy and wonderment at God's great goodness—once we see all that, we wouldn't want to change one single detail of what they suffered. It is always this way, my King. You are always working to make us truly good and completely happy. If we don't see this in our sorrows or sufferings, the fault lies in our shortsightedness, in our lack of faith and trust, not in Your goodness or loving care.

DEAR LORD, If I lived by faith, I'd see the whole story right from the beginning and I'd have such peace. If my trust were what it should be, I'd enjoy the final outcome even while I was suffering the trials—and they'd be so easy to take. "Lord, that I may see!" In every trial and sorrow, my King, let me go back and watch the raising of Lazarus from the dead. Let it be a living proof that for those who love God "all things work together unto good."

JESUS RAISES LAZARUS (2)— INTELLECTUAL BASIS FOR FAITH

John 11:36-46

1. *Lazarus coming forth from the tomb.*
2. *The grace, my Lord, to realize that You proved Your divinity.*

JESUS WAITED a few minutes as the crowd expressed their various reactions, and then He nodded to some of the Apostles: "Unbind him, and let him go." They removed the face cloth from Lazarus and the bindings from his hands and feet. They were almost afraid to speak to him. He looked at Jesus and his sisters. In his eyes there was deep gratitude to Jesus — especially for the happiness He brought to Martha and Mary. He walked over then to where Jesus stood and tried to express his thanks. Martha and Mary stood up. He took them in his arms and warmly embraced them and kissed them. He was the same Lazarus — the same smile, the same warm and gentle brother and loyal friend.

DEAR LORD, as beautiful as this was as an act of kindness to Your friends, it has even a greater meaning to the world as a proof of Your divinity. Lazarus had been dead for four days. Since the Jews didn't embalm their dead, his body was already decomposing. And yet, at just a word from You, his soul returned from Limbo, revivified the decaying body, and he was alive! No power, my King, absolutely no power, except God's, could have done this!

Nor can anyone deny that it happened. There were hundreds of people who saw it. They had seen the dead body, and had helped seal the tomb two days before when the odor began to get oppressive. The Apostles couldn't have lied about the facts even if they wanted to, for these people were still living when the Apostles preached and wrote. Nor would they have had any motive to lie. Most of them suffered persecution and martyrdom for what they taught. Only an insane person would die to defend a story he made up. Not even Your early enemies could deny that it happened, my King. They said that You did it with the power of the devil — which is of course ridiculous! But they couldn't deny the fact that it happened! The proof is so overwhelming, my Jesus, for those with intellectual honesty. Those who don't see are those who won't see!

MY LORD, there are times, I must admit, when all the suffering in the world, all the evil and injustice tempt me to wonder whether God sees—or cares. Evil seems so real and near, and God seems so far away. In those moments of emotional distress and temptation, my King, let the reality of Your life and the clear proof of Your divinity be the steel to keep me strong and faithful and true. I believe in You, my King. And "even if You should slay me, still I will trust You"!

JESUS CURES TEN LEPERS—GRATITUDE

Luke 17 : 11-19

1. *The cured man bowed to the ground before Jesus in humble gratitude.*
2. *The grace, my Lord, to live always in a spirit of gratitude.*

JESUS and the Apostles were making their way to Jerusalem for the feast of the Passover. As they neared a little town along the way, ten victims of leprosy recognized Jesus and called out to Him for mercy. They were forbidden to come near, so they begged from a distance: "Jesus, Master, have pity on us." Jesus stopped and looked at them. They were a pitiable sight. "Go, show yourselves to the priests," He said. Only those who were cured showed themselves at the Temple for a certificate to prove they were well. But they believed that they would be cured as He implied. So they started for Jerusalem, and as they went along they were cured. They were so happy they almost jumped with joy. They must get their certificates quickly and then bring the joyful news to their loved ones. One of them, a Samaritan, suddenly realized Who was responsible for his cure. He turned and ran back to Jesus and "fell on his face at His feet, giving thanks." The Face of Jesus was sad: "Were not the ten made clean? But where are the nine?"

MY KING, lack of gratitude isn't a positive fault, like stealing or unkindness or impurity. The ungrateful person is simply thoughtless; he doesn't mean to hurt. And yet his thoughtlessness does hurt, almost as though it were an intentional insult. The lepers who were cleansed were naturally excited. It was only normal that they should be overcome with happiness and want to show themselves to their relatives and friends. And yet You were hurt, because they took their cure for granted; they failed to appreciate the love and kindness You had poured out to them; they clung to their gift and forgot the Giver.

DEAR MASTER, I'm afraid that lack of gratitude is one of the biggest failings of my life. I take so much for granted! I marvel that the cleansed lepers didn't return to thank You. Yet do I? Are You any less good in giving me health all the time than You were in restoring health to them? Are You to be less thanked, less appreciated because You've never let me lose my sight, than You should be appreciated when You restored sight? O my King, each faculty of body and soul is a gift from You. All the love that has been poured into my life—from parents, brothers and sisters, devoted friends—it is all Your doing. The restraining influence that has kept me from doing the most foolish things and committing the worst sins—it's all the work of Your protective grace.

Lord, don't let me take my gifts for granted! Let me appreciate them, love them, enjoy them—and constantly be grateful to my Father!

JAMES AND JOHN SEEK HONORS—BIGNESS

Mark 10:35-45

1. *The ten Apostles indignant and murmuring about James and John.*
2. *The grace, my Lord, of bigness, the gift of greatness of soul.*

THE MOTHER of James and John was keenly aware of the strong love her sons had for Jesus. She knew them so well that she could decipher every expression on their faces and lips, could figure out their desires even when left unsaid. So she approached Jesus for them, pleading that He grant them the places closest to Him in the Kingdom. It embarrassed James and John at first. But Jesus seemed to take the request seriously. Turning to them, He asked: "Can you drink of the cup of which I drink?" They were quick to answer: "We can!"

The other Apostles overheard the conversation. They felt sure that James and John had prompted their mother to speak for them. They grew indignant, muttered uncharitable things about the brothers, were bitter at what they considered ambition and cowardice. Jesus knew better. He made no promise of favoritism, but assured the brothers that they would have their chance to be near Him at least in His sufferings.

DEAR MASTER, the indignation of the ten proved that they still hadn't learned to be big. The whole incident recalls to mind the story of the shrinking man. As he grew smaller, everything else seemed bigger—the cat, the broom, the door. Even things we consider small—a pencil and scissors—to him they looked huge.

The same is true of our feelings and prejudices, my Lord. The smaller we are in moral stature, the bigger little things become for us. Petty insults, unkind words, being ignored — even the way a person looks at us — all these things become tremendous problems, making us lose our self-control. We get unbelievably disturbed, and shout our indignation or else pout in a corner. It would be a different story if these were matters of principle for which we should fight. But they are only petty, insignificant things.

It's very different for the man who is big, who stands tall and strong in moral stature. Throughout all these petty annoyances, he is calm and peaceful, because he hardly even notices them! It's not a question of principle, my King; it's a question of size!

MY KING, with all my soul I pray for bigness. I know that I have often been small, really disturbed over ridiculous trifles. And in every case there was no peace — no victory. I was charging valiantly against toy cannons, wielding my sword viciously against soldiers of straw! "A tempest in a teapot" — I was just as small as the things that made me angry.

My Lord! Teach me how to take little annoyances with serenity. Let me save my anger for the cause of justice, my fire for Your glory!

THE CONVERSION OF ZACCHAEUS (1)— RESPECT FOR INDIVIDUALITY

Luke 19 : 1-10

1. *Jesus calling Zacchaeus to descend from the tree.*
2. *The grace, my Lord, to take people as I find them and love them as they are.*

EXCITEMENT ran high in Jericho as Jesus and the Apostles came back after being across the Jordan so long. News about the raising of Lazarus had spread and all were anxious to see Jesus again. One person in particular felt a strong desire to see the Master. But he was Jericho's leading publican and therefore its most hated man.

Zacchaeus felt that he couldn't mix with the crowd and face all the insults. Besides he was very short and wouldn't be able to see much anyway. So he climbed a tree near the road where Jesus must pass. He was excited and nervous as the crowd drew near. Then he saw Jesus and thoughts poured in upon him. The Master was so poor, so simple and unaffected. Zacchaeus began to feel ashamed of his greed and ill-gotten goods. Wealth hadn't made him more a man. Then Jesus looked up—looked right into his eyes. He was calling him by name: "Zacchaeus, make haste and come down; for I must stay in thy house today." Zacchaeus was so happy he almost tripped coming down from the tree. Jesus smiled as he stood before Him. Zacchaeus no longer felt an outcast.

DEAR MASTER, it's a beautiful thing to watch You at work with souls! What perfect respect You had for each one's individuality. What reverence for each one's temperament, problems, needs! You knew that Zacchaeus was tired of being an outcast from the community, that he was fed-up with wealth that couldn't bring happiness. What he needed most was understanding and encouragement — someone who wouldn't be

shocked or repelled by his past — someone who knew he was capable of better things. What a joy to him, then, when You, Who were holiness itself, passed over all other homes to stay in his! It was just what he needed! In that one lovely act of kindness, You gave him faith in himself—and You won his heart.

MY KING, probably the biggest hindrance to charity for me is my lack of respect for the individuality of others. I have my own temperament and disposition, my own way of doing things—and I imagine that this way is the only way. And when others are different, I tend to be critical and unkind—as though human beings, like lead soldiers, were all poured into the same mold. They are not, my King! You made each one different and unique.

Teach me then, dear Master, to have great reverence for each one's temperament and personality. Let me see that each one is good in his own way, that each one has his own work to do for You—whether he be haphazard or systematic, cheerful or sour, stern or lenient, shy or forward, refined or coarse. No narrowness, my King! No smallness! Let me take people as I find them, and love them—

not as I imagine they should be, or as I would like them to be—but as they are! Then I will love them rightly. Then, and only then, will I know how to approach them and bring them closer to You.

THE CONVERSION OF ZACCHAEUS (2)—HUNGER FOR GOD

Luke 19:1-10

1. *Zacchaeus making Jesus comfortable in his home.*
2. *The grace, my Lord, to hunger and thirst for You.*

ZACCHAEUS was thrilled beyond measur when Jesus noticed him and asked t stay at his house. The embarrassment o being seen in the tree didn't bother him a all. The Master was to be his guest! As h started to show Jesus the way to his home however, a new fear came over him. Th people all about were murmuring disgrunted ly. Some were complaining openly: "He ha gone to be the guest of a man who is a sin ner." Zacchaeus was afraid that his hono would be short-lived. The Master would giv in to so much pressure from the crowd Zacchaeus watched Him. Not a change Joy returned. And with joy a most generou resolve. He would save the Master embarrassment by announcing publicly his repentance. Half his wealth to the poor! And to those he defrauded a fourfold return! At his home Zacchaeus couldn't do enough for Jesus and His Apostles — the kiss of peace, water for His feet, oil for His head, a fine dinner and a quiet place to rest. Jesus let Zacchaeus do all that he wanted — it seemed to make him so happy to anticipate Jesus' wants and to show Him every courtesy.

DEAR MASTER, You couldn't help but contrast this royal welcome from Zacchaeus with the treatment You had received at the home of Simon the Pharisee in Magdala. And yet Simon was supposedly a holy man, a Pharisee, a man educated in refinement and good manners; whereas Zacchaeus was a lowly person, a publican, a sinner, a charlatan who would steal from anyone. He certainly wasn't as refined as Simon, didn't have the know-how of good manners or taste for nice things. But, my Jesus, Zacchaeus had a great need. He had experienced the utter emptiness of sin and wealth, had known the loneliness of being an outcast, had felt the cruelty of man's unkindness and misunderstanding. His heart was hungry for what would really bring it peace and joy. When he found You, he truly appreciated You. And he showed You a courtesy beyond the cold, metallic refinement of proper manners. Simon failed because Simon had no great need. He was too satisfied with himself, too smug, too convinced that he knew everything worth knowing, too content with his wealth and reputation. He toyed with You because he felt You had nothing to give him. "To comprehend a nectar requires sorest need."

LORD, what a powerful lesson I learn from those two men. I simply cannot have the pride of smugness and self-sufficiency if I expect to love You completely. The man who felt he had everything, felt he didn't need You. And he was left with his miserable little toys of self-conceit and worldly trinkets. It was the man who knew he was poor, the humble man who knew his limitations and sinfulness, who knew that his heart was made for a love which the world couldn't give — it was he who welcomed You. It was Zacchaeus with the great need who found You.

O my Lord, I realize now why You often send sorrow and suffering into our lives. It is to highlight our need of You. Dear Master, make me aware of my great need. Don't let

me settle for the glittering trinkets which the world offers me — praise, attention, wealth, pleasures. If You send them, I can use them, but only if I remember that I am still poor, still hungry, still in great need — a need that You alone can fill. And if having them will cause me to forget my need, then, dear King, take them, take them all and leave me only my hunger for You.

THE SUPPER AT BETHANY (1)— SPIRITUAL OUTLOOK

John 12 : 1-11

1. *The beautiful look on the face of Mary as she pours the precious ointment.*
2. *The grace of a spiritual sense of values.*

JESUS and the Apostles made the journey from Jericho. The Good Shepherd was happy that another stray sheep, Zacchaeus, was back in the fold. Bethany was all set for Him when He came. Simon, a former leper, wanted to thank Him; Mary and Martha and Lazarus looked forward so much to seeing Him again. Simon prepared a banquet for Jesus and the Apostles and invited all His close friends at Bethany. It promised to be such a perfect meal; no sharp-eyed Scribes, no complaining Pharisees, no cold, unbelieving Sadducees — just friends and loved ones. Jesus was so much at ease. There was perfect understanding as His Eyes met those of Lazarus—the only one besides Himself who had seen the other world. He was happy to see Martha serving with a new spirit of joy—no complaints now, no anxieties. Something new had been added. Now her work flowed from contemplation and love, and her manner radiated peace. Simon the Leper, too, made Jesus happy. Jesus could feel his gratitude in every little act of hospitality. And then Mary — Mary above all gave Him delight. Mary, impetuous Mary, who couldn't give her love by degrees. Taking a jar of precious ointment, she broke it completely, and poured it on Jesus' Head and Feet, wiping His Feet with her hair. It is a scene too beautiful for words—a total giving, the lavishness of love!

DEAR LORD, anyone with even the smallest bit of spiritual depth would have been thrilled and edified at such a beautiful act. What a sad disappointment to You, then, my King, when the Apostles, and especially Judas, missed the point completely and only thought of the price of the ointment. Such spiritual blindness—after all this time with them! They knew the price of things, but not their value.

DEAR MASTER, I know I disappoint You just as much as they when I have a worldly point of view and fail to see spiritual values. You send me someone to laugh at me or humiliate me, and it is just as beautiful an act of love as Mary's was, because You know I need it to make me humble and meek. And all I do is resent it and get annoyed—just as though I didn't have any faith or spiritual sight. I am blind to the spiritual advantages in suffering, sorrow, sarcasm and neglect. I miss the sheer beauty of soul that would come if I welcomed being overlooked and ignored. O my King, open my eyes. Let me judge everything from the same point of view that I'll have on Judgment Day. I promise prayer and recollection as helps to gain it; You do the rest!

THE SUPPER AT BETHANY (2)— THE HYPOCRISY OF JUDAS

John 12 : 1-11

1. *The enraged look on the face of Judas as he watches Mary "waste" the costly ointment.*
2. *The grace to be true.*

THE SUPPER at Bethany was a beautiful get-together for Jesus and the Apostles.

The company was composed of friends and loved ones and grateful ones, who had received much from Jesus. All were in a delightful frame of mind and in a happy mood, until Mary took the costly spikenard and poured it on the Head and Feet of Jesus. Every eye was upon her in amazement. She had taken them all unawares. There was a deathlike silence. For those who truly loved Jesus, it was a scene of joy and beauty—an exquisite, delicate act of pure love. Tears welled up in their eyes and ran down their cheeks. But for those who loved the world, like Judas, for those without a true spiritual sense of values, it was all a foolish, childish act of an immature girl, an unnecessary waste. Quickly, he calculated how much the spikenard would bring in the market place. A great sum. And it was being wasted. The sentimental girl was pouring out every drop of it! He could restrain himself no longer. In a bold voice, the voice of one demanding attention and an answer, he exclaimed: "Why wasn't this sold for 300 denarii and given to the poor?"

DEAR MASTER, it's a wonder that this hypocrisy of Judas didn't sicken You. It certainly sickened John as he sat next to You. Even though he is writing his Gospel years later, the thought of this scene makes his blood boil, and he, the gentle Apostle, writes: "Now he said this not because he had care for the poor, but because he was a thief." Judas wouldn't dare tell his real motive in being angry; everyone would have despised him. So he assumes the role of a lover of the poor, to cover up his avarice which made him hold back from the poor. And he makes believe that Jesus doesn't really care for the poor the way he does. His hypocrisy is worse than his avarice.

DEAR LORD, every time that I give an excuse or an explanation of my actions which is not the real motive, I am untrue like Judas. Even if there are several motives (as is usually the case), and I only give the good one to others, I am a hypocrite. I'm appearing as something pure white, when at best I am a dirty gray, with many selfish motives mixed in with the good. And yet, my King, how often do I do this—make excuses, explain, defend myself, talk about what others did and what I did just to gain sympathy or admiration. Help me to see that such is the sin of Judas. Let me never explain or give excuses, except where absolutely necessary. Dear Jesus, make me true!

TRIUMPHANT ENTRY INTO JERUSALEM (1)— TAKING PEOPLE AS I FIND THEM

Luke 19 : 29-44

1. *Jesus meekly seated upon the ass, coming down the narrow road from Olivet to Jerusalem.*
2. *The grace to take people as I find them and love them for what they are.*

JESUS and His Apostles were coming up the other side of Olivet from Bethany. When the people realized it, a sort of spontaneous demonstration began to occur. News of the raising of Lazarus had spread and the people were wild with joy and with Messianic hopes. They ran to meet Him and welcome Him. Many cut palm branches and other green branches. The excitement spread; a great crowd gathered all over both sides of Olivet. Jesus had the Apostles get a young donkey from Bethpage, one so young and meek that they had to bring its mother with it. The Apostles were caught up in the enthusiasm also. They spread their cloaks on the little donkey and asked Jesus to mount it. The crowd cheered and waved their branches. They sang psalms and hymns with great joy. They professed their faith, "Son of David,

Hosanna! Blessed is He Who comes in the name of the Lord."

DEAR MASTER, Your calm joy and gladness in their procession and praise is a beautiful tribute to Your perfect humility. You knew how short-lived would be the triumph and the praise. You realized that in five short days, some of these very people would be shouting, "Crucify Him!"—or, at best, feeling sorry for You but afraid to help You. And yet, You don't let that bother You! You don't despise them and indulge in pitying Yourself. You accept them as they are, with all their faults and weaknesses as well as their good points. What perfect humility and bigness and charity!

LORD, You know how small and narrow I am on this point. I refuse so much to make allowances for peoples' weaknesses. And so when I see faults, especially faults that inconvenience me, I tend simply to write these persons off my book. I reject the good in them along with the bad. Dear King, teach me to change. Let me be big and take people as I find them. Let me look at their good points, and treat their faults in the same way I would treat bad thoughts — not give them a chance to enter my mind.

TRIUMPHANT ENTRY INTO JERUSALEM (2)— CALMNESS UNDER CRITICISM

Luke 19:29-40

1. *The angry Pharisees demanding that Jesus make the crowd stop calling Him by Messianic titles.*
2. *The grace, my Lord, of calmness under criticism.*

THE ENTHUSIASM of the crowd was like a shock that electrified all around. Each one wanted to praise Jesus like this for so long, but somehow never got started. Now each rejoiced in His triumph and called out and sang with such zeal and happiness: "Hosanna to the Son of David!" As the procession was halfway down Olivet, the Pharisees by the side of the road heard the cheers and shouts of glory to the Messiah. They were beside themselves with rage. How dare they usurp those titles and apply them to this poor Carpenter! How dare He let them!

And yet there was no stopping this surging, earnest crowd, so they wedged their way through it to Jesus. Indignantly, they spoke, with fire in their eyes and on their lips. "Master, rebuke Thy disciples." It was not a request but a demand. Jesus faced their angry looks. He was calm and deliberate as He answered: "I tell you that if these keep silence, the stones will cry out!"

O MY KING, I admire You here so much! It is so easy for us to be deterred from what we know is right by the anger and indignation of others. Our lack of courage can make us distrust our convictions and begin to give way. Not You, my King, You Who could suffer and be ill-treated without complaint. You knew how to be what You were—every inch a King, and to be a King without fear and anxiety about what others would say or do. This is humility and courage — to be what we are with all calmness, no matter who or what opposes us.

O MY LORD, I am really so different from You in this matter! How easy it is for me to become nervous and fidgety! Even when I do what I feel is right, I'm nervous about criticism and adverse opinions. Give me the grace to be different, my King! First, let me consider the opinions of others and weigh them fairly against my own. But then, when I know I am right, give me the courage to stand by my principles, come what may. Let no fear of human respect cause me to

move one inch from my convictions. Firm and strong like You, my King, with serenity and peace, no matter how fierce the opposition!

JESUS WEEPS OVER JERUSALEM—ABANDONMENT TO GOD'S HOLY WILL

Luke 19:41-44

1. *Jesus standing with His face buried in His hand, as He weeps for His city and His people.*
2. *The grace, my Lord, to welcome all of my Father's visitations.*

AS THE triumphal procession came over the summit of Mt. Olivet and began to descend, the beautiful city of Jerusalem lay before them. Jesus stopped for a few moments. He grew very pensive and sad. The Apostles could see tears coming down His cheeks before He finally buried His face in His hand. They heard Him sob: "If thou hadst known, in this thy day . . . the things that are for thy peace! But now they are hidden from thy eyes. For the days will come upon thee when thy enemies . . . will dash thee to the ground and thy children within thee . . . because thou hast not known the time of thy visitation!" Only once before had the Apostles seen Jesus weep. In both cases, it was because something He loved very dearly had died. But the death of the people of Jerusalem was much more sad than the death of Lazarus. Theirs was a spiritual death, and therefore a death from which He could not call them back. God wanted their love, but love cannot be forced—even by God! It must be given freely, from within.

DEAR LORD, Jerusalem didn't recognize You or accept You because the Pharisees and most of the people had their own ideas on how the Messiah should come and what He should be like. They pictured You as a worldly king with a great army and fabulous riches. And when You didn't fit in with their ideas, when You came in Your own way, they didn't recognize You, and they didn't want You.

And oh my King, what they missed! They lost out on all the spiritual treasures of Your wisdom and Your grace. They lost out on the truth about life and the peace that the truth can bring. They were so interested in conquering the Romans that they lost the much more important lessons on how to conquer themselves. And, my King, in the end they didn't even conquer the Romans. For the Romans came, as You prophesied, in 70 A.D.

and destroyed the city that had rejected its God.

DEAR LORD and Master, I'm so ready to blame the Pharisees for not recognizing You or receiving You, and yet how often I'm guilty of the same fault! Everything that happens to me is a visitation from God, if only I had the proper faith to see it—the people I meet, the joys and sorrows each day brings, success and failure, rain, snow, illness, pain, injuries to loved ones. All of these, Lord, are visitations. My Father is working through them to form me in virtue and make me a saint. But like the Pharisees, so often I have my own ideas of how things should go. And when my Father's plans are different and He comes in His own way, I rebel, I get impatient or despondent. I do not "know the time of my visitation!" Dear Lord, open my eyes and my heart. Teach me to welcome my Father and love Him, no matter what might be the manner of His coming!

THE WITHERED FIG TREE—HYPOCRISY

Matt. 21 : 18-19; Mark 11 : 13-14

1. *The leaves of the fig tree withering under the condemnation of Jesus.*
2. *The grace, my Lord, to be the Christian I claim I am.*

JESUS and His Apostles were coming from Bethany to Jerusalem one morning. Just outside the wall of the city, He saw a fig tree with its leaves in bloom. Jesus went over to it to get some figs, but it had no fruit. "May no one ever eat fruit of thee henceforward forever," He said. The Apostles heard Him, and that evening as they returned they were shocked to see that the tree was withered and its leaves were gone.

O MY KING, You were a man of absolute self-control and reasonableness, so it wasn't unsatisfied hunger that made You condemn the barren fig tree. Nor were You blaming the tree, since it was not yet the season for fruit. You blamed it for professing to be something it was not! Your action was a parable in action. The fig tree with blooming leaves and no fruit was typical of pharisaical hypocrisy—all show and no interior virtue, all appearances and no fruit! You couldn't stand such hypocrisy. You cursed the empty appearances, the lying leaves that promised fruit it didn't have. Now that it was withered, at least it was true!

DEAR LORD, I dare not be a hypocrite! You preferred the withered fig tree and publicans to the lying fig tree and Pharisees. I must be true—or face Your eventual curse. I profess to be a Christian and thus I put forth such fine green leaves. But do I have the virtues of a Christian: the humility of accepting joyfully to be what I am? The sincere charity of loving all men and wishing them well? Cheerful, loving acceptance of all that You send? At least, Lord, do I have a burning desire to have these virtues, a firm determination to pay the price?

THE GRAIN OF WHEAT—UNSELFISHNESS
John 12 : 20-33

1. *Jesus standing in the Temple, His eyes seeing the awful vision of His suffering and death.*
2. *The grace, my Lord, to be self-effacing and unselfish in every way.*

THE TRIUMPHAL entry of Jesus into Jerusalem on Palm Sunday had caused great excitement among the people. All the sincere

people were so glad that He had finally allowed Himself to be hailed publicly as the Messiah. On the following day, as Jesus was surrounded by the happy crowd, some Gentiles were caught up by the enthusiasm. They wedged their way through the crowd and talked to Philip: "Sir, we wish to see Jesus!" Philip relayed the message to Andrew, and Andrew to Jesus. Jesus realized that the enthusiasm of the Gentiles might have come from their seeing the triumphal entry. Perhaps they were interested in Him only as a worldly king and a public hero. So He was quick to explain that His triumph would be on Calvary, where He would die so that others might live. "The hour has come for the Son of Man to be glorified . . . unless the grain of wheat falls into the ground and dies, it remains alone. But if it dies, it brings forth much fruit."

DEAR LORD, what an important lesson for us. Those people who live for self, who seek their own comfort and plans, who put self first and others last—these all gain their own little petty selfish ends, but no more! They have no growth. They remain just what they have always been—self-centered, small people. But if they die to self, if they put themselves out for others' comfort, be hurt themselves rather than hurt others' feelings, praise and honor and serve others rather than be praised and served themselves—then they become big! They grow up into the "fullness of the stature of Christ." Then they yield the rich fruit of radiating Christ to others.

MY KING, how often I say this to others; and yet how little I practice it. Do I not fail to adapt myself to the mood of those with whom I am? When they are cheerful, I fail to make myself join in the fun. And when they are sad, I fail to be quiet and sympathetic. Again, how I urge others to prefer to talk about the topics of conversation proposed by their companions, to relish the subjects of interest to them. And yet don't I get enthused about my own interests, while remaining dull, or at best, halfhearted about the interests of others? And so often I fail to give time to others, falsely feeling that they are interrupting my plans and schedule. Dear King and Lord, make me see that in all such "intrusions," my day has been interrupted by none other than You! Make me self-effacing and let me always put others first. Teach me to die to self that I may really begin to live — to live the Christ-life.

THE COIN OF TRIBUTE (1)— FLATTERY AND PRAISE

Matt. 22 : 15-22; Luke 20 : 20-26

1. *Agents of the Pharisees pretending to ask a sincere question about taxes to Caesar.*
2. *The grace, my Lord, to be true.*

THE PARABLES of the vineyard workers and the royal marriage had left the Pharisees in a furious state. In both parables Jesus had shown up their stubbornness in rejecting His divine authority. And both foretold their ultimate punishment. He had to be put out of the way! But how? During the day He was surrounded by crowds who loved Him. And at night He left the city and they didn't know where to find Him.

Finally they hit on a plan. Why not let Rome do their work for them! They would get Him to denounce the paying of taxes to Caesar, and then let the Roman Governor take care of the rest. They laid their plans carefully. They wouldn't go to Him themselves. He would recognize them and suspect a plot. So they chose certain agents who pretended to be holy men with serious qualms of conscience. These men approached Jesus. How could they pay taxes to Caesar, they asked. They knew that He would tell them the truth, they added, because He was honest and truthful and didn't care what people thought about Him. The eyes of Jesus were sad, not happy as they had imagined. It surprised them no end when He exclaimed: "Why do you test Me, you hypocrites?"

MY KING, it takes a lot of humility to be serene under criticism and correction. But to be undisturbed and balanced under flattery or praise — this takes the greatest humility of all! Even the most important men can be swayed by flattery—especially if it's expressed well and mentions the virtues they like to think they have. It can make the hardest man soft; the sternest man easy. Not You, my King, for You had perfect humility! You knew what You truly were — apart from peoples' opinion. So neither opposition or flattery disturbed Your equilibrium one iota.

DEAR MASTER, it's so difficult for me to take praise graciously. I imagine I have to deny everything that is said—even if it is true. Peoples' opinions are so important to me that I'm afraid they won't think I'm humble if I accept the praise. So I get all upset denying it, secretly hoping that they will think more highly of me. How far away from the beautiful peace of true humility! Once I really know my virtues and my limitations and am glad to be what I am — once I have this true humility, then it doesn't matter what praise or flattery is said. I will smile and be happy about the praise which is true. I'll peacefully decline the flattery which is false. It will not matter then what people think. I am what I am—no more, no less—no matter what they think! That's how You felt, my Lord. Make me true, like Yourself!

THE COIN OF TRIBUTE (2)—LOYALTIES

Matt. 22:15-22; Luke 20:20-26

1. *The coin of tribute with Caesar's image and inscription.*
2. *The grace, my Lord, of great loyalty to my country and my Church.*

THE AGENTS of the Pharisees were completely taken back by the keenness of Jesus in seeing through their plot, and by the wisdom of His answer. They were forced to admit that the denarius, the Roman coin they used constantly for business and trade, bore Caesar's image and inscription. They carried Caesar's coin; they enjoyed the protection of Caesar's legions, the justice of Caesar's courts, the prosperity of Caesar's peace, plus the freedom to worship God as they pleased. It was only just and fair that they pay taxes for these material and political benefits, as it was fair that they worship God for His goodness. "Render, therefore, to Caesar the things that are Caesar's and to God the things that are God's."

DEAR LORD, You thus taught with a brilliant stroke that there is no conflict between our loyalty to our country and our loyalty to our Church. You taught, and Your Church teaches with You, that there are two necessary and perfect societies: the State, which is supreme in the temporal sphere, and the Church, which is supreme in the spiritual sphere. It is only when the State steps out of its sphere, as it did in Communist Russia, and takes away human rights or infringes on the spiritual privileges of its members, that the Church must step in and correct the State. Otherwise, both are independent and supreme in their own sphere. We can be completely loyal to both. A good Catholic is a good American.

DEAR MASTER, love for my country isn't an extra — it's a real part of Christian piety. Just as I must be grateful to my parents for all they gave me, so I must love and honor the land which gave me so many opportunities —peace, education, protection, justice and priceless freedom.

And I must love the Church — the Church which is Your Mystical Body, the Church that watches over me like a mother and gives me Your grace and Your truth.

Make me a splendid American Catholic, my King. Let me sincerely "render to Caesar the things that are Caesar's, and to God the things that are God's."

PARABLE OF THE TALENTS (1)— THE GOOD HEART

Matt. 25:14-30

1. *The disgruntled man with one talent hiding it in the earth.*
2. *The grace, my Lord, to accept Your gifts as seeds—to be developed by good will.*

JESUS was teaching His favorite theme from a new point of view. He was telling the crowds the parable of the talents. God was like a master going away on a journey who gave a different amount of talents to each of

His subjects—to one five, to another two, to another one. He told them to trade with the talents until he returned. The first two obeyed and they gained in turn five more and two more. And on his return the master praised them with equal honor and reward. But the third man hid his talent. He returned it to the master—but nothing with it. And he was condemned!

Jesus was showing so clearly that it is the heart that matters. Our talents are given to us, not fully developed but as seeds. It is only when we work them with a sincere heart and strong will that we bring them to full maturity. No matter how brilliant our talents may be they do not grow automatically. The finest intellect, the most attractive personality, the very spark of genius—can all end up in drunken abandonment or vicious misuse unless developed by a strong, sincere will.

DEAR MASTER, what an important lesson for us. We understand our talents rightly only when we see that all our talents, both of nature and of grace, come unassembled as it were, undeveloped, incomplete. It is the good heart that pleases You. You send all Your gifts incomplete so they can be worked on by the sincere heart. Our mind has to be trained and disciplined or it will never reach its peak; our flare for art and writing have to be worked on with tireless energy and practice or it will never inspire; the same with our gifts of grace, my King. Our talent for prayer must be used again and again, our gifts of faith, hope and charity given in Baptism must be nourished and made strong by repeated acts, by faithfulness in the dark hours, by study and prayer. Your gifts are beautiful, but they are not magic! They are seeds, which need the rich fertile soil of a sincere, energetic will.

DEAR LORD, how often I have expected to get Your gifts in finished form. I prayed for patience. And when You sent trying persons and unnerving circumstances, I complained. I felt somehow my prayer wasn't answered. How wrong I was, my King! The very annoyances were the answer to my prayer! These were the things that could produce beautiful, serene patience, if I just had the good will to take them rightly. Like all Your gifts they were the seeds of patience—the good heart could make them grow!

Divine Master, I give You my heart for Your service. Sincerely I thank You for every gift; sincerely I will work to make them grow.

PARABLE OF THE TALENTS (2)— TRUE HUMILITY

Matt. 25 : 14-30

1. *Jesus explaining the parable of the talents.*
2. *The grace, my Lord, to be glad to be what I am.*

IN THE parable of the talents Jesus notes that both the man with five talents and the one with two talents receive the exact same praise and reward from the master. He wanted us to know that God judges us on our own individual merits and not in reference to anyone else's merits or accomplishments. This was such an important lesson for them to understand if they were ever going to understand true humility. Our natural tendency is to look down on those who are less talented, either in nature or in grace, and to feel inferior in the presence of those who are more talented. Both attitudes are wrong. Both offend against true humility. It is we who make the comparisons, not God!

DEAR KING, make me realize that humility is complete and absolute honesty—honesty of mind and of will. It means recognizing what we are—just what we are with our talents and our limitations; and it means being glad to be what we are, and not feeling one bit of resentment about what we are not. Such humility brings tremendous peace. The truth of the matter, my King, is that our Father makes us individuals. He gives us the qualities of body and soul that we need to do the particular work He has planned for us. The talents we don't need, we don't receive. No one receives all the talents. One has a sense of humor, another a fine mind, another true sincerity and simplicity. One is physically attractive, another has a beautiful voice, another the ability to lead, another the docility to follow. Each one has what is best for the unique and special work in life that our Father has given us to do. Success in life isn't measured therefore by comparing ourselves to others or weighing our accomplishments against theirs; success is measured by how we used the talents God gave us. A good office boy is a much bigger success than a bad vice-president.

DEAR MASTER, when will I ever learn this humility of being glad to be what I am! I get so discouraged when I make mistakes. I forget what I am. I'm a human being and all human beings make mistakes. It's pride to resent it. It's not accepting to be what You made me to be.

The same is true when I see others with great talents and accomplishments. I get jealous and try to minimize their accomplishments—as though somehow they were a threat to me. Or I strive to equal their accomplishments without having the talents—and I fail miserably and become despondent. Dear Jesus, teach me that no one is a threat to me, that no one's accomplishments can hurt my chances of success or greatness. Greatness consists in being perfectly what I am, not what someone else is!!

Let me appreciate the talents You have given me and work hard within the framework of what You have made me to be. Let me delight in being the living fulfillment of Your Holy Will!

THE LAST JUDGMENT—POSITIVE CHARITY

Matt. 25:31-46

1. *Picture of myself standing before Jesus in the last judgment, in the presence of all who ever lived.*
2. *The grace, my Lord, of positive charity—kind words, kind deeds.*

THE THOUGHT of the slothful servant's condemnation in the parable of the talents led Jesus to tell them about the final judgment of all men at the end of the world. He described how He would come with great power and majesty together with all His angels. He would sit on a splendid throne of glory. All the people who ever lived would be gathered before Him. On His right hand would be the just—those who used their talents rightly in the service of love. On His left hand would be the wicked, who refused to love. He told how He would address the just in warm gentle tones of reward: "Come, blessed of My Father, take possession of the kingdom . . . for I was hungry and you gave Me to eat. I was thirsty and you gave Me to drink." For the wicked love and forgiveness were no longer possible. 'Depart from Me, accursed ones, into the everlasting fire . . . for

I was hungry, and you did not give Me to eat; I was thirsty and you gave Me no drink." They will act surprised and ask "When did we see Thee hungry or thirsty or a stranger?" "Amen I say to you, as long as you did not do it for one of these least ones, you did not do it for Me."

MY KING, this tremendous scene of the general judgment has such important lessons for us! You make it very clear that the basis for reward will not be great external works or worldly success—but the presence of charity and grace in our hearts. Love is the fulfillment of the law, so we are judged on love. And You show us it must be positive charity, love in action and service, not merely negative charity of avoiding unkindness. It's a staggering realization, but an important one that both the servant with the one talent and those on the left side in this scene are not condemned for positive acts of malice. They are not condemned for doing evil, but rather for not doing good! Heaven is for those who have learned to love and serve!

DEAR MASTER, I'm so liable to think of holiness in negative terms—not missing Mass, not breaking the Commandments, not being unkind. Teach me to realize, Lord, that when I love someone, I don't simply avoid being unkind to him—I do much more. I enjoy his company, I rejoice over his goodness, I love to hear him praised, I love to do things for him that will prove my respect and admiration. Love is positive; it rejoices over good, it serves cheerfully. Teach me this true love. Let me give all I have in cheerful service. There are so many who are lonely, confused, hurt, so many hungry and thirsty. Let me go out to them, my Jesus; let me feel privileged to serve.

LAST SUPPER—TRUE CHARITY

Luke 22:14-18, 24-30

1. *Jesus standing in the doorway of the Cenacle, looking upon "His own," His Apostles.*
2. *The grace, my Lord, of true charity for my neighbor.*

THE CENACLE was a picture when Jesus and the Apostles arrived for the Last Supper. On the U-shaped table, Our Lady and the women had arranged the paschal lamb and unleavened bread, the wine and bitter herbs. Thirteen divans had been placed along the outside. The soft candlelight gave it all a warm, homelike appearance. Jesus was the last to enter the room. He stopped for a moment in the doorway. For the others it was just another paschal meal, but not for Him. His great Heart was charged with emotion. This was a parting, the ending of two and a half years of close, wonderful friendship. And like all partings, it was also a beginning—the beginning of His redeeming Passion. He stood in the doorway to take it all in before taking His place. St. John, who was so close to Him, seemed to know what He was thinking. "Jesus . . . having loved His own, who were in the world, loved them to the end." Jesus entered the room then, and reclined with them at the table. When He spoke it was with deep feeling: "I have greatly desired to eat this Passover with you before I suffer."

MY LORD, what exquisite courtesy and charity You show us here! The privilege was theirs, my King, not Yours! They are the ones honored by Your divine company; they are to receive the Eucharist and be ordained priests. They and we are the ones who would be saved by the events of this night and the following day. Yet You say that You are honored, that You have looked forward to it with great desire. What unspeakable courtesy and graciousness! To make the ones whom You are helping feel that they are honoring You!

MY LORD, teach me that my charity must be gracious and cheerful, or else it is not charity at all! Charity which is done only from a sense of duty is so hard on the person who receives it. He feels inferior. He resents terribly his poverty and need. He actually finds it hard to forgive the person for the favor he receives. It is only when I love the receiver of my kindness very much—only when the receiver feels that he is honoring me as much as I am honoring him—that receiving becomes easy and my kindness is Christlike. Let me love dearly all those who need me, that they may forgive me the favors I do for them.

JESUS WASHES THE APOSTLES' FEET—SERVICE TO OTHERS

John 13:1-17

1. *Jesus on His knees before His Apostles.*
2. *The grace, my Lord, to serve others out of love.*

JESUS had just spoken with such deep feeling and solemnity that all the Apostles began to realize that there was something special about this Passover. They watched and listened intently as He blessed the bowl of wine for the first of the four ritual drinks. "Take this and share it among you . . . I will not drink of the fruit of the vine, until the Kingdom of God comes." They caught their breath. The Kingdom was near at hand! The Kingdom! Immediately they seemed to forget Jesus and think about themselves and their place in the Kingdom. They spoke in whispers at first, then louder. Some said that Peter was the head. Others noted that John was closer to the Master. What about Judas? He held the purse! They were so engrossed in their argument that at first they didn't notice Jesus get up from the table and lay aside His outer robe. Then they saw Him and they became silent. He wrapped a towel around His waist, poured some water into a basin, and then knelt before the first Apostle at the table. Their faces dropped. A terrible shame came over them. They were deathly silent.

O MY KING, You had once told them that they were not to be like worldly leaders, lording it over their subjects and fighting for honors. Now You show them by the visual aid of Your own magnificent example that in Your Kingdom the greatest was to be the least. You know that they will remember every little detail of this great night later on. You want them to remember that being like You meant deep humility and loving, generous service to others. After You finished, You emphasized that You were their Lord and Master, yet You served them. They must do the same to others. You didn't ask them to serve others out of fear, like a slave. That kind of service is degrading. You asked them to serve as You did, out of love, with deep respect for the personal dignity of each human being. This kind of service is ennobling and beautiful.

DEAR LORD, the early Christians learned this lesson and the beauty of their service illumined the darkness of that pagan world. "See how those Christians love one another." Teach me to learn it, too. Don't let me go by likes and dislikes, my King—thus running now hot and now cold in my service to others. Don't let me be repelled either by ingratitude or surliness. Let me see through the camouflage of distasteful qualities, see through to the precious soul for which You died. And then let me serve out of love!

JESUS WASHES PETER'S FEET—RESPECT FOR INDIVIDUALITY

John 13 : 1-17

1. *Peter pulling back his feet in protest.*
2. *The grace, my Lord, to respect the unique individuality of each person.*

JESUS went from one Apostle to the other. They were ashamed, but kept silent. When Jesus came to Peter, however, Peter could not be silent. "Lord, dost Thou wash my feet?" Peter felt so unworthy, felt that it was undignified for Jesus. Jesus explained that he would understand eventually. When later they recalled this night of His capture and death, they would have such a vivid memory of His lesson of humble service. But that answer didn't satisfy Peter. Impulsively, he pulled back his foot from the hand of Jesus, and jumped to his feet. "Thou shalt never wash my feet!" Jesus was silent for a moment. The air was tense. Then He looked up at Peter. "If I do not wash thee, thou shalt have no part with Me." The words struck Peter with force. He sat down again on the divan. His tense body and face relaxed. He put out his hands toward Jesus. "Lord, not my feet only, but also my hands and my head."

MY LORD, I love this scene. It shows so clearly how You treated every single person as an individual, with his own individual personality and temperament. Anyone else but You would have been so exasperated with Peter! You were teaching a most beautiful lesson, a parable in action rather than in words—and he interrupted the whole continuity, destroyed the whole atmosphere that You had created. You knew what good there was in Peter. You understood that it was really His respect for You that made him look and act disrespectfully. You accepted him as he was. You worked with what You had. You taught him the way he could learn. Love prompted him to rebel. You used that love to get him to obey!

MY KING, what souls I could influence for good once I learned to respect their individuality. Some people are talkative, others are quiet. I can't put them in the same mold or approach them in the same way. Some are very sensitive, others not; some courageous, others weak; some idealistic, others sour. I can't treat them as heads of cabbages, as though they were all the same. Indeed, Lord, even heads of cabbages are different! Teach me, then, to love and respect the sacred, unique individuality of each person. Let me take each as I find him, work with him in his way, and lead him thus to You!

THE SACRIFICE OF THE HOLY EUCHARIST (1) —LOVE OF JESUS

Luke 22:19-20

1. *Jesus holding out the chalice to the Apostles to drink.*
2. *The grace, my Lord, to love You as You deserve.*

THE PASCHAL meal was almost over. Jesus and the Apostles had celebrated the memory of that night in Egypt long ago—the night on which their fathers were saved from the land of slavery through the blood of an innocent lamb. God commanded the Jews to celebrate this feast in a very realistic way each year. It would remind them that some day another Lamb would shed His Blood to free them from the slavery of sin. Jesus and the Apostles went through the beautiful prophetic banquet for the last time. Then, as it drew to a close, Jesus took a portion of the unleavened bread in His Hands: "Take and eat; this is My Body, Which is being given for you." And then He took the cup of wine: "This is My Blood of the new covenant, Which is being shed for many unto the forgiveness of sins." Shadows and prophecies were over. Here was the Lamb of God!

MY KING, help me to fathom the significance of this tremendous offering! If You had been killed on Good Friday against Your Will, Your death would have had no meaning, no value. It would have been a murder, like any other murder, except so much worse because of Your great dignity! What changed Calvary from being a murder to being a most beautiful act of redeeming love was Your complete acceptance of Calvary there at the Last Supper. "My Body, Which is being given for you . . . My Blood . . . Which is being shed for many . . ." What could that mean except that You were accepting to be the Lamb of God and die for our sins? Your acceptance is what turned the whole Passion into love!

DEAR LORD, how do I act when I am faced with a cross? When people misunderstand me, when they are sarcastic and cruel, when my ideas are ridiculed or my plans rejected, how do I feel? Or when someone else is preferred before me, when I am fired and have no recourse, when I am told that I have cancer and nothing can be done, am I not tempted to let these things make me bitter and resentful? Teach me to be like You instead. For me, as for You, acceptance of His Will can put meaning into every cross, can turn every Calvary into an act of redeeming love. I do accept Your Will for me, my Father. This is my body . . . my blood. I accept whatever You send me. Take all my sorrows and heartaches and joys. Make them all part of His Passion.

THE SACRIFICE OF THE EUCHARIST (2) —HOLY MASS

Matt. 26:26-29; Luke 22:19-20

1. *The Sacred Host raised aloft at Mass.*
2. *The grace, my Lord, to pray the Mass, not simply attend.*

JESUS knew that there would be untold millions of Christians who could not be present on Calvary. So He arranged to bring Calvary to them in a renewal of the Last Supper—the Holy Sacrifice of the Mass. "Do this in commemoration of Me." Do this! Yes! the very thing He had just done! Consecrate bread and wine into His Body and Blood, and thus offer Him—the Victim of Calvary—to His heavenly Father. Now all men of all times and places

could come to Calvary! The prophecy of Malachias, some five hundred years before, was thus fulfilled: "From the rising of the sun unto its setting, My Name is great among the Gentiles; and in every place there will be sacrifice to My Name . . . a pure oblation."

MY SAVIOUR, make me remember that it was Your willing offering of Yourself at the Last Supper that put meaning and value into Your death on the Cross! Your acceptance turned Calvary from being a murder to being the most beautiful act of love ever known.

So also, in the Mass, my Lord, it is Your continuous offering of Yourself again and again through Your priests that renews Your sacrifice. "This is My Body . . . this cup is the new covenant in My Blood, which shall be shed for you." In these words, my King, You offer up again to Your Father Your death on Calvary. It isn't just a Passion play, where we might be moved to tears, but would know that it was just acting. At Mass it is all real! You are truly present. Your death is represented by the separate consecration of Body and Blood, and Your death is truly offered to the Father—the same beautiful act of redeeming love which took place on Calvary.

When we offer Mass, my Jesus, we offer God a gift worthy of God!

MY KING, how little I have appreciated Holy Mass up to now! I would speak about attending Mass, not praying the Mass. And yet, my King, for the Mass as for Calvary, it is the offering that counts. If I were to attend Mass without giving myself with You, it would not be my gift, it would not be my act of love. I must say with You, and mean it, "This is my body . . . my blood. Take me, take me for whatever Calvary You wish for me this day. I accept the sorrows, the crosses, the disappointments, the failures, the joys and the successes. I accept them cheerfully and willingly, my King. I offer them in this Holy Mass!" Ah, my Lord, then my life, like Yours, becomes an act of redeeming love, consecrated by my offering at Mass.

THE SACRAMENT OF THE EUCHARIST (1) —HOLY COMMUNION

Matt. 26 : 26-29; Luke 22 : 19-20

1. *Jesus seated apart from the crowd, enjoying a few moments with His own.*
2. *The grace, my Lord, to let You abide in me, that I may abide in Thee.*

IT STARTLED the Apostles for a moment when Jesus consecrated the bread and wine into His Body and Blood. But then they remembered the Passover of the previous year when He had multiplied the loaves and fishes. The crowds had pursued Him looking for bread and He had told them: "The Bread that I will give you is My Flesh for the life of the world . . . He who eats My Flesh, and drinks My Blood, abides in Me and I in him." It had seemed so unreal then. But now it had happened. Reverently, silently, they received His precious Body and Blood. They closed their eyes in gratitude and silent prayer.

DEAR LORD, they realized then that the Eucharist was not only a Sacrifice by which You offered Yourself to the Father, but a Sacrament of Love in which You would be our spiritual food. Everyone who is in love desires to be with his loved one. And the stronger the love, the greater the obstacles it can overcome. What must Your love be that it burst asunder obstacles that no other love could pierce—centuries of time, untold distances of space—to be with Your loved ones. No wonder You say "abides in Me and I in him." This love is so great, this union so perfect that You and Your loved ones rest in one another in Holy Communion.

MY LORD, I believe that in Holy Communion I receive You—Body and Blood, Soul and Divinity. I believe that until the Sacred Species corrupt by digestion You "abide in me." You abide in me under the sign of food, food which works for the health and strength of the person who takes it. Jesus, my spiritual food, You work each moment in Holy Communion to strengthen me and build up virtue in me—until I am so like You that it can be said that I abide in You.

Why is it then, my Lord, that I am still so far from this ideal? Nothing is lacking on Your part. You do Your work in each reception of Holy Communion. It's I who am lacking. I fail to appreciate how great is the love which brings You to me across the centuries.

I fail to realize that You're with me. And I dissipate my thoughts in petty distractions, my feelings in petty annoyances and resentments.

O Lord, take and receive as Your own my thoughts, my feelings, my heart, my will. Abide in them, work in them—until I abide in Thee!

THE SACRAMENT OF THE EUCHARIST (2) —HIS ABIDING PRESENCE

Matt. 26 : 26-29; Luke 22 : 19-20

1. *Jesus stretching forth His arms from the tabernacle to welcome us.*
2. *The grace, dear Master, to love Your Sacramental Presence.*

"I HAVE greatly desired to eat this Passover with you." Now that Jesus had given them the Holy Eucharist, the Apostles understood what He meant by those words at the Supper. He had loved that closeness and intimacy with His own. Despite their faults, their slowness to learn, their spiritual dullness, He loved them, enjoyed their company. Soon that intimacy would be over. There would be only the occasional visits of the resurrected life, and then the complete departure of the Ascension. But no, it would not be a departure. He longed for that night, because that night would be the time when He would guarantee that they could be in His company forever. Through Calvary and the Mass, He would gain Heaven for them. Through the Eucharist, He would be with them and all others whom He loved even while they were still on earth.

DEAR MASTER, is it not so that Your presence in the Eucharist gives us the closest approximation to the privilege of the Apostles to walk in Your presence and have You for Teacher and Guide? To kneel before You there with the Gospels before me — what a privilege! How closely I come to seeing "what prophets and kings have desired to see and have not seen"! I have You, the living God made Man, in Your words and actions—and You are not far away, You are here!

BEING near You, my Lord, turned the Apostles into saints and gave them a vision of life so beautiful that they were able to inflame the world. And yet how I neglect Your presence! I let such trifling things interfere with my daily visit to You there in the tabernacle. Especially the "holy temptations," the entanglements of things that seem good—

but in reality are so unimportant compared to time with You!

O my Lord, I need the refreshment of Your presence each day as my lungs need air and my heart needs joy. I dare not stop breathing in order to do something else. Then let nothing, except necessary works of charity, interfere with the time I would spend before You for my soul.

THE NEW COMMANDMENT—FRATERNAL CHARITY

John 13:33-35

1. *Jesus emphasizing a point which He considered so important.*
2. *The grace, my Lord, to see the good in others and love them as You love me.*

THE APOSTLES had just received their first Holy Communion and had just been ordained to the Sacred Priesthood. While they closed their eyes in silent prayer and thanksgiving, Jesus couldn't help but think of how much He loved them. It would hurt Him terribly if they didn't always love one another. Now was the time to tell them. In a voice that was charged with emotion and emphasis, He said: "A new commandment I give you, that you love one another." He paused a moment; He must give them a precise standard—"that as I have loved you, you also love one another. By this will all men know that you are My disciples, if you have love for one another." They had seen vivid evidence of His love for them that night. On the next day they would realize that there was "no greater love." It was this great love that He now set up as a standard for their own love and reverence for one another.

DEAR LORD, You don't command us to "like" one another, but to love one another. The first is a natural feeling that we have for those whose personality and temperament are attractive to us. Some people will fit in this category for us and it will be easy for us to like them and to love them. Others will not. These may be very distasteful to us, have qualities we simply cannot like, and perhaps real faults that we should not like. But we can love them, my King, because love is above the natural; it is supernatural. Love means seeing them as souls — precious souls for whom You died. Love means wishing them well, praying sincerely that they will overcome their surly disposition and distasteful habits. And love means striving to overlook their bad qualities and trying to discover their good ones.

DEAR MASTER, I feel so ashamed when I realize how easily I indulge my natural likes and dislikes! I strive to avoid those I don't like. I make no effort to discover their good qualities. I let my mind go over their faults and the things they did to hurt me, until my feelings are on fire with indignation and hate! Dear Lord, make me stop my unkindness. Let me know that everyone has to have some faults—everyone including myself! But love doesn't go looking for the faults, love looks for the good—"is patient, is kind . . . bears with all things, believes all things, hopes all things, endures all things." Make me love like this, my King. Let me see the good in others, feel for them and love them as You love them and me!

"I AM THE WAY, AND THE TRUTH, AND THE LIFE"—PERSONAL LOVE FOR GOD

John 14:1-14

1. *Jesus in earnest discussion with His Apostles.*
2. *The grace, my Lord, to see the Father in You and love Him completely.*

JESUS prepared His Apostles now for the shock they would soon have in seeing Him put to death. He was only going in order to prepare a place for them. "Where I go you know and the way you know." Thomas was confused. They didn't know where He was going, so how could they know the way to get there? The answer of Jesus was magnificent. "I am the way, and the truth, and the life...he who sees Me sees also the Father." It was a summary of the entire spiritual life. The way to find heaven and eternal life was to know Jesus and to imitate Him.

MY KING, we don't have to be taught to love what is beautiful and good — the golden sunshine, a smile, the innocence of childhood. Our hearts just go out to it naturally; all we have to do is to see it and we will love it. In the case of visible things—the things of the world—and other human beings,

their beauty and goodness appear to us right away. But in the case of Beauty Itself, our Father in heaven, we cannot see His Beauty immediately or directly. So to know Him and to love Him, we have to realize that all other beautiful things are just a tiny reflection of His Loveliness. This is the work of prayer and meditation, my King. Prayerfulness makes us to see Beauty at its source—aware that the loyalty of our friends, the majesty of the night sky, the breath-taking sunset are all just a tiny sparkle of His unspeakable Beauty. Once we see it, once we get the big picture of God, we cannot help but fall in love with Him.

But as much as these other things of the world can reflect His Beauty, my King, the one perfect reflection of the Father is You in Your human nature. "If you had known Me, you would also have known My Father ... he who sees Me sees also the Father." Your unselfishness, my King, Your wisdom, Your absolute fearlessness in fighting for what was right, mixed so wonderfully with Your unutterable tenderness and gentleness and charity—what a picture You give us of the Father! We don't have to be taught to love Him once we see You, my Lord! We simply will! Our hearts will be captured!

DEAR MASTER, it's persons that attract us and influence us — much more than ideas or things. How good of You to give me in Your personality the image of my Father—"the way, the truth, the life"! Dear Lord, let me love to pore over Your life, Your words, Your actions. Let me see Your thoughts, feel Your feelings. Let me be hopelessly involved with You! As St. Patrick expressed it:

"Christ as a light illumine and guide me.
Christ as a shield overshadow and cover me.
Christ before me, Christ behind me,
Christ about me on left hand and right."

THE AGONY IN THE GARDEN (1)— PATIENCE IN SUFFERING

Mark 14:32-42

1. *Jesus' Face drawn tight in sadness as He calls Peter, James and John aside.*
2. *The grace, my Lord, to realize Your sorrows and pain, and to try to bear my own with something of Your manliness and patience.*

JESUS emptied Himself of gifts at the Last Supper. Generously, lavishly, He gave them His example of humility, the Eucharist and the Priesthood. After the Supper, He walked with them to Gethsemane. He grew sad as they went along. The approaching agony and death began to lay like a pall on His soul. He Who had such perfect control over His feelings now admitted to them His overwhelming sorrow: "even unto death." They saw Him almost confused, wanting to be alone and yet asking the three to go with Him—needing them.

MY LORD, You bore every sorrow and suffering human nature can know. And You were so perfectly human, so sensitive to joy and pain, that You felt sorrow just as much as we do—and more. You sensed so keenly the dull, heavy feeling, the loss at the desertion, the agony of the disloyalty, the confusion, the heartsickness, the awful longing to fall down and die. And yet You bore it so bravely; You let it do its work in Your soul.

DEAR MASTER, I'm so afraid of sorrow. I so resent disloyalty and desertion, I who certainly don't deserve loyalty the way You deserve it. I lack Your calm, manly bearing under trial. I cry out, I fight, I tell my whole tale to others in an effort to gain sympathy.

How wrong I am, my King! How can I ever expect to be like You unless I suffer as You suffered, with patience and serenity. Be near me in these moments of suffering, dear Lord. Let Your example be my ideal!

THE AGONY IN THE GARDEN (2)— GOD'S WILL

Mark 14:36

1. *Jesus, overcome by suffering, flat upon the ground.*
2. *The grace, my Lord, to be patient in every trial and setback.*

UPSET and overwhelmed with sorrow, Jesus asked the three chosen Apostles to wait and, going on further, fell to His knees and prayed. The sense of the impending agony became so great that He felt His strength leave Him completely and He fell flat on His Face. He moaned: "Father, if it is possible, let this cup pass away from Me." And then, with a superhuman strength, He breathed: "Yet not as I will but as Thou willest."

YOUR sufferings and pain, my King, were terrible things in themselves. All the powers of evil combined to break and hurt

You. Not a faculty of Your Body or Mind escaped the scalding agony. How unjust that You, Who were so faithful, should be betrayed and deserted and denied! How wrong that Your kindness and love were misunderstood and twisted! How sad that the beauty of Your teaching and the splendor of Your example should be ignored! And yet, all this You turned from evil into love, into good. Even the devil can be made to serve God's purpose. Even evil can be baptized and used! There is absolutely nothing that is wholly bad, nothing that cannot be transformed into good. If only we see our sufferings as God's Will for us, and love them as that, then we make them one with Your Passion; we turn them into love.

DEAR MASTER, how little have I realized all this in my life! I pay lip service to God's Will. I speak of it to others, but how little I have benefited from its soothing and healing wisdom. I ruin everything—because I have my own ideas about how things should be, and I refuse to accept His way. When He lets things happen His way, I resent it and fight it, and think that I could do much better. And the result is anxiety and discontent and loss of peace. And worse still—I spoil what He is trying to accomplish in my soul. Teach me, dear King, to see His Will in all things and to accept all patiently, peacefully, gladly. Teach me to turn all things into love. Show me that nothing is to be lost, even the apparent evil. All, all may be turned to good.

THE APOSTLES ASLEEP—REPARATION

Mark 14 : 37-42

1. *The Face of Jesus, lined with pity and disappointment as He looks upon the sleeping Apostles.*
2. *The grace, my Lord, to love reparation as true loyalty.*

WHEN JESUS said, "not as I will, but as Thou willest," He regained a bit of His strength and composure. Rising, He returned to His beloved three — only to find them asleep. It hurt Him a little—especially now when He needed them so much. Simon above all! Simon, who had promised to go "to prison and to death" with Him. The words escaped His lips: "Simon, dost thou sleep? Could you not, then, watch one hour with Me?" It was disloyal of them. The sense of His danger and sorrow should have made them wide-awake, no matter what their weariness might be—if they really loved Him as they said they did. He felt that disloyalty. And yet, even here He found an excuse for them. With magnificent patience and understanding, He said: "The spirit indeed is willing, but the flesh is weak."

COULD you not, then, watch one hour with Me?" Undoubtedly, dear Lord, You would have been pleased had You found them awake and watching with You. It would have indicated that they had sensed Your pain and danger, that they had understood Your sorrow and longed to relieve it—or at least to suffer it with You. What tremendous comfort that would have meant for You! Love so longs to be understood completely! So longs for the loyalty of shared joys and shared sorrows. It is no wonder that the agony came on You again and that You returned to Your lonely vigil.

DEAR MASTER, You have chosen me apart as a Christian in Baptism, as a soldier in Confirmation. And yet how little I have understood this loyalty of watchful reparation! My sleeping has been a complete lack of awareness that You are suffering still in Your Mystical Body, that You are lonely in the tabernacle for souls that do not come. If I only realized how much sheer joy just one faithful, watchful, loyal friend gives You! Oh make me see, dear King. Teach me how to "watch and pray." Make me so aware of Your sufferings, so understanding and sympathetic of Your pain, that I will lose all drowsiness and weariness and force my sleepy eyes to watch with You. Help me to love reparation! Help me to see it as loyalty! And, dear Lord, be pleased as I watch.

THE BETRAYAL—HYPOCRISY

Matt. 26 : 46-56; Luke 22 : 45-48

1. *Judas saying, "Hail, Rabbi!"*
2. *The grace, dear Lord, of utter sincerity.*

AS JESUS was going through His agonizing prayer for the third time, Judas approached with a few hundred armed men. Jesus sensed their approach and went back to the Apostles and stood by them. The Apostles, hearing the crowd coming, feared for their Master and for themselves, so they entered the Garden and stood beside Jesus and the other three. Judas approached; the twelve were together again. And as he said, "Hail, Rabbi!" and kissed Jesus, one would have felt that he was the most loyal and true of them all. Yet the very kiss itself was the sign of the betrayal.

MY KING, it was a fitting climax to Judas' treachery that he should betray You with a kiss. For Judas was a hypocrite and this was his supreme act of hypocrisy. Hypocrisy is a lie in action. It is giving the appearance of goodness to something that is evil in order that we might be praised—or, at least, not blamed. Thus when Judas complained that Mary wasted the ointment at Bethany, saying it could have been given to the poor, he was a hypocrite. He wanted it not for the poor but for himself. When he sat at table with You at the Last Supper, sat there as a friend to You Whom he was about to betray, he was a hypocrite. And now the kiss, the sign of love, esteem, loyalty. And he used it to cover up betrayal!

DEAR LORD, while I profess to despise this sin, have I not been guilty of it? Do I not always put my best foot forward before others? Do I not always want them to think more of me than I am worth? Am I not always acting the part of the holy, the sincere, the real Christian, while in my heart I still nourish pride, jealousy, rash judgments, real uncharitableness?

O my King, teach me utter simplicity—the ability to be true, true to Thee, true to my neighbor and true to myself. Help me by Your light to see myself as I am, and to profess myself to be that and no more. Teach me to avoid false condemnation and hypocritical criticism of self on the one hand, and the constant temptation to put on an act on the other hand. I resolve to speak as little about self as possible—and then only with complete honesty and sincerity.

THE ARREST—MORAL COURAGE

Matt. 26:46-56; John 18:4-12

1. *Jesus, calm and strong, directing the action of His own arrest.*
2. *The calm of self-possession, of moral courage.*

AFTER His last quick effort to win Judas, Jesus turned to the soldiers and the mob and asked them whom they sought. When He told them that He was Jesus of Nazareth, they fell to the ground. And so when He directed them to allow the Apostles to leave, no attempt was made to stop them. In the excitement, Peter cut off the ear of Malchus. That could well have touched off a free-for-all had not Jesus saved the situation by His calm, deft action. Moral courage based on prudence is so much greater than physical courage. Then Jesus turned to the mob and logically, bravely made the issue clear to them, that they were the agents of the prince of darkness. Then, with physical courage equal to His moral strength, He freely gave Himself into their hands.

DEAR MASTER, even Your enemies would have to admit that the outstanding figure in this whole scene of Your arrest, the only true leader and director of the whole affair, was Yourself. What was it about You that so impressed them in spite of themselves? What was it that made them obey the One they had come to command? What was it except the magnificent spectacle of Your indomitable courage and self-possession. Men, like animals, gain courage the moment they sense the weakness of their prey, the moment they feel that they are the stronger force. And yet this mob and the soldiers never felt that way in this scene until You actually let them tie Your Hands.

MY KING, I love Your indomitable courage and long for it and the perfect peace and self-possession which it brings. You gained it, Lord, in Your heartfelt prayer in the Garden. That prayer straightened out all things. All was right between You and Your Father; all was offered for Him and accepted beforehand! So what evil could befall You? Men could do their very worst—but they could not harm You or Your Cause.

I am weak, dear Lord, because I am not prepared as You were. I, too, could have Your beautiful vision and the courage which it brings, if I were like You in the Garden—praying so sincerely and completely accepting the Father's Holy Will! Let me pray like You. I promise You in my daily meditation and each day at Mass I will accept whatever the Father has in store for me. Then all else will be well.

JESUS BEFORE ANNAS (1)—SELF-CONTROL

John 18:12-13, 19-23

1. *The Sacred Face of Jesus marked with red welts from the soldier's hand.*
2. *The grace, my Lord, of self-control under misunderstanding, hatred or derision.*

JESUS was bound and then half-dragged, half-pushed across the brook Cedron to the house of Annas. Annas, crafty, unscrupulous, was the real power in Jewry. He had arranged to have his five sons and then his son-in-law as High Priest. He could question

Jesus while Caiphas summoned a quorum of the Sanhedrin and coached the witnesses. Cleverly, he asked Jesus apparently harmless questions about His teaching and followers. Just as cleverly, Jesus answered. Nothing was hidden, all was open. The fox who could cross-question other men and discover all he wanted to know now suffered the discomfort of meeting a superior intellect. Jesus answered respectfully, but told him nothing. Then one of the sycophants of Annas' court, sensing his master's defeat, struck Jesus a cowardly blow on the cheek. There was silence for a moment! And then Jesus turned to him: "If I have spoken ill, bear witness to the evil; but if well, why dost thou strike Me?"

O MY KING, what magnificent self-control You manifested to that cowardly court. The surprise of the blow, so uncalled for, would have upset the equilibrium of anyone except You. But You were always so self-disciplined, always so closely united to the Father in prayer, that anger or impatience could never surprise You or catch You off guard. With what splendid deliberateness You turned to the guard and showed him the cowardliness of his action. Only the meek and the humble are so strong!

DEAR LORD, what a pale image of You am I in this regard. I'm so quick to take offense, imagine insults, feel hurt—and so often without justification. And even when I am really slighted or hurt, instead of taking it manfully like You, don't I indulge in self-pity and pout? Or else, don't I tell others exactly what was said and just how I was wronged?

O my King, give me the strength of self-discipline and meekness. Let me love to stand with You and take all blows and relish them—because then I am like You. The blows across my face are needed, if I am to resemble my King!

JESUS BEFORE ANNAS (2)—PURE INTENTION

John 18 : 13-14, 19-23

1. *The deep-set eyes of Jesus Christ searching the eyes of the soldier.*
2. *The grace, my Lord, of a pure intention and absolute simplicity in all I do.*

FOR THE hangers-on at the court of Annas, the meeting between Annas and Jesus was fascinating. Annas was a genius at questioning men and unveiling all their secrets. At the same time, the Nazarene was clever, too. Neither the Pharisees nor the Sadducees had been able to trick Him or ensnare Him—even though they had almost foolproof plots. Now Jesus faced the master-schemer. It would be a good contest! Annas asked Jesus about His followers and His doctrine. He knew all this from his spies; he asked only to catch Jesus in some misstatement. In a most disarming manner, Jesus let Annas know that He saw through the whole scheme. "Why dost thou question Me? Question those who have heard what I spoke to them." Jesus, of course, knew how carefully Annas had done this very thing. Thus, beautifully, did He rip the mask from the hypocrite's face.

The hangers-on were disappointed. They sensed Annas' embarrassment. To the soldier nearest Jesus, it was a chance to ingratiate himself with Annas. He looked shocked as though Jesus were in the wrong and had said something awful. With all the cowardice that goes with hypocrisy always, he struck Jesus and spat forth his hypocritical surprise: "Is that the way thou dost answer the High Priest?" There was a moment of deathless silence. The eyes of Jesus burned into his: "If I have spoken ill, bear witness to the evil; but if well, why dost thou strike Me?" As Jesus had unmasked the hypocrisy of words in Annas, now He unmasked the hypocrisy of action.

O MY KING, You hated hypocrisy — our tendency to hide our evil behind good, to think one thing and say another, to make excuses for ourselves which give us wonderful motives we don't have! "Why?" was the question You asked both Annas and the soldier. "Why" unveils the motive. And it is the motive that really counts in every act.

MY KING, teach me to hear Your "Why?" deep in my soul. "Why" my words and my actions? To honor You, or to gain praise? To be considered good? To have others love me? To grasp the crumbs of praise? Or, the only worthy why — that You may be loved and praised forever! Lord, make me true!!

JESUS BEFORE CAIPHAS—PREJUDICE

Mark 14 : 53-65

1. *Jesus standing before a quorum of the Sanhedrin in the house of Caiphas.*
2. *The grace, my Lord, to bear prejudice with calmness and resignation.*

JESUS was pushed into the center of a large room. He was made to stand facing a few

rows of seats as the Pharisees and Sadducees filed in to take their places. Those hypocrites then went through the regular formal procedure of a legal trial, although the witnesses had been coached and the verdict determined beforehand. Jesus had to listen to the mockery, as they questioned the witnesses. They tried hard to get at least two witnesses to agree since the Law demanded exact agreement by two witnesses. The hypocrisy of it so disgusted His sincere and truthful soul! Yet He stood there in silence—strong and calm.

MY KING, You were a victim of prejudice. They judged You before they heard the witnesses, before You even came to trial, before they gave You a chance to explain Your doctrine. Prejudice means to prejudge. How it hurt You! And how much they missed! If they had given You a hearing, they would have learned that You came "not to destroy but to fulfill," not to take away but to give, not to kill but to give life in untold abundance. They would have found such peace and joy and happiness.

O MY KING, when I am the victim of prejudice, then I am like You. The "servant is not above his Master." If they prejudged You, they must prejudge me. Don't let me resent it, Lord. Let me embrace it willingly, as an instrument of Your grace to transform me into Your image. No pouting, Lord, no self-pity — but eyes to see it all as Your way of making me like You.

And Lord, don't let me prejudge others. When I have done so in the past, how wrong I have been! Let me meet each person along the road of life face to face, accepting him as I find him, and loving him for the good that I make myself find in him.

JESUS BEFORE THE SANHEDRIN— PEACE OF SELF-DISCIPLINE

Matt. 26 : 67; Mark 14 : 63-65

1. *The members of the Sanhedrin milling about Jesus and spitting into His Sacred Face.*
2. *The grace, my Lord, of self-discipline in all my feelings.*

ONCE Caiphas had won his point of getting Jesus to declare under oath that He was the Son of God, the hypocritical Pharisees and Sadducees of the Sanhedrin put on a great act. They made believe that they were shocked, held their ears so as not to hear "blasphemy," and rent their garments in protestation of Jesus' guilt. And then their wild passions of envy and hatred took over. They rushed out of their places and milled about Jesus. They blindfolded Him and began to strike Him with all their might across the Face. "Who is it that struck Thee?" they screamed. And then, the lowest of all things, they spat into His Face. Jesus remained silent. He uttered not a single cry of pain or hatred. Gradually, they began to feel ashamed; they began to slink away into the night.

MY OUTRAGED King, You seemed more royal than ever as You endured that torment. Even those Pharisees began to see it. As You stood there, silent and tall and strong, they began to realize that they were the victims of their own uncontrolled passions, victims of their own envy and jealousy, cowardice and hatred! And those passions were brutal masters. Your calmness made them realize that You were the only One there Who was free. Self-control had made You the Master of Yourself. Their lack of self-discipline had made them slaves to their emotions.

DEAR MASTER, I hate to imagine myself in this picture! But if I am to be honest, I must admit that I belong there. Have I not let my feelings and moods dominate me—and make me sulky and hard to live with? And all because I lack self-discipline. All because I just ride the tide and go along with my moods. Have I not let myself think over and over again about incidents which only make me mad and resentful? Have I not let myself be oversensitive and get hurt at things I never should have noticed? How Your majestic calm shames me, my Saviour! Teach me, then, this bigness and calmness of humility and self-discipline. Teach me to stop the bad and negative emotions right at the start. Let me see that they are not worthy of You! Humility and self-discipline! These will help me to live by faith and not by feeling!

PETER'S DENIAL (1)—SELF-KNOWLEDGE

Luke 22 : 54-65; Mark 14 : 67-72

1. *Peter swearing to the maidservant that he did not know Jesus.*
2. *The grace, my Lord, to be faithful to daily examinations of conscience.*

AFTER the initial fright in the Garden, Peter and John came to their senses. They should be with their Master. They retraced their steps until they were in sight of the band of soldiers that held Jesus prisoner. When

Jesus was brought in to Annas and Caiphas for questioning, Peter and John gradually moved in closer, until they were with the group of servants and bystanders in the courtyard. A maidservant recognized Peter as an Apostle, but he was able to deny it and move away. At the door of the garden, another maidservant pointed at him: "This is one of them." Peter felt something he had hardly known before; he felt fearful as all eyes turned on him. Nervously, he shouted that he didn't know Jesus. He called God to be his witness that he was not a disciple of the Nazarene. This seemed to convince them and they let him alone for a while. Peter had a sickly feeling, but he still didn't recall the prophecy. He was separated from John also in the confusion and felt uneasy by himself.

An hour dragged by. Still no news about Jesus. The cold night air made him shiver. He drew near to the servants' fire to get warm. Suddenly a finger was pointing right at him. It was a cousin of Malchus, whose ear Peter had cut off. "Did I not see thee in the garden with him?" The terrible fear was gripping at Peter's heart again. He called down curses from God on himself if he were a friend of Jesus. There was just no truth in it! And then he heard the cock crow; and he remembered!

DEAR LORD, no one in this world could doubt that Peter loved You! He said that he'd go to prison and death with You and he really meant it. In the Garden he would have fought the whole cohort all alone! He didn't lack love; he lacked self-knowledge. He knew where he was brave; but he didn't know where he was weak! Because he had physical courage, he assumed that he had moral courage—the ability to stand criticism and ridicule. But he didn't! This was one of his big weaknesses. And since he didn't know it, he walked right into the trap and denied his Master Whom he really loved.

DEAR LORD, self-knowledge is an absolute prerequisite for serving You well. I have an Achilles' heel like Peter—one or more predominant weaknesses, where I am most vulnerable to attack. I must know them if I am to surround them with the armor of grace and avoid the dangers. And yet, my King, how careless I am about daily examination of conscience. I either neglect it altogether or skim over the day so lightly that I don't see my faults. Even when I notice faults and list them, I fail to ask why I fell, or where the real source of weakness is, or where my motivation was most poor. O my King, make me work at self-examination. Don't let it be superficial. Each day I will list my faults and the reasons for them with all the specific details, so that I'll know my weaknesses and thus be strong.

PETER'S DENIAL (2)—TRUE SORROW FOR SIN

Luke 22 : 54-65; Mark 14 : 67-72

1. *Peter almost staggering from the courtyard, overcome by grief.*
2. *The grace, my Lord, to see sin as a betrayal of You, my Friend.*

THE COCK crowing the second time made Peter remember the prophecy of Jesus: "Thou shalt deny Me thrice." Peter could hardly believe it. Suddenly it was all over. The terrible thing had been done. He was guilty of denying the One he swore to uphold. An ugly mass of dark emotions seized his soul. He almost staggered from the garden, unable to stifle the sobs and low gasps of agony. His Friend Who loved him, his Friend Who took him from a reeking fishing boat to make him a prince — he had betrayed his Friend! He leaned against a wall, his head pressed against his arm: "Jesus, forgive me," he sobbed, "forgive me, forgive me."

DEAR LORD, Peter's sorrow was a very touching and beautiful thing. In his own impetuous, blundering way, he understood so well that religion is love for a Person. And when he fell into sin, it wasn't the ugliness of his soul that hurt him, or what people would think of his sin—it was deep regret for the sorrow that he caused his Father and his Friend. What a difference between the remorse Judas would feel that night and the sorrow that Peter felt. One couldn't stand the vileness of his deed; the other was so sorry that he had hurt a Friend.

MY LORD, I need this lesson of true sorrow for sin so very much. I tend to get so despondent when I fall into sin or even commit faults against charity, humility or patience. I feel depressed and am tempted to give up trying. "What's the use!" I say, "I'm just impossible!" How wrong is such an attitude, my King! It comes from an over-concern with self. My pride is hurt that I've fallen again. The false picture I've painted of myself has to be revised. Self! Self! And my Friend, Whom I've betrayed by my sin, I forget. I forget You, my Jesus!

Teach me to have Peter's sorrow, dear Lord. Let me see sin for what it really is—an injury to You. And let me go to You to express my sorrow. I know what will happen, my King. I'll realize right away that You forgive me—and that realization will throw my heart in chains! I'll start again like Peter, determined never to hurt my Friend again!

JESUS MOCKED BY HIS GUARDS—INSULTS

Luke 22:63-65

1. *Jesus, blindfolded, being slapped in the Face.*
2. *The grace, my Lord, never to cause pain just to hurt another.*

THE GUARDS who stood by Jesus during the trial were amazed to see the reaction of the Pharisees when Jesus was condemned. It amused them to see that these dignitaries could lose all their dignity and act as they themselves might act — with viciousness, hatred and jealousy. When they escorted Jesus to a dungeon for the rest of the night, they felt fully justified in imitating their masters. They mocked Jesus with vile and vulgar insults. They blindfolded Him and struck Him in the Face. "Prophesy," they taunted, "who is it that struck Thee?" Jesus was numb and sick from the blows, but He said not a word. Gradually, they grew tired and gave up their cowardly sport. They locked the dungeon gate and left Him. It was such a relief to be alone again. Although the cell was damp and cold, He welcomed it as a blessed respite from the insults and noise. He sank to His knees as in the Garden, with eyes raised to Heaven: "Father, not My Will but Thine be done!"

MY KING, it's a dreadful fault, deliberately to insult another human being. Dreadful because insults can cause pain as few other wounds can. Insults can so shake a man that he will become uncertain of himself, confused, hurt in the very depths of his personality. How dreadful then were the insults heaped on You that night in the prison. They mocked Your royal silence, saying You were too stupid to speak. They laughed at Your dignity, saying that You were an actor making believe You were a King. They taunted Your claim to divinity by blindfolding You and asking: "Who is it that struck Thee?" Each insult was calculated to hurt, to break down Your self-respect, to make You feel foolish and confused. What horrible cruelty! My King, if charity is the highest virtue because it wishes well and rejoices over another's good, then surely these insults were the most reprehensible faults because they wished evil and rejoiced over another's pain.

MY KING, I hate to think that I have ever deliberately insulted another human being. But blindfolding myself to the facts won't help me to do better. The truth is that I have! I've hurt others — and deliberately. I've brought up their faults just to cause them pain. Sometimes jealousy caused me to do it; sometimes the desire to "get even" for what they did to me. No matter! I was wrong — dreadfully wrong! I really made myself part of that uncouth mob who insulted You so shamefully that night. For what I did "to these the least of Your brethren, I did to You."

O my King, no matter what I suffer in the future, never, never let me insult another human being. If I have to correct another, let my correction be constructive and private and kind. Never let me insult; never let me cause pain just to see the other person suffer. To atone for what You suffered that night, I pledge myself never to cause a needless pain!

THE MORNING TRIAL BY THE SANHEDRIN—DIVINITY OF JESUS

Luke 22 : 63-71; Mark 15 : 1

1. *Jesus, Face to face with Caiphas.*
2. *The grace, my Lord, to realize that You are divine.*

CAIPHAS knew that the evening trial was completely illegal. He was determined not to have any such "technicality" brought up by Pilate or by Pharisees like Joseph and Nicodemus who were friendly with Jesus. At the crack of dawn, therefore, he had the Sanhedrin assemble for another trial. At this one he didn't even try to get false witnesses. The one thing he could rely on was the absolute sincerity and truthfulness of his Prisoner. As soon as Jesus was led into the Hall of Hewn Stone and was turned to face His judges, Caiphas asked without any further ado: "If Thou art the Christ, tell us." But Jesus wanted them first to realize their own insincerity. "If I tell you, you will not believe Me . . . or let Me go." Even then He was anxious to win some of them by making clear their deceit. Then He answered their question. "But henceforth the Son of Man will be seated at the right hand of the power of God."

He was saying it! They all jumped up, anxious to have it stated clearly. "Art Thou, then, the Son of God?" they asked. Bravely, unequivocally, came the answer: "You yourselves say that I am." They were delighted. "What further need have we of witness?" And they hurried Jesus off to Pilate.

DEAR LORD, I admire so much Your clear, open profession of Your divinity. You were on trial for Your life. You were before the highest court of the land. And You were under oath. No one could ever doubt that You meant every word most sincerely. So when You told them and the world the tremendous truth, that You are the eternal Son of God, equal to the Father, the only logical reaction is to accept it as true.

Men have tried to discount Your words, saying that You were a dreamer, or a megalomaniac with delusions of grandeur. How completely empty are all these accusations! A megalomaniac is fanatical, nervous, ruthless. But You—You, my King, were the most self-possessed Person in that whole court, even though You stood alone against them all. You tried to win their souls even then when they were being so deceitful and hateful in trying to destroy you. Ah, my King, Your bigness and beauty of soul is the best witness for the truth of Your words.

MY LORD, do I realize what Your words mean? The eternal Son of God, unlimited in power, exhaustless in beauty and wisdom, God Himself, walking this earth in human form, with a body and soul just like our own! If once I realized what I believe and know, then I'd never stop studying about You, my King. I'd love to pore over each page of the Gospels, listening attentively to the words God is speaking, watching with love and admiration everything God did, in His human nature. And, Lord, how I would try to be just like You — to think big, to love strongly, to radiate You to others. Let me realize, then, my King, what You are! And let the knowledge and love of You be a burning thirst in my life. My heaven will thus have begun. "Now this is eternal life, that they may know Thee, the only true God, and Him Whom Thou hast sent, Jesus Christ."

THE DESPAIR OF JUDAS—LONELINESS OF SIN

Matt. 27 : 3-10

1. *Judas seated on a rock in Gethsemane, all alone.*
2. *The grace, my Lord, to see the utter desolation of mortal sin.*

WHEN Jesus was tied securely, the Apostles slipped away into the shadows and fled. As the soldiers led Jesus away, the representative of the High Priest turned to Judas and handed him a small purse with the thirty pieces of silver. He made some remark about easy money. But Judas didn't reply or count the coins. His eyes followed Jesus and the soldiers down the path to the brook Cedron. The representative of the High Priest turned then and left also. Judas was alone. The tramp of the soldiers and the clanging of their armor had faded. There was a deathly stillness. He entered the Garden and sat down. He should be happy, he told himself. He was well rid of that group of dreamers. Someone had to be practical! The Pharisees would have captured Jesus anyway, and then no one would have gained. But it was no use. They were just words, and they couldn't stop the tide of disgust and sorrow that overwhelmed him. If only he had someone to talk to!

O MY KING, there is just no loneliness like the loneliness of being in mortal sin. To whom could this poor wretch go? He didn't dare go to the Apostles. He couldn't even go back to the Pharisees and soldiers; he was despised and unwelcome even there! He was alone in the still night—alone with no one who cared how he felt or what he did. He was alone with his thoughts and feelings until they nearly drove him mad.

MY KING, teach me to understand this horrible loneliness of mortal sin. Let me experience it beforehand—before temptation leads me astray. Let me see that my sin is mine and mine alone. It isolates me from You and from Your friendship and love. Though others try to console me, though they be in sin with me, it's no use. My sin is still only my sin. I am guilty; I must pay for it. I must suffer the isolation and the awful loneliness.

Teach me then, my Saviour, to have a strong and healthy fear of mortal sin! And when sin begins to look alluring, when the devil makes temptations attractive, let my mind go back to that poor, miserable creature in Gethsemane. Let me feel his loneliness and awful desolation, and then I'll be strong.

THE SUICIDE OF JUDAS—DESPAIR

Matt. 27 : 3-10

1. *The awful sight of the body of Judas hanging from a tree.*
2. *The grace, my Lord, never to despair.*

JUDAS was nearly mad with grief when he ran from the Council Chamber. Thoughts and feelings rushed upon him in such rapid succession—hatred for those hypocrites, sorrow for Jesus, regret, bitter regret for what he had done. They raced around within him until his whole being became a screaming whirlpool of agony. If any feeling was stronger than the others, it was an awful hatred for himself. How could anyone who was so favored turn on his Benefactor! How could anyone who was treated with such kindness . . . ! He found himself in the Valley of Hinnon below the southern wall of the city. "Look you to it," they said. They were right. It was his fault, no one else's. He couldn't endure himself. Nervously, he fixed his cincture around his neck. He tied the end to an overhanging branch. He wouldn't let himself think. He threw himself down.

DEAR LORD, what an unspeakable tragedy! Not so much his awful agony and misery—but the tragedy that he came so close to true repentance and still despaired! If only he had stopped looking down at his sin and looked up to You, to Your mercy. But he was so proud. He couldn't bear to think that he could commit such a horrible crime. And when the realization came to him that he had, it was more than he could take! He was just nauseated by his own ugliness, hated what he saw. Humility would have saved him. Humility would have told him that all human beings make mistakes, that God is bigger in mercy than we are in sin.

DEAR LORD, I hope I never presume. But, above all else, never let me despair. Despair attacks You, my God, in Your most lovely attribute—Your mercy, which "is above all Your works." Help me, then, my King. You know how pride makes me think I've conquered certain sins. You know what happens when I fall again—how despondent and miserable I am, how terribly upset—and more because of the sight of my ugliness than the thought of You. Lord, make me humble. When I fall into sin, let me have sorrow — great sorrow—because I love You. But let me know that when I have perfect sorrow, You forgive me right away! And then I'll be so grateful for Your forgiveness, I'll really love You more. Make it so, my King! No despair! Let even my faults teach me to love You!

JESUS BEFORE PILATE (1)—DETACHMENT

John 18 : 28-32; Luke 23 : 2

1. *Jesus, tall, silent, a picture of stillness against the noisy background of the crowd.*
2. *The grace, dear Master, of deep peace based on detachment.*

TRIUMPHANTLY the members of the Sanhedrin led the band of soldiers who dragged Jesus through the streets to the Fortress Antonia. His hands still tied, Jesus was pushed inside the Praetorium and handed over to the Roman guards. Pilate came out to meet them. He sat near Jesus to hear the charges. The trumped-up political charges came flying up from the crowd, provoked by the Pharisees and chief priests. They shouted loud to make an impression of real indignation: "perverting the nation, refusing to pay taxes, etc." All lies! Pilate knew that they

SPQR

were lies. He looked over at the Accused, expecting Him to shout back and revile them —at least feeling that He would deny the charges. But not a word! He truly looked like a King.

DEAR MASTER, how beautifully You demonstrated silence under false accusation! You could do it because You were so detached from what they were saying and thinking about You. You were what You were, whether they recognized it or not. How strong and virile that detachment made You! There was no vacillation, no cringing or crying, no shouted defense or pleas! Just perfect silence and perfect calm and peace.

DEAR LORD, how greatly I fret and worry when falsely accused! How concerned I am when misunderstood! How disturbed and upset interiorly when shown up for faults or weakness — either before my own conscience or before others. Like Judas, I am more concerned about the ugliness of the fault in my soul and what people will think than I am for the One Whom I have hurt.

Teach me detachment, dear Lord—detachment from the thing I cling to most—my complacency and my wanting to be understood and loved. When others misunderstand me, I am more like You. What more could I want! Grant me, dear Lord, detachment and peace. Let me realize that You are closest to me and love me most, precisely when others misunderstand me and reject me.

JESUS BEFORE PILATE (2)—REJECTED GRACE

John 18:33-38

1. *The searching eyes of Jesus piercing the soul of Pilate.*
2. *The grace, my Lord, to accept Your graces now — and not put them off.*

IT WAS a delight to the Heart of Jesus when Pilate asked Him into his own study and put to Him the question: "Art Thou the King of the Jews?" Our Lord had given Pilate many graces—His strong silence, His serenity under attack when all His accusers were in a frenzy, His bigness in not descending to hate and self-defense. And the graces were now beginning to tell. Pilate was really interested in knowing more about Jesus. One more grace Jesus would now give Pilate, the grace to be true to himself and true to God — the chance to admit that his question was not simply the formal duty of a Procurator, but the question of a searching mind and heart.

"Dost thou say this of thyself?" Jesus said as His eyes penetrated the eyes and heart of Pilate. Pilate was caught! The Man saw right through him, recognized his question for what it was—his own personal interest. How dare an insolent Jew, a prisoner—majestic though He appeared—how dare He suggest that Pilate could be interested in Him or consider Him a King! Flustered, annoyed, he almost yelled back the answer that really was no answer: "Am I a Jew? Thy own people and the chief priests have delivered Thee to me." Jesus was saddened. The grace was rejected. Pilate's pride was too great for him to be true.

O MY KING, Your method of dealing with Pilate as well as with so many others in the Gospel makes me realize that You continually are working for souls. You never stop trying to win them over, or to lead them higher. "My Father works until now, and I work." Everything that happens is just Your work in the soul, a grace to lead us higher.

DEAR MASTER, I know this in theory, but how blind I am when it comes to living it! How much like Pilate! My life is one stream of rejected graces, like dead soldiers on a battlefield after the fight is over. Let me see, my King, that there is no real opposition in my life, no cause for disappointment or regret. Let me see that everything that happens to me is a grace—You at work. The sarcasm of others, teasing that is mean and sarcasm that hurts, prejudice that burns me, the dislike and neglect that wounds me—they are graces like the graces to Pilate. They are Your work. And so are the joy and love and kindness and gentleness that You send me—graces, my King, to be used. No more interfering with You! No more neglected graces! Do with me what You will; I will take all with joy!

JESUS BEFORE PILATE (3)—INTERIOR PEACE

John 18:33-38

1. *Jesus, silent as the crowds shout their accusations.*
2. *The grace, my King, of interior peace.*

JESUS waited until the flustered Pilate had expressed his annoyance. Then, calmly, clearly, He explained that His Kingdom was not of this world. If it were, He could and would win the battle. But His Kingdom was to be a spiritual kingdom of souls. As Jesus was speaking, Pilate was drawn again — almost in spite of himself. Our Lord's unperturbed manner, even under Pilate's anger, just fascinated him. He found himself asking again: "Thou art then a King?" Jesus answered him: "Thou sayest it; I am a King." This was why He came into the world — to teach truth. But to Pilate, confused by the maze of conflicting philosophies, finding truth seemed impossible. He stood up. "What is truth?" he asked, with a shrug of his shoulders, and went back to the crowd.

"I find no guilt in Him," he said. But the Pharisees were ready. There was a terrible uproar from the crowd; they shouted their accusations and lies. Pilate looked at Jesus. Not a word! "Hast Thou no answer to make?" Silence. Pilate almost shouted, "Dost Thou not hear how many things they prefer against Thee?" Pilate shook his head. He couldn't fathom this spiritual King Who seemed to have no fear.

MY KING, Your royal silence tells us so much. It was an outward proof of Your interior peace. Everyone else was noisy. The Scribes and Pharisees were shouting and yelling their lies, deathly afraid that this "empty-headed" Governor was going to spoil their plans. The soldiers at the Praetorium were nervous. They would be badly outnumbered, if this caused an open rebellion. Pilate was on edge. He hated to see the vaunted Roman justice flouted; yet he couldn't see risking his political career by opposing Caiphas. The only One at peace was You, my King. You show us that peace is from within. No one can hurt us except ourselves. If we are living to please our Father, then it doesn't matter what people say or think or do. Inside us, we'll have the precious gift of interior silence and peace.

LORD, even though I admire so much Your royal silence and peace, how often I am anxious and nervous. And why, my King? Because I was hurt by an unkind remark, crushed because my words or actions were misunderstood and twisted, disturbed about what people say and think about me! What clear proof that I lack the beautiful simplicity of serving God alone! Let me see, dear Master, that nothing, absolutely nothing, can hurt the peace of one who has learned to love and serve the Father! Teach me to live for Him alone, to refuse to be anxious about any human respect or opinions. Give me Your silence of heart and Your peace!

JESUS BEFORE HEROD—PEACE OF TRUE HUMILITY

Luke 23:7-12

1. *Jesus wearing the white robe of a fool.*
2. *The grace, my Lord, of true humility, of taking humiliations for Your glory.*

AS THE PHARISEES persisted in their demands for Jesus' death, Pilate heard them mention that Jesus was from Galilee. A wonderful break of fortune! He would send Jesus to Herod to be judged. It would be a chance to flatter Herod and thus win back his good will. And at the same time, it would take this sorry mess off his own hands.

For Jesus, it meant another terrible spectacle of being dragged through the city streets to the palace of Herod. For Herod it was good news. He had been so anxious to see Jesus—ever since he began to suspect that Jesus might be John the Baptist risen from the dead. Besides, it would be such a new diversion for his courtiers, a fine chance to show off his wisdom before the Pharisees, the intelligentsia of the land.

Herod began to question Jesus. No answer. He suggested different miracles that Jesus might perform—mock serious at first, then laughing openly, then annoyed and challenging! The perfect silence and serenity of Jesus made Herod seem like a fool in comparison, and no one was more conscious of it than Herod. He must save face. He would make Jesus look like a fool. He commanded that He be adorned in the fool's white robe and dismissed Him with an attempt at laughter.

DEAR LORD, what unspeakable humility You showed us in this scene! Eternal Wisdom treated like a fool! It is precisely this insult that our pride rejects most vehemently, my King. We would rather be considered evil than be rated a fool. How Your humility shames us! There was no bitterness in Your manner as You donned that robe; no terrible indignation, no feelings of hatred or longing for revenge! Humility was dear to Your heart; Your role was then the role of Saviour—One Who was to suffer in our place. So in humility You accepted to be what You were and what the Father wanted You to be. And that acceptance turned even humiliation into love and robbed it of all its bitterness!

MY KING, I admire You with all my soul in Your white robe of a fool! Nowhere are You more kingly and royal and worthy of all praise.

My King, You know how pride eats at the core of all that I do. You see how I love praise and recognition; how I hate being considered a fool! Let this picture of You, then, burn a place deep in my heart. Teach me to imitate You in Your role as Saviour—as well as in Your hidden and public life. Help me to accept and welcome humiliations, unkind joking and criticism, as Your holy Will. If Your glory or the good of souls might be compromised by silence, then give me the courage to speak and to fight. But apart from those cases, let me take all that comes with peace and serenity—being happy to stand at Your side in this role of a fool.

JESUS BROUGHT BACK TO PILATE—COMPROMISE

John 19:4-15

1. *Jesus covered with blood and spittle — "like a worm and no man."*
2. *The grace, my King, to see my duty and fulfill it.*

WHILE Jesus was being scourged, Pilate had time to sit and think. He hated this nasty business of punishing an obviously innocent man. He felt somehow that he was letting Rome down. He felt a little that he was letting himself down also. But what could he do, he argued in his own defense. He couldn't oppose the Sanhedrin and have another bad report go back to Rome. He had to provide for his future. And yet he couldn't condemn an innocent man to death. So he was really finding the best solution — a fair compromise. The Nazarene should be glad that Pilate was finding a way to save His life! Just then Jesus was brought back from the courtyard. Pilate heard the crowd shout, "Crucify Him!" He went out to them again and saw Jesus. The stately Figure that faced him before with majestic bearing was now brutally disfigured and covered with blood and spittle. Pagan though he was, Pilate's eyes closed in a surge of remorse and revulsion.

MY KING, maybe Pilate realized then that compromise with duty is cowardly, and like all actions that are cowardly, it ultimately leads to complete collapse. His duty was an unpleasant one, but his duty was clear! You were innocent! But Pilate couldn't face the possibility of political disgrace. So he took the coward's way out. He tried to salve his conscience and yet avoid the unpleasant consequences — he compromised.

But when the scourging was over, my King, and he looked at Your bleeding, swollen Face, when he heard the mob still shouting for Your death, he realized that his compromise accomplished absolutely nothing!

I NEED this lesson so very much, my Lord. Many times I stand in Pilate's place and must make Pilate's decision. My duty is clear. I know what You want of me—the sinful occasion I must give up, the distasteful person I must treat kindly, the unpleasant task I must do cheerfully! But the consequences are hard to take. I'm not ready yet—maybe later. But I'll do something else, Lord, so You'll be pleased. O my King, that's compromise with duty! And it's as cowardly as Pilate's. Never let me betray You like this, my King! Let me be true! True to see what my duty is and absolutely unflinching in fulfilling it.

JESUS OR BARABBAS—VIRTUE OR SIN

Luke 23 : 13-25; Matt. 27 : 15-22

1. *Pilate laying down the ultimatum: Jesus or Barabbas.*
2. *The grace, my King, to resist all temptations because sin is disloyalty, is choosing Barabbas rather than You.*

PILATE was disappointed when he heard the mob returning from Herod. He thought he had solved the problem. As he went out to meet them again, he determined on another plan to save Jesus. He would have the soldiers scourge Him and make Him look like such an abject and pitiable sight that their anger would be satisfied and they would have mercy on Him.

But as he began to state his plan to chastise Jesus, a new element entered the conflict. A large delegation from the people had arrived to ask for the customary release of a Jewish prisoner — the traditional act of generosity given by the Romans to Jews on big feasts. Pilate's shrewd mind hit upon another plan. Why not play this new group against the old group? The new group were sincere men; they would want a good man released, not a criminal. So Pilate chose the worst criminal he could find and narrowed their choice down to the two men: Barabbas or Jesus. Quickly, the clever Caiphas perceived Pilate's strategy. He screamed out before anyone could say a word: "Not Jesus, but Barabbas!" His cronies took up the cry. They shouted loud and ferociously, to impress everyone with their indignation. And they swept the weak mob with them.

O MY KING, what a shameful choice! What must have been Your feelings then! How could men be so weak, so disloyal! Barabbas was guilty of all crimes including murder. And You—You "went about doing good and healing all kinds of sickness." Even Your enemies had to say: "He has done all things well." And yet, my King, I shouldn't be so surprised, because all sin is exactly the same disloyalty; all sin is choosing Barabbas instead of You. The same with not doing the good that I could do—e.g., letting laziness or feelings keep me from acts of kindness to the aged or sick. This is disloyalty, too!

DEAR MASTER, I hate to think of it now, but my memory tells me that I have been right in the middle of that weak crowd that I despise. I have known all along that sin hurts You so much, and yet I have toyed with temptation, been swept along by human respect into lies, deceit, unkindness; been blinded by some bright temptations and just refused to look at You there with Your pleading eyes.

Lord, make me hate sin with all my strength and soul! Give me the strength to turn away from the slightest temptation, the bigness not to be guilty of the slightest disloyalty. Let me not commit a single venial sin ever again. And, O my King, let me die rather than commit a mortal sin!

THE SCOURGING—REPARATION FOR IMPURITY

John 19 : 1-7; Matt. 27 : 28-30

1. *The pitiable scene: Jesus bent over a low pillar, His back a mass of red welts.*
2. *The grace, my Lord, of never allowing the slightest immodest thought to stay in my mind.*

WHEN Pilate failed in his scheme to save Jesus by offering Him in contrast to Barabbas, he decided to try his other plan—to have Jesus scourged and treated shamefully. He hoped thus to satisfy the blood-thirst of the crowd and Pharisees. So Jesus was taken to the soldiers' courtyard, stripped of

His outer garments, made to bend over a low pillar. Two soldiers with weighted scourges stood over Him and began to bring them down upon Him with all their strength. The arms of Jesus convulsed in pain and pulled against the chains on His wrists until the skin and blood came from His wrists. His Sacred Back screamed in an agony of pain.

MY SAVIOUR, You had to suffer so much in Your Sacred Flesh for all our sins of giving in to the flesh. We pamper ourselves, so You had to pay the price. We refuse to be pleasant when we are weary, refuse to hide our feelings and be kind when we dislike someone; refuse to be abstemious when some food or drink is tasty; worst of all, we refuse to turn away when something impure attracts our attention or imagination. And so You had to suffer for our indulgences: "He was bruised for our iniquities; He was wounded for our sins. The chastisement of our sins was upon Him, and by His bruises we are healed!"

MY KING, I pity You in Your agony of pain! Forgive me for my part in it, for all my selfishness and impurity. Forgive me for toying with temptations that were dynamite. I feel so ashamed now, my King, that

I acted like a pampered member of the Mystical Body — the Body with a thorn-crowned Head and a Scourged Back.

Give me the grace, dear Master, of stern and firm discipline over my feelings and senses. Take my eyes and ears, my imagination and memory and feelings. Take and receive as Your very own all I am and have and hope to be. May I never again allow even the slightest selfish or impure thought.

JESUS IS CROWNED WITH THORNS— REPARATION FOR PRIDE

Matt. 27 : 28-30

1. *The pitiable sight of Jesus being mocked by the soldiers.*
2. *The grace, my King, always to be humble and true.*

THE TERRIBLE scourging was over. Jesus hung limp over the half-pillar. Even when they unchained the skinless and bloody wrists, He couldn't pull Himself erect. Two of the soldiers half-lifted Him and sat Him on a bench against the wall. Men with even the slightest pity would have been deeply moved at the sight. But these were pagans, and their Prisoner only a despised Jew Who gave Himself airs. A King was He! All right, then let Him be crowned! One of the soldiers put together some thorns. The brutal attempt at humor pleased the others. They got an old purple robe for His shoulders, a stick for His sceptre, and then the crown of thorns for His Head. The pain was terrible for Our Lord. But their attitude was worse. They hurled their vile and coarse jokes at Him; they knelt in mock adulation and then, vilest of all, they spat into His Face. And Jesus said not a word!

MY KING, what unspeakable humility! What splendid self-control that You didn't wither them with a glance, bring them to their knees at a display of Your majesty, overwhelm them with Your logic! You could have done all that, but You didn't. We have given in so much to pride and conceit that Someone had to pay the price of our forgiveness. We desire so much for others to praise us, to think highly of us, to notice us in a crowd and pay attention to us—that You had to suffer just the opposite to win our ransom. You wanted us never to forget that we were members of a Mystical Body that had a thorn-crowned Head!

WHEN I see You thus humiliated, my King, I feel such a great shame for my conceit and self-complacency and pride!

More than any other fault, it has led me to hurt You. More than any other tendency, it has led me to a bad disposition, resentment, pouting, unkindness and self-pity. But don't let shame be the end of it! Let my shame lead me to conversion and humility. Whenever I am tempted to look for praise, let me see Your thorn-crowned Head. Whenever I feel resentful or sulky or conceited, let me know that I am mocking You again as the soldiers did in the courtyard that morning. And then I will feel Your suffering, and I promise that I will change.

PILATE'S LAST EFFORTS—RATIONALIZATION

John 19 : 4-16; Matt. 27 : 24-25

1. *Jesus standing beside Pilate before the crowd.*
2. *The grace, my Lord, to be true to myself and to You.*

SICKENED though he was by the brutal beating Jesus had received, Pilate hoped that the sight of it might move the mob to pity. "Behold, the Man!" he said to them as he called Jesus out for the crowd to see. But hatred had made the chief priests keen and resourceful. They screamed out, "Crucify

Him! Crucify Him!" and the mob soon joined in the chorus. It was all so obviously the trumped-up work of a few! Again and again Pilate tried to be firm and dismiss Jesus. Each time they argued back until they finally found the argument that hit home. "If thou release this Man, thou art no friend of Caesar; for everyone who makes himself a king sets himself against Caesar." It was too much. They could ruin his political career. He was furious with them, and furious with himself that they had found his weakness. "Shall I crucify your King?" he shouted at them, in final defiance. Did they want a Roman to put their King to death? "We have no king but Caesar." Pilate stopped. What a sorry mess! He couldn't bear to think that he was part of it. He called for water. Then, dramatically, symbolically, in front of all he washed his hands. "I am innocent of the blood of this just Man."

MY KING, Pilate thus became the forerunner of all those who would rationalize about their guilt and do away with sin. They are torn between the desire for sinful pleasure and the awful feeling of guilt and self-blame which sin will bring. They want the pleasure, but can't stand the blame. So they rationalize: Such pleasure is natural. There's no such thing as sin. We mustn't cause frustration! They use quotations from Freud just as Pilate used the water: "I am innocent!" But it can't be done, my King. The water didn't remove Pilate's guilt. And all their rationalization doesn't remove theirs. Deep within them the guilt remains and festers. Peace comes from self-discipline and love, not from self-indulgence and false thinking.

O MY LORD, how often I have tried to rationalize. Everyone is reading the cheap, impure novels, I claim, so I must read them also. I have to know what others are thinking and doing. And my lack of ambition! I really can't be blamed for that. Look at the number of heart attacks. Better that I go slow and live longer. And my unkind conversations! I can't be expected to be a "dead-head" in the group. Everyone else is doing it! And on and on!

Ah, my Lord, make me true! If I'm doing something wrong, at least let me face it honestly. Don't let me wash my hands — trying to make it something good. Let me be true at least to myself! I promise faithful, sincere examination of conscience, that I might know myself and bring myself to You in all simplicity.

JESUS CARRIES THE CROSS TO CALVARY— LOVE FOR JESUS

Matt. 27 : 31; John 19 : 17

1. *Jesus stooped beneath the weight of the Cross.*
2. *The grace, my Lord, of a love for You that is faithful unto death.*

THE SOLDIERS took the soiled purple cape from the shoulders of Jesus and gave Him back His own robe. Then they brought Him His Cross. The weight of it seemed crushing in His weakened condition, but He made Himself hold it up, and with a great effort started forward towards Calvary. Each step became a sickening, painful agony. Several times He reeled with weakness as His strength left Him, and He fell forward to the ground. The soldiers finally realized that He might die on the way, so they picked out a man from the crowd and made him help Jesus. Simon seemed to resent it at first — until he looked at Jesus, and a sense of pity came over him.

Jesus saw His Mother by the side of the street. He couldn't stop; they couldn't speak.

He looked into her eyes for a moment. He felt so much sorrow for what she was suffering — but He knew she would understand. They didn't have to speak in order to understand each other.

At last the tortuous half-mile was traversed. The soldiers ripped off His garments, opening again the red wounds of the scourging. Jesus sat down upon the Cross. For a moment He rested His head between His arms. "This is My Body . . . My Blood." He stretched out then upon the Cross, and they hammered the nails through His sacred flesh. The pain screamed through every nerve in His Body.

MY KING, it was with mixed emotions that You accepted Your Cross. You were so deeply hurt by Your rejection by Your own people, the desertion of Your friends, the weakness of Pilate, the agony of Your Mother. And yet You were peaceful somehow, because Your final great work was about to be done. All the souls that You loved so much could now be reconciled to the Father and come home.

DEAR SAVIOUR, how can I thank You for such great love! The sins were mine, Lord, not Yours. I should have been mocked and scourged and spit upon, not You! It was

I who cut and hurt others by my speech, I who grew surly and arrogant in time of stress. It was I who selfishly indulged sinful pleasures. They should have crucified me! But, my King, You knew that I could not pay back the debt of sin. Like a child who breaks a watch but cannot fix it, I incurred an infinite debt that I could never repay. So You paid it for me. Let me always wonder at such generosity. And, dear Lord, let me repay Your love. Let me repay in the only way that love can be repaid—by loving You in return, by loving You faithfully unto death!

JESUS FORGIVES HIS ENEMIES— MERCY AND FORGIVENESS

Luke 23:34

1. *The Face of Jesus looking up towards Heaven, "Father, forgive them!"*
2. *The grace, my Lord, to make excuses for people in my own mind and in my words.*

THE GOOD He had done was twisted by false accusations to look like evil. What they couldn't twist, they lied about, said that He did evil things He never thought of doing. They treated Him like a fool, they spat at Him, struck Him, enjoyed it when the soldiers beat Him and mocked Him. And now, nailed to the Cross in great agony, Jesus listened while they mocked Him and taunted Him. Yet He uttered no harsh words, made no sarcastic reply, said nothing that would show up their hypocrisy and inconsistency — just beautiful self-control and silence! And then, suddenly, His lips began to move. A hush came over the crowd. What would He say to curse them? What would He say to try to explain away His "guilt"? "Father, forgive them, for they do not know what they are doing." For a moment even this mob was shocked and surprised and silent.

O MY KING, were You ever more royal and wonderful than at that moment! You were the Prisoner, being put to death, and it was You Who dispensed mercy and pardon! And it was so right that You should! For they were the criminals, they the victims and prisoners of their own unmortified passions and hates, they the blind victims of ignorance. So kingly and big were You to understand their weakness, so tremendous to find an excuse for them and forgive them!

MY SAVIOUR, I am so lacking in mercy. When others are mean to me, or sarcastic, or make me look foolish, I can no longer think straight in their regard. I want

nothing to do with them. I write them off my books. They become a blind spot in my eyes so that nothing they do is good. Their faults and shortcomings pound in my mind like a heavy pulse. How Your merciful spirit shames me! What are my tiny sufferings compared to Yours? Where is my blood shed? Where are my thorns and nails and public shame? I have no such wounds! Just petty little insults and hurts. If You could forgive what was done to You, dear Master, let me forgive the tiny injuries done to me. No self-pity, Lord! Big! Merciful! Forgiving! Like my King!

THE GOOD THIEF—CORRESPONDENCE WITH GRACE

Luke 23 : 35-43; Matt. 27 : 39-44

1. *The gentle look on the tortured Face of Jesus as He turned to Dismas.*
2. *The grace, dear Lord, to cooperate with the divine order, to reverence the moment-by-moment manifestations of the Divine Will.*

THE CROWDS were watching the ghastly spectacle. The passers-by, struck by the title over the Cross, jeered at Him. The high priests and Pharisees had a field day. They were so relieved now that He was dying and not saved by any of His miraculous powers or a tumult from the people. They found it much easier now to convince themselves that they were right. How could He be a prophet or the Son of God? Their jeering was marked by biting sarcasm and laughter. Even the soldiers joined in the mockery and taunts—even one of the thieves, one of His fellow-sufferers. And from Jesus, not a word!

Dismas took it all in. He knew that he was not bright, but he had just never seen such tremendous self-control, such royal silence, such majesty, even on this ignominious throne of the Cross. He began to believe in Jesus. He saw the accusers as slaves of their own hatred and jealousy, prisoners of violent passion and envy. The only Man at peace, the only Man in complete control of Himself, was Jesus.

So when the other thief began to taunt Jesus, it was more than Dismas could stand—it was a disloyalty he couldn't stomach. And so he spoke the only words on Calvary said in Our Lord's defense. And then, unashamed, he showed Jesus his belief: "Lord, remember me when Thou comest into Thy kingdom."

And then, what a reward! "Amen, I say to thee, this day . . . paradise."

DEAR LORD, how pleased You were when men accepted Your grace! And how tremendously generous when they met You halfway. You gave Dismas the grace of Your beautiful silent patience. And when he had the spiritual insight and courage to respond to it, You were so happy that You gave him Heaven. What a gentle look on Your Face as You turned to him! What assurance of love You gave him in approval of his contrition and his faith!

O MY LORD, I am fearful when I think of all the graces You have given me — the Sacraments, the Gospel, my Church, my work, beautiful examples all around me, the love of family and friends, inspiring books — and I remain so cold and unaffected! Dismas puts me to shame! My Lord, open my eyes. Give me the overwhelming grace to appreciate all Your graces. Lord, remember me now; draw me to You now.

MARY BENEATH THE CROSS—SELF-DISCIPLINE

John 19 : 25

1. *Mary standing beneath the Cross, her head pressed against His knees.*
2. *The grace to discipline my feelings and moods into love of God and neighbor, and never to give in to self-pity.*

OUR BLESSED LADY was there on Calvary when the soldiers drove the nails through Jesus' Hands and Feet. She saw them raise Him up on the terrible gibbet of the Cross, and the sight of it nearly tore her heart in two. She made her way closer to the Cross then with St. John and Mary Magdalene. The soldiers had held them all back at first. Now she was near, right beneath the Cross. He could see her and know that she understood and loved, that she was near at the end as she had been at the beginning. She buried her head against His knees and the tears flowed freely.

DEAR LORD, You must have been so proud of her then. Any other woman would have been overcome at the sight of Your sufferings, would have broken down and given in to her feelings. Anyone else would have screamed at the Pharisees, pleaded with the

soldiers, pulled at their uniforms and made a scene. Not Mary! She didn't even fall on the ground in a fit of sobbing. She "stood" beneath the Cross. She was in perfect control of herself even then; she was strong and at peace even there. By self-discipline her strong emotions were directed to the only objects worthy of her love—God and neighbor—and never self.

O MY LORD, You know how easily I can lose control of my feelings and give in to self-pity and prejudice, to irritability and surliness and smallness in a thousand ways. How her strength and peace shame me! Teach me, my Lord, to discipline my feelings. Let me never give in to self-pity and never consent to smallness. Teach me to channel all my feelings into love. Negative thoughts are the big obstacle—allowing myself to mull over what is said against me or done to hurt or slight me. Let me never tolerate such thoughts! Teach me to substitute for them big thoughts—especially the picture of Our Lady standing beneath the Cross!

THE THIRD WORD: "BEHOLD THY SON . . . BEHOLD THY MOTHER"

John 19 : 25-27

1. *The faces of John and Mary lifted up to see Jesus as He spoke to them.*

2. *The grace, my Lord, of perfect personal loyalty to You.*

MANY THINGS crowded in on the mind of Jesus as He hung on the Cross. His physical sufferings were excruciating and called often for His attention. But His great Heart felt so much for others that He made Himself think of their needs. He forgave His enemies and asked His Father to forgive them. He won the good thief's soul and promised him Heaven. And now, despite all the agonizing pain in His Body, He made Himself pay attention to His friends beneath the Cross. The sight of them touched Jesus deeply. His closest friend, John; His mother; Mary Magdalene; Mary Cleophas, His aunt. He called Mary's attention and John's. "Woman," He said, and then, nodding towards John, "behold thy son." Then with tender eyes that spoke volumes to John, telling him to watch over her well, He said, "Behold thy mother."

THERE are few things more beautiful in all literature and history than this scene, O my King! What comfort for You even in that pain-wracked agony to behold the loyalty of Your Mother and Your friend! How warm it made You feel! How wonderfully did their love and loyalty make up for all the hatred and curses and taunts of all the others. They deserved each other! It was such a comfort to You to give Mary into John's strong care. It was such a joy for You, now that You must leave her, to give her another worthy and devoted son.

O MY SAVIOUR, I realize now that personal loyalty to You is one of the most pleasing virtues in Your sight. It brings such joy to You when we refuse to abandon You or Your principles, even when others criticize and mock and hate us. Loyalty to You can also make us so strong. John that day was like the Rock of Gibraltar, and Mary like a beautiful tower of strength. Neither of them gave vent to hatred or fear, to excessive grief or anxiety. You were suffering, they just knew that they must be near You and suffer with You and let You know that they were there and understood. And O my King, what that meant to You!

Make me loyal, dear Lord. Make my faith in You so strong, my trust so firm, my love a tower of strength, that I may give You joy!

THE FOURTH WORD OF JESUS—LONELINESS

Matt. 27:46-47

1. *Darkness over Calvary.*
2. *The grace, my Lord, to share Your loneliness that I may know Your Heart.*

THE BODY of Jesus throbbed now in excruciating pain. The aching agony forced His attention, so that He could hardly notice His loved ones any more. Even the consoling presence of His Father seemed to leave Him as His mind struggled through the maze of pain to pray to Him. Suddenly He felt completely alone. It seemed unreal that anyone was near Him, impossible that anyone could understand the agony of it. He was alone — alone. In almost unbelievable desolation He cried out, "My God, My God, why hast Thou forsaken Me?"

MY SUFFERING, desolate King, of all that long list of sufferings foretold by David a thousand years before, this loneliness was the ultimate sorrow. Your cry of agony should have been enough to convince the hardest heart that the prophecies were fulfilled and their redemption accomplished. In the 21st Psalm, David foretold that they would pierce Your hands and feet and number all Your bones, that they would surround You like barking dogs, wagging their heads and shouting, "He saved others, Himself He cannot save," that the soldiers would divide Your garments among them and on Your vesture cast lots, that Your thirst would be so great that Your tongue would cleave to Your palate. All these things they had seen fulfilled. And now the worst agony of all, which David described in the opening words of the Psalm: "My God, My God, why hast Thou forsaken me?" When that cry of desolation came from Your lips, who could doubt, my King, that You were the Saviour of the world? Who could possibly fail to understand the depths of Your suffering, the immensity of Your love?

MY KING, I can never understand Your Heart, never imitate You completely, until this bitter cup of loneliness has been put to my lips and I have drunk of it—deeply! Following You means facing opposition. Imitating You closely, taking You at Your word and living by faith and trust — means being dubbed a fanatic. Even good people will say that I am "overdoing it." They'll cry out in words dripping with sarcasm, "Too much! Too much!" And I have to face a choice—either turn back on taking the Christ-life seriously, or go my way alone. That loneliness is so difficult, my King, so confusing, so empty. When it comes I almost feel abandoned by God. But, O my King, the comfort from going on—the insight into Your Heart—and in the end, the peace as my loneliness is dispelled by Your presence, and I am alone no more!

Lord, do not hold back. I want to be like You. Send what You will — even this desolation of going it alone.

THE LAST WORDS OF JESUS— SANCTIFYING SUFFERING

John 19 : 28-30

1. *The soft, parched cry from the cross, "I thirst."*
2. *The grace, my Lord, to run forth and embrace the suffering and the sorrow that will make me like You.*

THE DREADFUL loss of blood, together with the burning fever that wracked His Body, caused Jesus to have a fearful thirst. His tongue almost stuck to the roof of His mouth

and became swollen until He could hardly talk. It was with a low voice, almost rasping, that He called out: "I thirst." One of the soldiers put a sponge in some wine and then lifted it up on the end of a reed. The Jews tried to stop him, saying, "Wait, let us see whether Elias is coming to take Him down." But the soldier didn't mind them. He put the sponge to the lips of Jesus. Jesus took some of it and said, "It is consummated." All was fulfilled. He was ready to die.

DEAR MASTER, there are very few sufferings that are as intense as this pain of thirst. In many instances it has driven men mad. How tragic, my King, that You Who are the source of living water both of nature and of grace — that You should be consumed with fever and this agonizing thirst! But it was not in vain, my suffering King! From that moment of Your Passion onwards, suffering took on a new meaning and a new dignity. You made it Your own, You sanctified it by Your love and used it to redeem the world. And so You gave it a new depth, gave it new power to transform our souls—power to burn away the effects of our sins, to deepen our insight into life's true meaning, to broaden our hearts in sympathy for others. Suffering never had to be an enemy any more. If we only accept it with love, we make it part of Your Passion; we fill up what is wanting in the sufferings of Your Mystical Body. We help to heal and save the world.

DEAR MASTER, I'm such a coward in the face of suffering and sorrow. I run headlong from it, as though it were the greatest evil. Let me hear in the depths of my soul Your pitiable gasp, "I thirst." Let me see and feel what You felt. And, O Lord, give me enough love for You to want to go through it with You!

I don't have to seek sufferings, my Lord. Much better to let Your watchful Providence send me the kind of sorrow and the intensity of pain that I need. It's what I do with it that counts. Let me accept it cheerfully, knowing You have sanctified it. Let me offer it to You with love, knowing that thus I hang beside You on Your Cross. Dear Master, send me what You will!

JESUS DIES ON THE CROSS—SACRIFICE CONSECRATED BY LOVE

Luke 23 : 46

1. *The lifeless Body of Jesus.*
2. *The grace, my Lord, to love You with a deep, personal love all my life.*

THE LAST few minutes of His life were an agony of pain for Jesus. He was too weak to push Himself up with His legs — so His whole Body sagged, its full weight stretching His arms in indescribable pain. The sagging of His Body constricted His breathing. With exhausting effort He just managed to draw in a few gasps of air. "Father," He called out, "into Thy hands I commend My spirit." Then the last bit of strength left His pain-wracked Body. He couldn't breathe. All effort ceased. His Sacred Head dropped forward and He died.

MY KING, even in these last agonizing moments there was a strange, consoling peace in Your heart — the peace that can only be known by those who die for love. The realization of the untold good You were doing for souls gave You this peace.

St. Thomas More experienced that peace in the Tower before his death. His daughter,

Meg, begged him to give in to Henry and sign the oath of supremacy. But he resisted all her pleas. "All men must die sooner or later," he told her. "Those of us who are lucky die for love . . . I am one of the lucky ones, Meg. I, too, die for love!" Love gave meaning to the death of Jesus; love brought peace through it all.

DEAR MASTER, I'm so ready to complain about little crosses, so prone to wallow in self-pity about slights and petty insults and being overlooked. And why? Because I forget the meaning of life as You taught it; I forget love. These annoyances are the raw materials of a beautiful life in imitation of You, my King — an opportunity to put on Your humility and patience and serenity, a chance to die to self as You died. But love must be the key. I have to consecrate these little crosses by love for You if I am going to unite them to Your Cross. I have to die for love, if I am going to be one of the fortunate ones that has peace and serenity even in the darkest trials and most trying difficulties. My Saviour, let my daily dying to self be motivated by love for You!

THE BURIAL OF JESUS (1)— TRUE SENSE OF VALUES

John 19 : 31-40; Mark 15 : 43-45

1. *Anxious expression on the face of St. John.*
2. *The grace, my Lord, to be aware of Your sufferings in Your Mystical Body.*

ONCE JESUS was dead, Our Lady and John felt an overwhelming sense of relief. His pain was over; His work done. John then thought of the burial. It was unthinkable that Jesus should be buried in a common ditch with the criminals. He must somehow get permission to take His Body. Yet how could he possibly get an audience with the Governor? And where could he find a tomb before sunset? It seemed hopeless. Just then Joseph of Arimathea and Nicodemus came up. They were thinking the same thoughts as John. Joseph had influence with the Governor, and he had a new tomb nearby. He'd make the arrangements. John was relieved. While Joseph and Nicodemus started on their mission, he told the encouraging news to Mary.

DEAR LORD, how remarkable that Joseph and Nicodemus should appear on the scene now that You were dead — when they were so timid and afraid while You were

alive! And yet, my King, I suppose I should not be surprised. Had You not told Nicodemus on the first night he came to You that when "You were lifted up from the earth, You would draw all things to Yourself"! There was something about the intensity of Your suffering, something about the inspiring generosity of Your dying for others, that made their fears seem so petty and insignificant. They felt ashamed now that they had been afraid and selfish. The sight of the Cross changed in a flash their whole distorted sense of values.

MY KING, what a lesson for me! I can get so bogged down in my own petty sufferings and tiny problems; I can feel that the whole world is coming to an end just because some little plan was frustrated or some pet idea rejected. How I need to get out of my petty little world of self — and get away from my narrow confines of selfish interests! I need the sight of the Cross! Let me see what You suffered, my King. Make it vivid. Let me see what You still suffer in Your Mystical Body — the millions who are persecuted, the innocents who are slaughtered, the hearts that are aching with sorrow, the souls who don't even know You died to save them!

And, O Lord, then selfishness will end and smallness cease! And I'll leave my narrow world to serve You again!

THE BURIAL OF JESUS (2)—CORPORAL WORKS OF MERCY

John 19 : 31-40; Mark 15 : 43-45

1. *Removing the blood-stained nails which pierced the Sacred Hands.*
2. *The grace, my Lord, to "weep with those who weep and rejoice with those who rejoice."*

WHILE JOHN waited for the return of Joseph and Nicodemus, one of the Pharisees presented a sealed order to the Centurion. It was permission from the Governor to break the legs of the criminals, and thus hasten their death and the removal of their bodies from the crosses before the Sabbath. John saw the Centurion and a soldier approach the first thief. It gave him a sickening feeling to see the soldier swing a crowbar against the thief's legs, to hear the awful thud, the fearful scream. He held Our Lady close to him. "Jesus is already dead," he was saying, "they won't..." The Centurion was next to Jesus and saw that He was dead. He went to move away, but then turned as though by second thought. He took a spear from one of his men and drove it into the side of Jesus through to His Heart. A little Blood poured out and some water. Now there'd be no question about actual death when he had to report to the Governor.

Joseph and Nicodemus returned now. Several servants were with them. Gently they lowered the Body of Jesus from the Cross. They removed the Crown of Thorns and washed away the dirt of the congealed Blood. Then, wrapping His Body in a new linen shroud, they carried It to the nearby tomb of Joseph. Inside the tomb they anointed the Sacred Body with the spices and sprinkled It with the myrrh and aloes. They led Mary in that she might see Jesus for the last time. Each of them felt her sorrow with her. They handed John the relics for her — the nails and the thorns, wrapped in a small linen cloth. Slowly then, John and Mary Magdalene led her away to Bethany.

MY MOTHER, what a relief for you in your great sorrow to have the understanding and sympathy of loyal friends. They were just perfect. They didn't talk too much; they didn't make a fuss. They simply went ahead and made all the arrangements which you were too weak and confused by sorrow to make yourself. In that moment of great loss, when all else was confusing, you had the one sure thing to hold on to — you were loved and wanted.

MY KING, the corporal works of mercy are truly beautiful expressions of charity at work. I must re-examine my conscience on them. Do I really make myself available to those who need me? Am I a good listener for those who just have to talk out their problem? Do I put myself into the situation and the mood of those about me — do I "weep with those who weep and rejoice with those who rejoice"? I would love to have comforted Your Mother that day — love to have served You! Show me that I still can! "Whatever you do to these, the least of My brethren, you do unto Me."

THE RESURRECTION OF JESUS— THE SEAL ON OUR FAITH

Matt. 27 : 62-66

1. *The empty tomb on Easter morning.*
2. *The grace, my Lord, to believe and to rejoice in the truth!*

THE CHIEF PRIESTS and the Pharisees ate their Passover meal in peace Good Friday evening as the Body of Jesus lay in the tomb. But the next day they became uneasy again. They remembered the prophecy of Jesus that He would rise again on the third day. A fear took hold of them. The Nazarene had such unexplainable power. What if . . . ? They must ask Pilate to guard the tomb carefully with soldiers. They wouldn't admit the real cause of their fear to each other. They even tried to hide it from themselves. It was the Apostles they feared — not Jesus. The Apostles might steal the Body and claim that Jesus had risen.

Pilate told them to do what they wanted with their own Roman guard. So taking personal charge, they set up a Centurion and a squad of men at the tomb. They also sealed the tomb with tape and wax, stamping the wax with their official seal — so the soldiers couldn't be bribed to open it. But early Sunday morning their worst fears were realized. The tomb and seal were burst open, not from without but by an angel from within to show that the tomb was empty.

O MY KING, they acted out of fear and hatred — and yet they couldn't have served Your cause more perfectly. No honest person now could ever doubt about the reality of Your Resurrection, or about the evidence

it gives for Your divinity and for our own resurrection from the dead.

The facts are so clear, my King. You were dead. The Centurion pierced Your heart before he'd let Joseph of Arimathea take You down from the Cross. If there were any possibility that You were still alive, Mary and Your friends never would have let You be buried. As it was, You were enclosed in a small tomb with the entrance sealed. Secondly, there is no question about the identity of Your tomb. The Pharisees saw to that. It was guarded carefully and sealed by men whose hatred and fear would let them take no chances of making a mistake.

And yet, my King, on Easter Sunday morning the tomb was empty! Dead bodies don't move. Some unbelievers will say that the Apostles stole Your Body. But how — with the guard of soldiers there? And why? If they were afraid to fight for You when You were alive, how would they have the courage to risk their lives when You were dead? Other rationalists will claim that an earthquake swallowed Your Body. But Peter and John found the linen shroud and face cloth wrapped neatly in the tomb. It would be a most considerate earthquake that would swallow Your Body and neatly fold the shroud!

There's only one explanation of the empty tomb, my King! The angel expressed it perfectly to the women: "Why do you seek the living One among the dead?" You had risen as You said, glorious and immortal!

O MY LORD, the miracle of Your Resurrection overwhelms me—once I realize what it means. When a man is dead, we speak of him in the past tense, so incapable is he of any action. Yet Your soul came back through Your own power to Your Body and You were alive again. The empty tomb, Your many appearances are overwhelming proof. Let me realize what I know. The most beautiful part about Your teaching is that it is true. It's absolutely so that You are God incarnate, that You love me so much that You died for me, that You care for me, forgive me, want me — that You want my help in bringing others to You — that in the end there will be a glorious resurrection and life and peace forever! Let me just love to think of it! Our faith is absolute truth; our biggest battle has been won. Alleluia, alleluia, alleluia!

THE WOMEN AT THE TOMB—TRUE CHARITY

Mark 16:1-4

1. *The women starting for the tomb at the crack of dawn, anxious to anoint Jesus.*
2. *The grace of true charity — love that is completely selfless.*

WHILE JESUS was in the tomb, the women prepared spices and ointments of all kinds. In their sorrow they had to keep themselves busy, and it was good to be busy about something that would be a service to Him. Very early on the first day they were permitted to go to the tomb (Sabbath rest forbade it on Saturday) they started for the sepulchre. A few of them went to buy whatever spices they were lacking.

MY KING, Your Sacred Body didn't have to be anointed. Nicodemus had brought a hundred pounds of myrrh and aloes on Good Friday. Every respect had been paid to You. It was with the greatest care that they wrapped Your Body in clean linens and laid It carefully in the rich tomb of Joseph. Nor could You appreciate this extra attention since, as far as the women knew, You were still dead. Neither could they count on any favors. Apparently You were defeated. The only thing they could expect would be insults and derision. But they had to do something! That's the way love is. They had to find some service for their Beloved; and they had to be near You! Truly love serves; truly love is stronger than death.

DEAR MASTER, I feel ashamed when I contrast their beautiful, selfless, undying love with my fickle and feeble affection. I say I love You and yet so much of my service is only a service of myself. I look for praise even in the work I think I am doing for You. I am disappointed when I seem to fail — even though You have such different standards of success and failure, and only judge by the greatness of the effort and the love which prompts it. All disappointment and worry and fretting means that I am more concerned with myself than with You and Your service.

Give me clear vision, Lord! Give me a great heart! Let my eyes see only You and my heart love only You! And thus let my every moment be spent in Your service. Take my efforts, my thoughts, my joys, my success, my failures. They can all serve You. I give them all to You.

No more fretting or worry! So what if I fail according to worldly standards! It is only You

I want to please, and You are pleased even by failure. Love is service; love is total abandonment. Take me — all that I am and do and think and say!

THE RESURRECTION ANNOUNCED TO THE WOMEN—TRUST

Luke 24 : 3-8; Matt. 28 : 8-10

1. *The guards terrified at the sight of the angels in dazzling brightness.*
2. *The grace, my Lord, to trust in You throughout the dark hours.*

THE SUN was just coming up over the Judean hills near Jericho as the women made their way to the tomb of Jesus. Just before they arrived, an earthquake rocked the tomb, marking the time that the Soul of Jesus again took possession of His Body. Two angels then appeared and rolled back the stone to show that the tomb was empty. The guards were transfixed with fear at the earthquake and the sight of the angels. Only gradually did they gain enough composure to back away from the tomb and then run headlong from the place.

When the women arrived at the tomb, they were amazed to see the stone rolled back. An awful fear came over them that it might have been violated. They hurried inside and there they saw the angels. "Why do you seek the living One among the dead? He is not here, but risen." They could hardly contain their joy. Their Beloved was safe! He was risen! They would see Him again!

When they left the tomb, however, the same fear came over them again. Perhaps their great sorrow had caused them to have hallucinations. Perhaps the tomb had really been violated. At that dark moment, Jesus Himself appeared to them. "Hail," He said, with great love in His eyes. They fell in adoration at His Feet. This was no hallucination! In their hearts was a joy so great it almost hurt!

MY REDEEMER, how wonderful that You appeared in all Your glory to these loyal followers! They deserved to share Your joy. They were completely unselfish and loyal, right from the beginning. And they remained true to You when even the bravest hearts were tempted to desert You. Now You rewarded them. You let the angels give them an inkling of the glorious truth so that Your appearance to them wouldn't overwhelm them. And then You came to them Yourself in all Your risen glory. You rewarded their love in the only way that love can be rewarded, by showing Your appreciation and Your own great love in return.

O MY LORD, shouldn't this happy scene convince me of Your ever-faithful love and care. You once said that even a cup of water given in Your name would not go without a reward. How much more, then, will You reward the sufferings, the cares, the weary everyday tasks, the dark hours of loneliness and pain! I'm so tempted to think that I'm alone in those dark moments — that somehow the sufferings are just accidents that are coming to me without Your seeing and understanding. How wrong I am, my King. You are with me every moment — even when the clouds are darkest — just as You were near the women at the tomb in all their desolation and fear. Let me trust, like them, and keep loving and serving. And then the moment will come when the angel of Your grace will tell me that the trial is over and I'll see You and be near You once again.

MARY MAGDALENE CALLS PETER AND JOHN—FAITH

John 20 : 2-10

1. *Mary, breathless, telling the Apostles about the open tomb.*
2. *The grace, my Lord, of such strong faith that I'll never waver or doubt.*

IN HER anxiety to be of service to Jesus, Mary Magdalene outdistanced the other women and arrived at the tomb first. She gasped when she saw the tomb opened. She was afraid to look, afraid that the Sacred Body of Jesus might have been desecrated or stolen. She ran as fast as she could to the Cenacle. Breathlessly, she poured out her story to the Apostles. Peter and John started for the tomb. They asked her to stay there and rest, but she begged them to let her come. Fast as they went, she kept up with them.

The angels were no longer there when Magdalene and the Apostles arrived. Jesus apparently wanted to reveal Himself to them directly. Peter entered the tomb and then John. The linen cloths in which Jesus was buried were lying there undisturbed. The napkin for His Face and Head was folded neatly in another place. This couldn't be the work of enemies. A sense of great relief and peace came over them. In their hearts, they believed now that Jesus had risen. He would come to them in His own time. Peacefully they returned to the Cenacle.

MY KING, You show me very clearly in this scene how You lead us on to faith in You. You could have shown Yourself to the Apostles immediately and they would have known You were alive. You would have proven Your divinity. But You wanted them to see the evidence for believing and to believe before You let them see the Reality. They saw the empty tomb. How did it become empty? It certainly was not the work of vandals or enemies who would wish to desecrate the Body of Jesus. Such a group would never have left the tomb and linens in such neat order. Nor could an earthquake have swallowed the Body of Jesus — for how then explain the headcloth folded neatly and in another place? Only one explanation made sense — the wonderful truth, almost too good to believe, that Jesus had risen from the dead.

MY KING, it is so good to see how You acted with the Apostles because this is the way You still act with us. If You appeared to me in the Eucharist, or showed Yourself to me by a vision — what credit could I possibly get for believing? What honor would I possibly be giving to You that I trusted Your words and accepted what You said as true? A vision would take away merit and faith. I no longer believe once I see.

Help me to believe, my Lord. I have the evidence of Your miracles and Your glorious Resurrection. They prove that You speak with the authority of God, that You are what You say You are — the Son of God. I believe, Lord. I believe every word You've spoken. I accept with a sincere heart all the truths taught by Your other Self — Your Mystical Body, the Church. Some day soon I'll see You face to Face. But now I'm grateful that I don't see, so I can take You on Your word! Make my faith so strong, that I'll never waver or doubt.

JESUS APPEARS TO MARY MAGDALENE—REJOICING IN GOD

John 20:11-18

1. *Mary at the Feet of Jesus, overcome with joy.*
2. *The grace, my Lord, to rejoice in all the good that is done for You.*

MARY MAGDALENE kept her vigil at the tomb, sorrowful, alone, her mind full of memories from the past two years. After a while, the angels appeared to her, and then Jesus. Both seemed to tease her — asking her why she wept and whom she sought — only that her joy might be greater when she found out that He was alive. Thinking that Jesus was the gardener, she begged: "Sir, if thou hast removed Him, tell me where thou hast laid Him and I will take Him away." Her eyes, red from crying, pleaded with Him. Jesus was deeply touched. Such loyalty! Such love! He kept her in suspense no longer. "Mary," He said, in the old familiar tone of voice without disguise. The light came back to her face. She fell at His Feet in a torrent of sobs. "Master . . . Master!" Jesus let her stay there for a little while, allowing her to borrow those moments from Heaven. Then

He stooped down and lifted her up. He told her then not to delay, but to go and tell the news to His disciples. In Heaven she could have that place at His Feet forever!

MY KING, so often we think of what Your love has done for us. It is seldom we stop to consider how much sheer joy our love gives to You! The Gospels give us short glimpses of it — how pleased You were by the signs of affection at Bethany, how moved by the rich young man, how delighted by the manly devotion of the Apostles at the Last Supper that, disguise it as You would, they could see it! And finally in this scene when You told Mary the good news, it was almost in a playful manner—as we would hide a child's present behind our back, making believe that we forgot his birthday, only to see his eyes dance more brightly in the end! It is almost in this same manner that You revealed the Resurrection to Mary — so pleased were You with her unselfish and devoted love! How very human and warm You were, dear Master! How good to be pleased by our simple, human love!

DEAR MASTER, let me always realize what great joy You receive from those who are good, and let me rejoice in it, too. I'm so tempted at times to be jealous of the good that is done by others! Tempted to be sorry that they seem to be so fine; tempted to discount the good that they do, or minimize it, or question their motives. Tempted to feel badly because I wasn't the one to do it!

O my Lord, don't let me give in to such smallness and pettiness! Let me be genuinely delighted over all the good that is done — no matter who does it. As Your great Apostle Paul put it: "So long as Christ is preached, in this do I rejoice, yes and I shall rejoice!" I realize now that "rejoicing in the good of others" is as much an act of love of You as loving and serving You directly myself.

DISCIPLES ON THE ROAD TO EMMAUS (1)—FAITH

Luke 24:13-35

1. *The anxious faces of the two disciples; the slow, weary gait.*
2. *The grace, my Lord, of strong faith, especially during time of trouble.*

THE TWO DISCIPLES left Jerusalem and headed for home with empty hearts. Their hopes had been so high when they saw the miracles of Jesus. Their hearts had thrilled to His words, His manner and His teaching. Surely here was the Saviour! And now they walked along with the darkest gloom in their hearts. The bottom had fallen out of their little world. They had seen Jesus defeated, put to death in torments. Every hope that at the last moment He would come down from the Cross and conquer was frustrated. He died. Evil had conquered. The Scribes and Pharisees had free rein for their jealousy and hatred. Jesus was beaten and their hopes died with Him!

MY SAVIOUR, these disciples felt so sad because they had such little faith. They didn't give You credit for being able to conquer by other means than the world uses. To them Your death on Calvary was just a horrible accident of fate. They never dreamed that it could be part of a divine plan! They couldn't see how humiliation could be used for good, or how suffering could be turned to love, or insults accepted for a purpose. And because by their worldly standards You had lost, they felt that the defeat was complete. And yet, my King, that very defeat on Calvary was Your greatest victory. By it You conquered sin, opened heaven. The tree of death became the tree of life!

O MY LORD, how much like those disciples I am! So weak in faith! I prefer my own plans to Your plan. I get angry over opposition and hurt by criticism. When suffering comes, or failure, I get depressed and almost ready to give up! And why? Because I lack faith! Faith to see that all these things are not obstacles to holiness but means. They are all part of Your plan to form me in Your own image. The only thing that cannot be used is bad will — the refusal to see Your plan and accept it. All else can be turned into love. Open my eyes, dear Jesus. Let me see!

DISCIPLES ON THE ROAD TO EMMAUS (2)—CERTITUDE OF FAITH

Luke 24 : 13-35

1. *Jesus explaining the prophecies to the wide-eyed disciples.*
2. *The grace, my Lord, of complete certitude of faith.*

JESUS approached the two disciples as they walked along disconsolate. Like a masterful teacher, He drew out the cause of their sorrow and disappointment, let them express it in their own way and with their own viewpoint. And then what a canvas He painted for them! He started from the point of their discouragement and went on through the prophecies showing how these very events at Calvary were all part of God's plan for our salvation. He reminded them of the paschal lamb in Egypt — innocent, slain without a bone broken, and its blood daubed on the door posts. Through the blood of that innocent lamb, they were saved from the slavery of Egypt. Was it not all a prophecy in action foreshadowing the Lamb of God Whose Blood would save them from the slavery of sin? The disciples nodded. Yes, it made sense. Then Jesus told them about Isaias' description of the Christ: "led as a lamb to the slaughter . . . bruised for our iniquities and wounded for our sins . . . and by his bruises we are healed." And then David's Twenty-first Psalm, describing the Crucifixion: "pierced My hands and My feet . . . they divided My garments among them and on My vesture they cast lots." Jesus recalled how the fourth word from the Cross was "My God, my God, why hast Thou forsaken me?" — the opening words of the Twenty-first Psalm, reminding all beneath the Cross that they had just fulfilled every prophecy in that Psalm. All the pieces began to fit together. The disciples were beside themselves with joy and hope. They wouldn't let Him leave.

MY SAVIOUR, six months before this incident, when the crowds in Jerusalem wanted to stone You for saying that You were One with the Father, You pointed to Your miracles as proof that You spoke the truth. Now in this scene You gave them another proof — the tremendous fact that various prophecies made over a period of thousands of years were all fulfilled in You! How could any fair-minded person doubt now Your claim to be divine. History knows of other men only after they have come into the world. But history knew You before You came! You were the only One Who was expected, Whose life was planned and foretold in detail before You came! No one knows the future except God! Only God could have foretold these events and fulfilled them!

DEAR MASTER, my "heart burns within me" also, when I realize that the Almighty Eternal God became Man and walked this earth! Your miracles and prophecies give me overwhelming proof that You are God made Man. Let me realize what that means! Every word You said is as true as God is true.

Your assurance of Heaven to those who believe and obey Your Commandments, Your assurance that You Yourself are with us in Holy Communion, Your word that my sins are really forgiven in Confession! How wonderful, my King! My faith isn't wishful thinking, or pious dreams. The most beautiful part about it is that it is true! Let me love Your teaching, my King! Let me love You!

JESUS APPEARS TO THE APOSTLES (1)— SPIRIT OF FAITH

Luke 24:36-43; John 20:19-23

1. *The looks of utter amazement on the faces of the Apostles.*
2. *The grace, my Lord, of a deep spirit of faith in all trials and dryness.*

IT WAS the evening of the day of the Resurrection. Peter had called a meeting of the eleven Apostles, and all except Thomas were there. The door of the Cenacle was locked; the discussion, nervous and anxious. Could the women be believed? Some of the Apostles felt the women were hysterical. Yet — if they were just hysterical, then how explain the empty tomb and the neatly folded burial shroud? Certainly the Pharisees would not have gone to that trouble if they had violated the tomb! Nor would they have had the time, for the women were there at the break of dawn, and the day before had been the Sabbath. And what about the report just a while ago from the two disciples who had been travelling to Emmaus? Certainly they weren't hysterical! And yet — it was all too good to be true.

And then, suddenly the room seemed to be illumined by a new light. They sensed a Presence. They turned toward the doorway. And there Jesus was standing with a smile on His Face! He was speaking now: "Peace to you. It is I, do not be afraid . . . Feel me and see; for a spirit does not have flesh and bones, as you see I have." They felt the wounds then, slowly, fearfully, without a word. "Have you anything here to eat?" He asked. And that seemed to break the spell. Yes, of course they did. Someone handed Jesus a piece of fish and then they all began to talk and surround Him and almost shout for joy.

DEAR MASTER, what a beautiful scene! What a triumphant return to Your chosen ones! Three nights before You told them You would not eat or drink with them again until the Kingdom had come. And now the work of redemption was accomplished. The Kingdom had come and You were back to rejoice in it with Your own. You had let their faith be sorely tried and now You let them see. You had let them suffer unutterable loss — and now You let them be rewarded. This is the pattern with them; this must be the pattern with me.

MY KING, make me understand that moments of darkness are a necessary part of Your plan. Teach me that until I seem to lose You in dryness and failure, I never really become a full-fledged apostle. Give me this deep faith, Lord. Let it be my comfort in trial, my light in darkness, my victory over pain. Even when it seems too good to be true that You love and care so much as to arrange every hurt in order to heal, let me believe and trust.

JESUS APPEARS TO THE APOSTLES (2)— SACRAMENT OF PENANCE

Luke 24:36-43; John 20:12-23

1. *The Apostles sitting in a circle in the Upper Room, their eyes glued on Jesus.*
2. *The grace, my Lord, to appreciate the Sacrament of Your mercy.*

ONCE THE APOSTLES realized that it was really Jesus present, Jesus as they had known Him and not just a vision, they could hardly contain their happiness. He let them enjoy the full wonder of it for a while. Then He explained to them that this was what He was trying to tell them all along — when He foretold His Passion and when He said to them at the Last Supper, "You shall be sorrowful, but your sorrow shall be turned into joy." They smiled as they recalled it all and realized what He had meant. Then He took them back to the Old Testament, through the writings of Moses and the prophets — just as He had done to the disciples on the road to Emmaus. The canvas He painted was huge. All the details about His birth, life, suffering and death — foretold and fulfilled! And the reason for it all — to redeem all men, to buy back Heaven with His Blood. They saw it now as they had never seen it before. They were speechless with wonder — even Peter.

And then came the supreme moment. They were to be the dispensers of the pardon and peace He had won. He spoke now with great solemnity: "As the Father has sent Me, I also send you . . . whose sins you shall forgive, they are forgiven them; and whose sins you shall retain, they are retained."

MY KING, it was most fitting that You should thus institute the healing Sacrament of Penance on the day of Your great victory. This is why You had fought the battle and won the victory — "to seek and to save that which was lost." What greater proof could we have that "Your mercy is above all Your works." The sweetest fruit of Your victory was the thought of all the billions of souls who would be cleansed and renewed in the saving graces of Confession. You seemed almost impatient to announce it, so greatly did it please You.

DEAR MASTER, how little have I appreciated this Sacrament of Your mercy! You are so thrilled to forgive me and welcome me back to Your friendship! And I go to Confession with such a matter-of-fact attitude, as though performing some routine, perfunctory duty.

Dear Master, let me see the big picture You painted for the Apostles that evening of Your Resurrection. Let me see that the whole scheme and plan of Your life—prepared and foretold in the Old Testament and fulfilled in the New Testament — was to win pardon and peace for me. Then I'll marvel like the Apostles. I'll approach Confession with the deepest sorrow for sin, with humility, with gratitude overflowing. O Jesus, risen Saviour, make me see!

JESUS APPEARS TO THOMAS—LEARNING FROM OUR FAULTS

John 20:24-29

1. *Thomas putting his finger into the wound in Jesus' hand.*
2. *The grace, my Lord, to learn from my faults how to love You and serve You more.*

WHEN THOMAS came to the Upper Room later on that evening of the Resurrection, he found the other ten exuberant. He could hardly make out what they were saying at first, because so many were trying to tell him all at once. Then he got the gist of the story—they thought they had seen the Lord! Thomas wasn't enthused. He sat down with his head between his hands. They had all the appearance of men who were deluded by their wishful thinking. They were insisting now! Jesus ate with them. They saw the wounds. He gave them the power to forgive sins. It was no use. He stopped them all with a wave of his hand. "Unless I see in His hands the print of the nails, and put my finger into the place of the nails, and put my hand into

His side, I will not believe." He wouldn't hear any more. He couldn't believe them; he couldn't even trust his own eyes. He must feel the wounds before he'd believe that the Body from the Cross had risen.

It was a hard week for Thomas. He seemed to be outside the Apostolic circle; he had no part in their joy and happiness. He told himself that he didn't care. Someone had to be sensible. And then suddenly a bright light filled the room. Thomas stood up in reverence and in fear. "Bring here thy finger and see My hands," Jesus was saying to him. Thomas felt the red wounds and the deep gash in His side. Instinctively, he fell on his knees, half in tears of sorrow, half in joy and wonder: "My Lord, and my God!"

MY KING, Thomas was wrong in not believing all the evidence for Your Resurrection. It was rash and stubborn not to accept the word of the other Apostles, of the disciples from Emmaus, of the women, besides the evidence of the empty tomb. And yet, my King, what a service his fault does for our faith! How could anyone ever again say that the Apostles were deluded by an imaginary vision, that they were misled by their desires and wishful thinking? Everyone of them was slow to believe, and Thomas was almost impossible. He wouldn't take anyone's word; he wouldn't even believe his own eyes and ears. The person might look like Jesus and talk like Jesus — but Thomas wouldn't believe until he felt the Body that died on the Cross and the wounds that accomplished Its death. What a bolster to our faith is Thomas' disbelief! How straight You write, my King — even "with crooked lines"!

DEAR MASTER, show me that all things can serve You — even my faults. It's so easy for me to become despondent over my sins and my mistakes, to give way to black remorse and corroding regret. Teach me, my Lord, that remorse is never pleasing to You, is never right. If I am sorry, then even my faults can serve You, for then they are no longer my faults — they used to be! And then I can go on to learn from them; I can profit by their mistakes; I can appreciate more Your tender mercy in forgiving and forgetting. "O Wisdom, proceeding from end to end, setting all things in order strongly and gently," take all, use all, even my faults, for Your greater glory.

JESUS APPEARS AT THE LAKE— TRUST IN JESUS

John 21:1-23

1. *Jesus standing on the shore.*
2. *The grace, my Lord, of humility and trust.*

THE APOSTLES had returned to Galilee as Jesus told them. These were strange days for them. They felt that they were "neither fish nor flesh." The last two years of their lives had been devoted entirely to Jesus. Their fishing trade, their regular life—all this they had left for Him. They had grown so used to the intimacy of His company and to sharing in His work of preaching the Gospel that they now felt uncomfortable and confused not to have Him with them all the time. And so in his usual impetuous way, St. Peter jumped up from the little group of Apostles and said: "I am going fishing." James and John were there, also Thomas, Nathaniel and two others. Willingly enough they joined him. But it was a fruitless task. All night long they dragged the nets, but to no avail.

As dawn was breaking and they headed in for shore, they heard a voice call to them: "Young men, have you any fish?" They just called back a disgruntled: "No." Then the lone Stranger spoke again: "Put down the nets on the right side of the boat." Peter began to get impatient. What difference did it make on which side of the boat they cast the nets! But then something struck him — the vague memory of how something like this had happened before. He and the others put over the nets and immediately they could feel the tug of the fish. John cried out what they all instinctively knew: "It is the Lord!" Peter grabbed his outer garment and jumped into the lake, wading ashore. When the others came, they saw a fire with a fish cooking and bread. The Master had made breakfast for them and He served them with His own Hands.

THIS IS a beautiful scene, my King! It looks as though You are trying to tell us again and again that results don't count with You; only effort and right intention. We can seem to be miserable failures, can labor so long without any visible results. As long as we act for love of You and do our best, You are pleased with us. You will come along in the end and we will make a great catch, and then feast with You on the shore.

O MY KING, somehow or other I think of success as depending on myself rather than on You and Your grace. That's why I get self-complacent feelings when I succeed. And that's why I'm depressed and confused when I fail. Won't You teach me humility and trust — humility to know that in the final analysis all depends on You, and trust to know that You will not fail. I must do my part, right! And don't let me shirk it. I must labor all the night if need be. And I must keep on working even when the whole job seems a mess and a failure! Above all I must have a pure intention — a good heart. But then! Then I can forget about everything else! It doesn't matter what happens then, because You will take care of it. No matter what You choose that it should be, my work will be a good work, and You will be waiting to greet me on the shore!

JESUS MAKES PETER THE FIRST POPE— "CHARITY COVERETH A MULTITUDE OF SINS"

John 21:15-23

1. *Sincere face of Peter as he professed, "Thou knowest that I love Thee."*
2. *The grace, my Lord, to love You deeply and sincerely.*

IT WAS a happy breakfast that Jesus and the Apostles shared by the lakeside. It was

good to have Him back with them. As they finished, Jesus turned to Peter: "Simon, son of John, dost thou love Me more than these do?" Peter was quick to reply: "Yes, Lord, Thou knowest that I love Thee." Jesus spoke solemnly: "Feed My lambs." A few moments passed. Jesus asked the same question and received the same answer. And then a third time: "Simon, son of John, dost thou love Me?" Peter felt hurt. Jesus seemed to doubt his love and loyalty. Then suddenly he recalled his threefold denial of Jesus. So this was it! The Master was only offering him the opportunity to profess publicly the One he had denied. It was with a grateful heart, charged with emotion, that Peter responded: "Lord, Thou knowest all things, Thou knowest that I love Thee." He bowed his head then as he heard Jesus confer on him complete authority: "Feed My sheep."

MY KING, Peter had his faults — but not loving You was not one of them. He wasn't the most prudent of the Apostles, he was impetuous, boastful to a degree. He lacked self-knowledge and moral courage. But he loved You, loved You greatly, loved You to the point where he would do anything to please You. He was striving sincerely to grow in virtue in order to please You; he was deeply sorry for his sins, because they hurt You. You were his ideal, his model; You were the one great moving force of his life.

So You loved him dearly, my Lord. And in spite of all his limitations, You could trust him to be Your visible representative on earth.

O MY LORD, You seem to show me again and again that it is love that counts with You. "Charity covereth a multitude of sins!" How true that was in Peter's case. The love he had for You seemed to blot out all his faults. Make it the same in my life! Charity is the short cut to holiness.

So often, my Lord, I feel that it's impossible for me to overcome my irritability, my prejudice against certain persons, my spiritual sloth and tepidity. And I get weary trying. Teach me the short cut. Nothing is hard for someone in love. Let me see Your goodness, Your manliness, Your unspeakable selflessness — as Peter saw it all that day — and my heart will go out to You. And then the smallness and faults will begin to fade away. Ask me the big question, Lord. I'm anxious to answer: "Lord, Thou knowest all things; Thou knowest that I love Thee."

JESUS' COMMISSION TO HIS APOSTLES— THE TRUE CHURCH

Matt. 28:16-20; Mark 16:15-18

1. *Jesus, seated with His Apostles on the familiar Mount of Beatitudes, above Lake Galilee.*
2. *The grace, my Lord, to love Your Church to the point of sacrifice.*

AFTER HIS FIRST appearance to them in Galilee when He prepared breakfast for them by the lakeside, Jesus showed Himself to them many times for a period of a month, instructing them about the Church and the Sacraments. Now He would appear to them for the last time in Galilee and confer on them their commission as Bishops of His Church. He told them to go to the Mount of Beatitudes, where He first set them aside as Apostles and where He preached His magnificent Sermon on the Mount. And now He appeared to them there. Instinctively they bowed down to adore Him. It gave Him great joy to see them coming closer to the realization of the truths He had taught. He spoke slowly and solemnly. "All power in heaven and on earth has been given to Me. Go into the whole world and preach the gospel to every creature. Make disciples of all nations, baptizing them in the name of the Father and of the Son and of the Holy Spirit, teaching them to observe all things that I have commanded you . . . And behold I am with you all days, even unto the consummation of the world." Never did so much depend upon so few and such frail human beings.

DEAR MASTER, what a clear picture Your words give me of the marks by which Your Church can be known. It must be a universal or Catholic Church, because it is to go "into the whole world . . . to every creature and all nations." It is to be apostolic, because the commission is to the Apostles and their successors only. You promised them, "I will be with you all days, even to the consummation of the world." They were going to die, my King, so You must be referring to their successors, the future Bishops of the Church to which the Apostles would hand on the commission by Holy Orders. Your Church was to be holy and united, for it was to teach men "all the things that You had commanded" — not just some truths, not just the soft teachings, but the wonderful, magnificent, unified whole — including the doctrine of the Cross and the high standard of morality.

O my Lord, what other church is completely united and teaches a holy doctrine; where is the universal Church, the Church that can make men saints — except the Holy Roman Catholic Church, Your Mystical Body, Your other Self!

DEAR MASTER, teach me to love the Church. Teach me to think with the Church and feel for her work and support her missionary efforts. For her thoughts are Your thoughts and her work is Your work.

I'm so ashamed when I consider how few converts I have won — worse yet, how few I have even approached — as though souls weren't so priceless that You died for them! I grow uncomfortable when I realize how little I have given to the Missions — compared with what I have spent on luxuries, like cigarettes, liquor and cosmetics — as though Your Church didn't need great funds to bring medicines to the sick and diseased. And how often I have let golden opportunities to explain Your teachings slip by because I didn't know the explanation and I was too absorbed in novels to study Your life-giving teachings.

Lord, I promise to change. I promise to love to the point of sacrifice, that Your kingdom may come.

ASCENSION OF JESUS (1)—WORLDLINESS

Luke 24 : 44-53; Acts 1 : 1-11

1. *Jesus at table with His Apostles for the last time.*

2. *The grace of complete trust, my King.*

THE FORTY DAYS of the Master's resurrected life were drawing to a close. Jesus had made His Apostles gradually used to the idea of His leaving them for good. He was not with them all the time now. He appeared to them at different times and different places, reviewed their studies in His teaching and laid down the guiding rules for the Church and the Sacraments. But now before He left them, He wanted to dine with them once more. So back they went to the old familiar setting in the Upper Room. Their joy was overflowing now. Jesus' success seemed so complete that they toyed again with thoughts of a worldly kingdom. As soon as Jesus reminded them to wait in Jerusalem for the Holy Spirit to come upon them with power, the unexpressed thoughts and ambitions were put into words: "Lord, wilt Thou at that time restore the kingdom to Israel?" It was such a blow to Jesus. After all His teaching! After all His efforts to make them spiritual men! And they still thought in terms of worldly success and material show! He was patient still. There was no complaint—He didn't even answer their question directly. The Holy Spirit would teach them all things. He just continued His instructions. It was not for them to know the times or the dates, not for them to know the results; just for them to do their part, "to bear witness to Him to the ends of the earth."

DEAR MASTER, worldliness is an insidious evil — like fine dust that can work its way into the cleanest room no matter how tightly we close the windows! It comes gradually but steadily until it covers the bright lustre of our faith and charity with its dull ugliness. And we begin to measure success in terms of comforts and money, in terms of appearances and worldly splash! We forget spiritual values — the good of souls, the redemptive value of suffering the success of failure. We forget the measure and the standard of the Cross.

O MY LORD, I must be honest with myself on this score. Haven't pure spiritual motives given way in me to the pull of natural likes and dislikes? Have not worldly honors and praise and flattery become very dear to me? And am I not very impressed by people with money and worldly position? The dust of worldliness has seeped into my soul and covered all the fine ideals. I consider that I'm a success when people praise me; that I'm a failure when my plans don't work out. And suffering I consider a sorrow! I have come to look upon them as the worst evils, things to be avoided at all costs.

Dear Holy Spirit, come with Your strong wind of refreshing faith and blow away the dust of worldliness. Let me see that sorrows can make me like Jesus. Teach me that only success is doing all for the love of Him. Let me live by faith once again!

ASCENSION OF JESUS (2)—HUMILITY

Acts 1:1-11; Luke 24:50-53

1. *Jesus blessing each one before His Ascension.*
2. *The grace, my Lord, of true humility.*

AFTER the supper in the Upper Room had ended, Jesus led the Apostles, Mary and the women and some of the disciples out of the city towards Olivet. They must have recalled the sorrowful journey along that same route on Holy Thursday. Now all was so different! And yet as they walked along, there was a bit

of sorrow. They couldn't help but feel that something was going to happen. The formality of the supper they had just finished, the discussions, all so reminiscent of Holy Thursday, made them feel that He was about to leave them again.

They came to the top of Olivet. All was beautiful in the warm sunshine; the trees and flowers were in bloom. Jesus went to each of them and said His farewell. They were choked up. They had so much to say, and yet somehow or other they couldn't say a word of it. Then before their eyes, He was lifted up. And as they gazed at Him, lost in wonder, a cloud took Him from their sight. And in His place came two angels to bring back their thoughts to this world and to the work that was yet unfinished.

DEAR MASTER, this scene gives me a good over-all picture of what life with You entails. In this one scene the Apostles have all the joy and thrill of victory and all the ache and loss of separation from You. You teach by action as well as by word that those who follow You must be ready for both joy and sorrow. True humility, my King, means accepting this wholeheartedly. We are creatures—in a world darkened by original sin—

and therefore must have our share of ups and downs, of success and failure, of friends and enemies. This is our lot, simply as creatures. And when we add to that the fact that we are followers of a crucified King, then suffering is a necessary part of our transformation into Your image. For Christians, there are greater joys and deeper sorrows—many times both on the very same occasion.

DEAR LORD, what peace true humility would bring into my life! How completely it would end resentment, anxieties, sulkiness and all those other negative emotions that kill peace in my heart. The obstacle is my pride, which just can't tolerate failure in myself or faults in others; pride which just can't see why things should go wrong when I took the pains to plan everything so well! Won't You teach me, my King! Let me stand there and watch You ascend into Heaven. Let me feel what they felt — all the joy of it, and all the sorrow. Lord, let me realize what it means to be a Christian, and then I'll be happy to receive all that You send me. Take me, risen, glorious King! Send me what You will!

WAITING FOR THE HOLY SPIRIT—SILENCE

Acts 1:12-14

1. *Apostles and Mary in the Cenacle, absorbed in silent prayer.*
2. *The grace, my Lord, to be silent and alone for at least one-half hour a day.*

AS THEY walked back from Mt. Olivet and made their way to the Cenacle in the southern section of Jerusalem, the words of Jesus began to take on greater significance for the Apostles. At the Last Supper, He had spoken so much about the Holy Spirit. And now He had told them to wait in Jerusalem until they would be "baptized with the Holy Spirit." And then they would be His witnesses "in Jerusalem and in all Judea and Samaria and even to the very ends of the earth." They were suddenly aware of a great longing for His coming. They discussed it openly and all agreed that they should be well prepared by silence and sincere prayer. So they went to the Upper Room, the familiar cenacle which had come to mean so much to them since the night of the Last Supper. And there they prayed as they had never prayed before. Their hearts were nothing but longing and desire that the Holy Spirit would come and make them ready to bear witness to their King and Master.

O MY KING, what a perfect preparation they thus made for the coming of the Holy Spirit. Silence made their hearts attentive and ready. It removed worry and anxiety and distraction. And their longing made their hearts hospitable for their Divine Guest. He would find them warm and receptive because they wanted so much for Him to come. All true holiness begins here, my King — with this strong desire to be holy and this willingness to pay the price of silent docility to the Holy Spirit.

DEAR MASTER, I have received the Holy Spirit in Confirmation. And yet I seem so cold, so unmoved by His inspirations, so little guided by His sevenfold gifts. My King, help me to realize the reason for it. It isn't that the Holy Spirit isn't speaking in my heart; it's just that there is too much noise there for me to hear Him. Outward noise of feverish activity, constant talking, television, radio, cheap and sensational reading. It drowns out His whispering. Inward noise, too, my King—anxieties, worry, fretting—all of it dissipates my attention and my love.

Dear Master, make me stop this noise! For at least a half-hour a day, let me leave it behind and enter the vast spacious hall of silence, where I can meet You and hear the loving inspiration of Your Holy Spirit. I want Him to come, my King. There's so much I need to know that only He can show me. Then let me pay the price of silent, longing prayer.

PENTECOST—THE BIG PICTURE OF GOD

Acts 2:1-41

1. *Tongues of fire above the head of each Apostle.*
2. *The grace, my Lord, of the vision of the first Pentecost.*

ON THE morning of Pentecost the prayerful longing of the Apostles and Our Lady was rewarded. As they knelt in silent prayer in the Upper Room, they suddenly heard a sound like a great wind. They looked up—and above the head of each were tongues of fire. No one spoke. But within their minds and hearts a wonderful change took place. Gradually, beautifully, like the sun coming from behind a cloud, all that Jesus taught them became vivid and clear. The beauty of it stirred them as it never had before. They wanted to shout it—to shout it to the whole world, and tell all men the good news! Almost deliriously happy, they started from the Cenacle for the celebration of the feast at the Temple. As they went along, others noticed their joyful singing and their praise of God in many different languages. Soon a huge crowd gathered about them. Peter raised his hand for silence. And then he spoke in a voice that was strong but vibrant with emotion and told all of them the good news about Jesus.

DEAR LORD, it's a lovely thing to contemplate their untold joy and ecstasy. They finally saw the big picture of God. Before You came, religion for them was just a series of unrelated laws, a great number of "do's" and "don'ts," without any real connection or meaning or purpose. But now the Holy Spirit brought to their minds all the things You had told them about the Father—above all, the Father's tender love and care for them—and they realized now that religion is love. Suddenly they knew that every quality they admired in their friends was only a tiny reflection of the Goodness of God; that all the attractive innocence of children, all the beautiful things of nature—the colored flowers and trees, the blue waters of the lakes and rivers, the golden sunshine, the vast, expansive sky—were all just trying to tell them of His loveliness. And Your care for them, my King, Your deep concern and feeling for each one, Your love that led You to Calvary, to save them—they knew now that You were the visible image of the Father, that it was His Goodness that they had experienced in You. They had true religion now, because they had awakened to this Beauty, were grateful for this care, were basking in the sunshine of this Love. They had the big picture of God, the true picture—and their hearts were lost in love.

DEAR HOLY SPIRIT, true Light, pure Love, I am so far away from this beautiful vision of God. I have such narrow and small thoughts of God—as though He were a stern taskmaster, ready to whip me when I do wrong—as though His laws were just arbitrary rules, making me give up what is pleasurable so He can test me. How I need this big picture of His Love and His Goodness—this vision that His Commandments and all that He sends are just Love at work, are just His Love molding me into the lovable likeness of His Son! Help me to see it, dear

Holy Spirit. Make me silent and prayerful so I can hear Your soothing, gentle wisdom. And then speak to my heart about my Father. Give me the big picture of Him — until my heart is lost in love and my service is a joy!

Contents

Contents

Page

Page

Page